# Teach Yourself®
# Photoshop® 5
# and 5.5

# Teach Yourself® Photoshop® 5 and 5.5

Jennifer Alspach and Linda Richards

**IDG Books Worldwide, Inc.**
An International Data Group Company

Foster City, CA • Chicago, IL • Indianapolis, IN • New York, NY

Teach Yourself® Photoshop® 5 and 5.5

Published by
**IDG Books Worldwide, Inc.**
An International Data Group Company
919 E. Hillsdale Blvd., Suite 400
Foster City, CA 94404
www.idgbooks.com (IDG Books Worldwide Web site)

ISBN: 0-7645-7503-1

Printed in the United States of America

10 9 8 7 6 5 4 3 2 1

1P/SR/QZ/ZZ/FC

Distributed in the United States by IDG Books Worldwide, Inc.

Distributed by CDG Books Canada Inc. for Canada; by Transworld Publishers Limited in the United Kingdom; by IDG Norge Books for Norway; by IDG Sweden Books for Sweden; by IDG Books Australia Publishing Corporation Pty. Ltd. for Australia and New Zealand; by TransQuest Publishers Pte Ltd. for Singapore, Malaysia, Thailand, Indonesia, and Hong Kong; by Gotop Information Inc. for Taiwan; by ICG Muse, Inc. for Japan; by Intersoft for South Africa; by Eyrolles for France; by International Thomson Publishing for Germany, Austria and Switzerland; by Distribuidora Cuspide for Argentina; by LR International for Brazil; by Galileo Libros for Chile; by Ediciones ZETA S.C.R. Ltda. for Peru; by WS Computer Publishing Corporation, Inc., for the Philippines; by Contemporanea de Ediciones for Venezuela; by Express Computer Distributors for the Caribbean and West Indies; by Micronesia Media Distributor, Inc. for Micronesia; by Chips Computadoras S.A. de C.V. for Mexico; by Editorial Norma de Panama S.A. for Panama; by American Bookshops for Finland.

For general information on IDG Books Worldwide's books in the U.S., please call our Consumer Customer Service department at 800-762-2974. For reseller information, including discounts and premium sales, please call our Reseller Customer Service department at 800-434-3422.

For information on where to purchase IDG Books Worldwide's books outside the U.S., please contact our International Sales department at 317-596-5530 or fax 317-596-5692.

For consumer information on foreign language translations, please contact our Customer Service department at 800-434-3422, fax 317-596-5692, or e-mail rights@idgbooks.com.

For information on licensing foreign or domestic rights, please phone +1-650-655-3109.

For sales inquiries and special prices for bulk quantities, please contact our Sales department at 650-655-3200 or write to the address above.

For information on using IDG Books Worldwide's books in the classroom or for ordering examination copies, please contact our Educational Sales department at 800-434-2086 or fax 317-596-5499.

For press review copies, author interviews, or other publicity information, please contact our Public Relations department at 650-655-3000 or fax 650-655-3299.

For authorization to photocopy items for corporate, personal, or educational use, please contact Copyright Clearance Center, 222 Rosewood Drive, Danvers, MA 01923, or fax 978-750-4470.

Library of Congress Cataloging-in-Publication Data

Alspach, Jennifer.
    Teach yourself photoshop 5 and 5.5 / by Jen Alspach.
        p.    cm.
    ISBN 0-7645-7503-1 (alk.paper)
    1. Computer graphics. 2. Adobe Photoshop. I. Title.
T385.A465   1999                                                    98-55000
006.6'869--dc21                                                         CIP

is a registered trademark or trademark under exclusive license

to IDG Books Worldwide, Inc. from International Data Group, Inc.

in the United States and/or other countries.

# ABOUT IDG BOOKS WORLDWIDE

Welcome to the world of IDG Books Worldwide.

IDG Books Worldwide, Inc., is a subsidiary of International Data Group, the world's largest publisher of computer-related information and the leading global provider of information services on information technology. IDG was founded more than 30 years ago by Patrick J. McGovern and now employs more than 9,000 people worldwide. IDG publishes more than 290 computer publications in over 75 countries. More than 90 million people read one or more IDG publications each month.

Launched in 1990, IDG Books Worldwide is today the #1 publisher of best-selling computer books in the United States. We are proud to have received eight awards from the Computer Press Association in recognition of editorial excellence and three from Computer Currents' First Annual Readers' Choice Awards. Our best-selling ...For Dummies® series has more than 50 million copies in print with translations in 31 languages. IDG Books Worldwide, through a joint venture with IDG's Hi-Tech Beijing, became the first U.S. publisher to publish a computer book in the People's Republic of China. In record time, IDG Books Worldwide has become the first choice for millions of readers around the world who want to learn how to better manage their businesses.

Our mission is simple: Every one of our books is designed to bring extra value and skill-building instructions to the reader. Our books are written by experts who understand and care about our readers. The knowledge base of our editorial staff comes from years of experience in publishing, education, and journalism — experience we use to produce books to carry us into the new millennium. In short, we care about books, so we attract the best people. We devote special attention to details such as audience, interior design, use of icons, and illustrations. And because we use an efficient process of authoring, editing, and desktop publishing our books electronically, we can spend more time ensuring superior content and less time on the technicalities of making books.

You can count on our commitment to deliver high-quality books at competitive prices on topics you want to read about. At IDG Books Worldwide, we continue in the IDG tradition of delivering quality for more than 30 years. You'll find no better book on a subject than one from IDG Books Worldwide.

John Kilcullen
Chairman and CEO
IDG Books Worldwide, Inc.

Steven Berkowitz
President and Publisher
IDG Books Worldwide, Inc.

*Eighth Annual Computer Press Awards 1992*

*Ninth Annual Computer Press Awards 1993*

*Tenth Annual Computer Press Awards 1994*

*Eleventh Annual Computer Press Awards 1995*

IDG is the world's leading IT media, research and exposition company. Founded in 1964, IDG had 1997 revenues of $2.05 billion and has more than 9,000 employees worldwide. IDG offers the widest range of media options that reach IT buyers in 75 countries representing 95% of worldwide IT spending. IDG's diverse product and services portfolio spans six key areas including print publishing, online publishing, expositions and conferences, market research, education and training, and global marketing services. More than 90 million people read one or more of IDG's 290 magazines and newspapers, including IDG's leading global brands — Computerworld, PC World, Network World, Macworld and the Channel World family of publications. IDG Books Worldwide is one of the fastest-growing computer book publishers in the world, with more than 700 titles in 36 languages. The "...For Dummies®" series alone has more than 50 million copies in print. IDG offers online users the largest network of technology-specific Web sites around the world through IDG.net (http://www.idg.net), which comprises more than 225 targeted Web sites in 55 countries worldwide. International Data Corporation (IDC) is the world's largest provider of information technology data, analysis and consulting, with research centers in over 41 countries and more than 400 research analysts worldwide. IDG World Expo is a leading producer of more than 168 globally branded conferences and expositions in 35 countries including E3 (Electronic Entertainment Expo), Macworld Expo, ComNet, Windows World Expo, ICE (Internet Commerce Expo), Agenda, DEMO, and Spotlight. IDG's training subsidiary, ExecuTrain, is the world's largest computer training company, with more than 230 locations worldwide and 785 training courses. IDG Marketing Services helps industry-leading IT companies build international brand recognition by developing global integrated marketing programs via IDG's print, online and exposition products worldwide. Further information about the company can be found at www.idg.com.

1/24/99

## Credits

*Acquisitions Editor*
Andy Cummings

*Development Editors*
Ellen Dendy, Chip Wescott,
Grace Wong, Kenyon Brown

*Technical Editor*
Ross Taylor

*Copy Editors*
Timothy J. Borek, Don St. John

*Book Designers*
Daniel Ziegler Design, Cátálin Dulfu,
Kurt Krames

*Production*
IDG Books Worldwide Production

*Proofreading and Indexing*
York Production Services

## About the Author

**Jennifer Alspach** is a nationally known artist and author. Her other books include *Illustrator Filter Finesse* (Random House), *Photoshop and Illustrator Studio Secrets* (IDG Books Worldwide), and *Illustrator Complete* (Hayden Books).

*To Dakota Kasey Alspach,*
*who inspired me throughout the writing of this book.*

# Welcome to
# Teach Yourself

Welcome to *Teach Yourself*, a series read and trusted by millions for nearly a decade. Although you may have seen the *Teach Yourself* name on other books, ours is the original. In addition, no *Teach Yourself* series has ever delivered more on the promise of its name than this series. That's because IDG Books Worldwide recently transformed *Teach Yourself* into a new cutting-edge format that gives you all the information you need to learn quickly and easily.

Readers told us that they want to learn by doing and that they want to learn as much as they can in as short a time as possible. We listened to you and believe that our new task-by-task format and suite of learning tools deliver the book you need to successfully teach yourself any technology topic. Features such as our Personal Workbook, which lets you practice and reinforce the skills you've just learned, help ensure that you get full value out of the time you invest in your learning. Handy cross-references to related topics and online sites broaden your knowledge and give you control over the kind of information you want, when you want it.

## More Answers . . .

In designing the latest incarnation of this series, we started with the premise that people like you, who are beginning to intermediate computer users, want to take control of their own learning. To do this, you need the proper tools to find answers to questions so that you can solve problems now.

In designing a series of books that provide such tools, we created a unique and concise visual format. The added bonus: *Teach Yourself* books actually pack more information into their pages than other books written on the same subjects. Skill for skill, you typically get much more information in a *Teach Yourself* book. In fact, *Teach Yourself* books, on average, cover twice the skills covered by other computer books — as many as 125 skills per book — so they're more likely to address your specific needs.

## ...In Less Time

We know you don't want to spend twice the time to get all this great information, so we provide lots of timesaving features:

▶ A modular task-by-task organization of information: Any task you want to perform is easy to find and includes simple-to-follow steps.

▶ A larger size than standard makes the book easy to read and convenient to use at a computer workstation. The large format also enables us to include many more illustrations — 500 screen illustrations show you how to get everything done!

▶ A Personal Workbook at the end of each chapter reinforces learning with extra practice, real-world applications for your learning, and questions and answers to test your knowledge.

▶ Cross-references appearing at the bottom of each task page refer you to related information, providing a path through the book for learning particular aspects of the software thoroughly.

▶ A Find It Online feature offers valuable ideas on where to go on the Internet to get more information or to download useful files.

▶ Take Note sidebars provide added-value information from our expert authors for more in-depth learning.

▶ An attractive, consistent organization of information helps you quickly find and learn the skills you need.

These *Teach Yourself* features are designed to help you learn the essential skills about a technology in the least amount of time, with the most benefit. We've placed these features consistently throughout the book, so you quickly learn where to go to find just the information you need — whether you work through the book from cover to cover or use it later to solve a new problem.

You will find a *Teach Yourself* book on almost any technology subject — from the Internet to Windows to Microsoft Office. Take control of your learning today, with IDG Books Worldwide's *Teach Yourself* series.

# Teach Yourself
## More Answers in Less Time

Go to this area if you want special tips, cautions, and notes that provide added insight into the current task.

Search through the task headings to find the topic you want right away. To learn a new skill, search the contents, chapter opener, or the extensive index to find what you need. Then find — at a glance — the clear task heading that matches it.

## Using the Pencil Tool and Other Options

The pencil is considered to be a painting tool even though it paints a hard-edged line that is visibly aliased. Use the pencil whenever you want a coarser look. All the brush sizes, painting modes, and opacity options apply, just as they do with the Paintbrush and Airbrush. Set the Fade and Stylus Pressure options for the pencil by double-clicking the pencil icon, just as you did for the Paintbrush and Airbrush.

We like to use the Pencil tool in Quick Mask mode to really tighten up selections. To switch to Quick Mask mode, click the icon, or press the letter Q. Zoom in on your selection. You can tighten up a selection border by using the Pencil tool to paint in pixels. If you make a mistake and go outside of your border simply press the X key (which toggles between foreground and background colors) and paint out that spot. Many times we use the Quick Mask mode to make the whole selection. You can change the Brush size to get the rough outline, then use a smaller brush to paint in the edge in Quick Mask mode. If you create a soft-edged brush you can get the feathered soft-edge mask. If you forget, you can always choose Feather from the Select menu.

Some of the other painting options we haven't mentioned yet are Airbrush and Eyedropper. Use the Airbrush for soft retouching effects, especially when colorizing grayscale drawings and photographs. The Airbrush paints a soft spray of color that is unequaled

for hazy glows and sheer overlays of hue. For some realism, use a pressure sensitive digitizing tablet.

The Eyedropper tool is fabulously helpful when working on any number of projects in Photoshop. It makes it easy to "grab" hard-to-mix colors from an existing document and very simple to match a specific color in a logo or other corporate identification. As well, the Eyedropper can be useful in straight-up manipulations. When you're smoothing a cheek, say. Or unruffling feathers.

Unlike the Paintbrush, with the Airbrush, paint builds up when you continue to hold it in one place and press the mouse button. It "puddles" just as a real airbrush does. You set Brush Options for the Airbrush as you do for the Paintbrush in the Brush palette. The Airbrush Options (Fade, Stylus Pressure: Color and Pressure) are the same as the Paintbrush. What is called opacity (on the Brushes palette) is called pressure when the Airbrush tool is active. Increasing pressure increases the darkness of the stroke.

Learn the concepts behind the task at hand and, more important, learn how the task is relevant in the real world. Timesaving suggestions and advice show you how to make the most of each skill.

> **TAKE NOTE**
>
> ### MAKING STRAIGHT LINES WITH THE PENCIL
>
> You can make a straight line using the Pencil tool by pressing the Shift key as you drag out a line. The Shift key constrains the line to 0 or 90 degrees.

After you learn the task at hand, you may have more questions, or you may want to read about other tasks related to the topic. Use the cross-references to find different tasks to make your learning more efficient.

**CROSS-REFERENCE**
For more on Quick Mask, see Chapter 3.

196

**FIND IT ONLINE**
Take a look here for some great Photoshop techniques:
http://www.pixelfoundry.com//techniques.

Use the Find It Online element to locate Internet resources that provide more background, take you on interesting side trips, and offer additional tools for mastering and using the skills you need. (Occasionally you'll find a handy shortcut here.)

# Welcome to Teach Yourself

The current chapter name and number always appear in the top right-hand corner of every task spread, so you always know exactly where you are in the book.

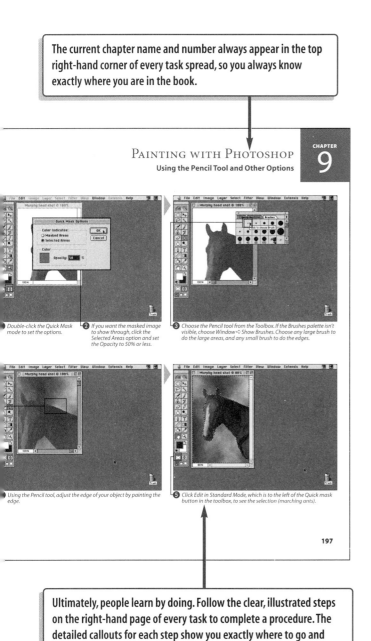

Painting with Photoshop
Using the Pencil Tool and Other Options

CHAPTER
9

① Double-click the Quick Mask mode to set the options.

② If you want the masked image to show through, click the Selected Areas option and set the Opacity to 50% or less.

③ Choose the Pencil tool from the Toolbox. If the Brushes palette isn't visible, choose Window ➪ Show Brushes. Choose any large brush to do the large areas, and any small brush to do the edges.

④ Using the Pencil tool, adjust the edge of your object by painting the edge.

⑤ Click Edit in Standard Mode, which is to the left of the Quick mask button in the toolbox, to see the selection (marching ants).

197

Ultimately, people learn by doing. Follow the clear, illustrated steps on the right-hand page of every task to complete a procedure. The detailed callouts for each step show you exactly where to go and what to do to complete the task.

## Who This Book Is For

This book is written for you, a beginning to intermediate PC user who isn't afraid to take charge of his or her own learning experience. You don't want a lot of technical jargon; you *do* want to learn as much about PC technology as you can in a limited amount of time. You need a book that is straightforward, easy to follow, and logically organized, so you can find answers to your questions easily. And, you appreciate simple-to-use tools such as handy cross-references and visual step-by-step procedures that help you make the most of your learning. We have created the unique *Teach Yourself* format specifically to meet your needs.

# Personal Workbook

It's a well-known fact that much of what we learn is lost soon after we learn it if we don't reinforce our newly acquired skills with practice and repetition. That's why each *Teach Yourself* chapter ends with your own Personal Workbook. Here's where you can get extra practice, test your knowledge, and discover ideas for using what you've learned in the real world. There's even a Visual Quiz to help you remember your way around the topic's software environment.

## Feedback

Please let us know what you think about this book, and whether you have any suggestions for improvements. You can send questions and comments to the *Teach Yourself* editors on the IDG Books Worldwide Web site at **www.idgbooks.com**.

---

> **Personal Workbook**
>
> **Q&A**
>
> **1** Name the Pen tools.
>
> _____
> _____
> _____
>
> **2** How can you add an anchor point where there wasn't one before?
>
> _____
> _____
> _____
>
> **3** What does the Magnetic Pen do?
>
> _____
> _____
> _____
>
> **4** What is a *path*?
>
> _____
> _____
> _____
>
> **5** Which gives you more saving options, saving with Paths, or saving selections as Alpha channels?
>
> _____
> _____
> _____
>
> **6** What is a *clipping path*?
>
> _____
> _____
> _____
>
> **7** Why would you use a clipping path?
>
> _____
> _____
> _____
>
> **8** What is a *clipping group*?
>
> _____
> _____
> _____
>
> ANSWERS: PAGE 339
>
> 216

After working through the tasks in each chapter, you can test your progress and reinforce your learning by answering the questions in the Q&A section. Then check your answers in the Personal Workbook Answers appendix at the back of the book.

Another practical way to reinforce your skills is to do additional exercises on the same skills you just learned without the benefit of the chapter's visual steps. If you struggle with any of these exercises, it's a good idea to refer to the chapter's tasks to be sure you've mastered them.

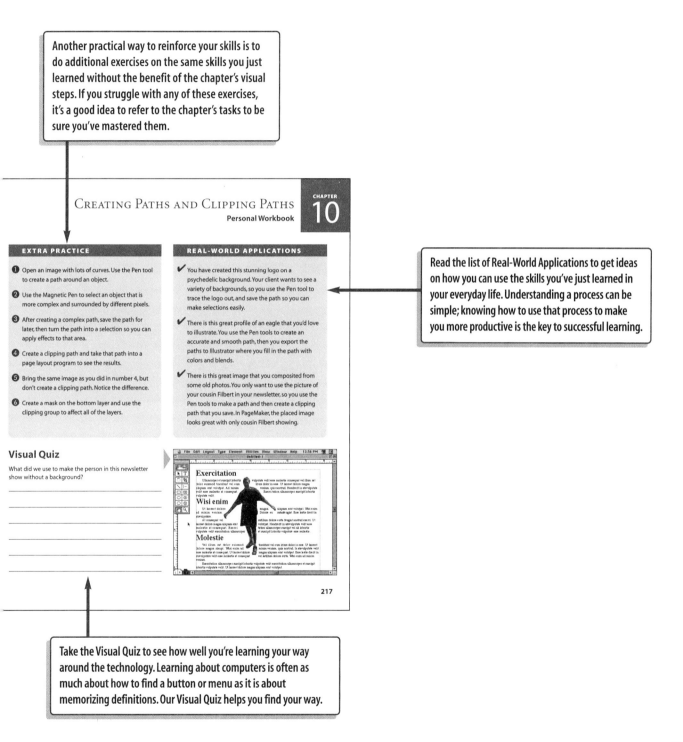

## Creating Paths and Clipping Paths
### Personal Workbook
**CHAPTER 10**

### EXTRA PRACTICE

① Open an image with lots of curves. Use the Pen tool to create a path around an object.

② Use the Magnetic Pen to select an object that is more complex and surrounded by different pixels.

③ After creating a complex path, save the path for later, then turn the path into a selection so you can apply effects to that area.

④ Create a clipping path and take that path into a page layout program to see the results.

⑤ Bring the same image as you did in number 4, but don't create a clipping path. Notice the difference.

⑥ Create a mask on the bottom layer and use the clipping group to affect all of the layers.

### REAL-WORLD APPLICATIONS

✔ You have created this stunning logo on a psychedelic background. Your client wants to see a variety of backgrounds, so you use the Pen tool to trace the logo out, and save the path so you can make selections easily.

✔ There is this great profile of an eagle that you'd love to illustrate. You use the Pen tools to create an accurate and smooth path, then you export the paths to Illustrator where you fill in the path with colors and blends.

✔ There is this great image that you composited from some old photos. You only want to use the picture of your cousin Filbert in your newsletter, so you use the Pen tools to make a path and then create a clipping path that you save. In PageMaker, the placed image looks great with only cousin Filbert showing.

Read the list of Real-World Applications to get ideas on how you can use the skills you've just learned in your everyday life. Understanding a process can be simple; knowing how to use that process to make you more productive is the key to successful learning.

### Visual Quiz

What did we use to make the person in this newsletter show without a background?

_____

_____

_____

_____

_____

_____

217

Take the Visual Quiz to see how well you're learning your way around the technology. Learning about computers is often as much about how to find a button or menu as it is about memorizing definitions. Our Visual Quiz helps you find your way.

# Acknowledgments

So many people helped get this book out the door. First and foremost, Andy Cummings, Senior Acquisitions Editor at IDG Books Worldwide, has been there above and beyond the call of duty. Ellen Dendy, Development Editor, helped shape this book and bend the rules. Chip Wescott, Ken Brown, Grace Wong, Timothy Borek, Paul Winters, and Colleen Dowling all helped in their own way in completing this book.

Utmost thanks go to Ted Alspach, for his unwavering support and thoughtful comments, as well as keeping Gage under control while I worked. Thanks to Gage for being patient and letting me get work done while he played contentedly by himself.

Ross Taylor gets many, many thanks for his great technical editing.

Finally, thanks to the furry group for their unwavering support: Linus, Toulouse, Pyro, Static, Sage, Yote, and Murphy.

# Contents

# CONTENTS

# CONTENTS

# CONTENTS

# CONTENTS

# CONTENTS

# Teach Yourself®
# Photoshop® 5
# and 5.5

# PART

## I

# Getting Started

# CHAPTER 1

**MASTER THESE SKILLS**

# Basics of Photoshop

As with any program, after you get past the basics, the rest comes easy. Photoshop provides windows, menus, palettes, and tools. In this chapter, we go over the Photoshop environment, using the pull-down menus, accessing palettes, and handling tools. When you get comfortable in the Photoshop environment, you'll increase your productivity tenfold. The next step in learning Photoshop is opening and saving files. Basic navigation of files on your computer is a breeze after you understand how you have filed your images.

The Photoshop window holds a few secrets that you may miss if you're not looking. You can easily access some great shortcuts and quick references from the window itself. The menu bar at the top of your screen is self-explanatory. By clicking and dragging your mouse to a function, you activate that function. The free-floating palettes are great to work with. They are palettes that you can open from the Window pull-down menu. You can move them around your screen at will. Using the tabbed names at the top, you can arrange and rearrange your palettes to your liking.

While opening a document may seem pretty basic, you can access an image from many different places. For instance, you can access an image from a CD-ROM, Zip cartridge, Jaz cartridge, floppy disk, optical drive, your hard drive, and so on. The same principal goes for saving an image. You can save a document to any of the previously mentioned devices and more. To go a step further, you can save a document not only to many different devices but also in many different formats as well. You need to be aware of difficulties when saving and opening a file from a Macintosh on a Windows system. The issues are largely due to the Windows system requiring a correct dot extension. On a Macintosh, you can pretty much open any file with or without a dot extension.

Every program includes a help feature. Photoshop's Help feature is found in the pull-down menu at the top of your screen. Every user, from beginner to the advanced, will access the Help features at some time in their use of Photoshop. Many of us use Help on a regular basis. If you press the help key on your keyboard, you access the Help feature.

# Understanding the Photoshop Window

When you open an image in Photoshop, it opens in a window that holds lots of information. The little square in the upper-left corner enables you to close the file with one click. The square at the far upper-right corner minimizes and maximizes your window. Another square opens the window to fit the image. If you click it, a second time, the window goes back to the original size. You can also drag the lower-right corner to resize the window. If the image is larger than your window, you see scroll bars to the right and bottom of the image. A quick way to move about your image is to press the spacebar, which accesses the Hand tool so you can drag to any area in your image.

The lower left-hand corner of an open window lets you know the percentage of your file as you view it, as well as the size of your open file in kilobytes (KB). Also shown in the box is the size the file will be when saved in compressed format. A pop-up menu is available that enables you to choose from actual document size or scratch size (the amount of memory or disk space that Photoshop needs to maintain both the file and copies needed to undo actions). Hold down the Option (Alt) key while you click the File Size box to see this display. It tells you the following: the height and width of the file, the number of channels the file contains, the mode (color or grayscale),

and the resolution of the image in pixels per inch. If you wish to see the height and width displayed in inches or centimeters, change the units in the Info palette (under the pop-up menu attached to the x, y box) or in the Preferences: Units submenu under the File menu.

Photoshop enables you to embed special file information (File Info) into any Photoshop, EPS, JPEG, PDF, or TIFF file on the PC. On the Mac you can embed it into any format.

**CROSS-REFERENCE**

For more on saving a document, see Chapter 2.

**FIND IT ONLINE**

You can find information about the Newspaper Association of America's standards at **http://www.naa.org/technology/standards/crest.pdf.**

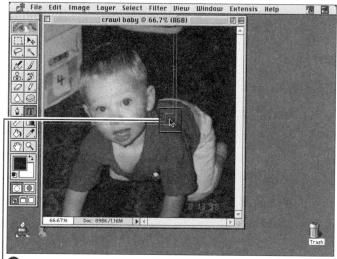

**1** Resize the window of your open document by dragging the lower-right corner of the window inward or outward.

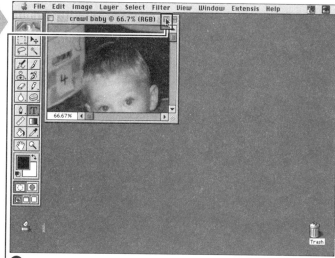

**2** Click the Zoom box (the inner square on the upper-right corner of your window).

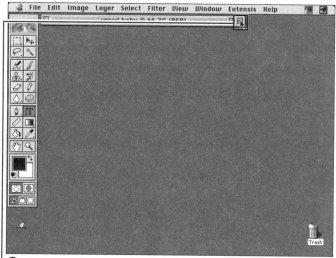

**3** Click the Collapse box (the outer square on the upper-right corner of your window) to reduce the image to just the title bar.

■ To get the image back, click the title bar.

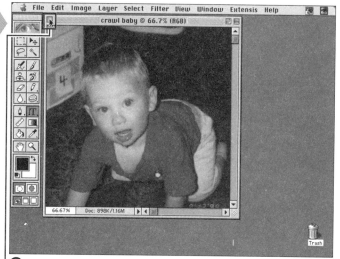

**4** Click the Close box found in the upper-left corner of your window.

# Working with Palettes

Photoshop has quite a number of palettes to access. You can access the palettes from the Windows pull-down menu. Lines separate groups of palettes in twos or threes. That means if you view one of the two or three palettes, the others are there and visible when you click their tabs. You can click the tab to view a hidden palette, or you can use the pull-down menu to access the palette you want.

The tabbed palettes are easy to use. You can click, hold, and drag a tabbed palette away from the group to stand alone. This is great, especially if you use only that one palette and are short on monitor space. The window surrounding the palette is very similar to the image window. You have a Close box in the upper-left corner, a Minimize/Maximize box in the upper-right corner, and a Resize box in the lower-right corner. If the palette is large and you have resized the window small, you see a scroll bar to access the hidden areas. If you click and hold the top bar of the palette's window, you can move the window anywhere on your screen.

The tabbed palettes can also be arranged or rearranged to your liking. You can click and drag a tab to move it away from the group. Then you can drag other palettes into a new grouping to customize your own palettes. You actually can combine all the palettes into one, but we wouldn't advise that unless you have a huge screen. To combine a palette with another, click and drag the tab of the palette you want to move into the window of the palette with which you want to combine. If you look closely, you'll see a black rectangle indicating that you are combining the dragged palette into another one. Don't release your mouse button until you see this rectangle, to ensure that you are combining with that palette. If you release your mouse button when the rectangle is not lit, fear not; it will only separate that dragged palette by itself. You then can redrag until you combine the palettes you wish.

## TAKE NOTE

### ▶ TRASHING PHOTOSHOP'S PREFERENCES

Another way to reset your palettes, as well as all of Photoshop's settings, back to default is to throw out Photoshop's preferences file. A quick way to find the file to throw it out is to do a Find for Adobe Photoshop 5 Prefs. Then, you can drag the file to the trash and remember to empty trash. Before you do any of this, you must first shut down Photoshop.

### ▶ RESETTING YOUR PALETTES

Now that you have learned the trick of combining and rearranging palettes, you probably are wondering how to get them back to their original states. In the General Preferences dialog box, you can click the button Reset Palettes Locations to Default, and the palettes automatically revert to their original positions.

### CROSS-REFERENCE

For more on Preferences see Chapter 2.

### FIND IT ONLINE

Use Windows more effectively. Check out the tips and tricks at **http://www.winplanet.com**.

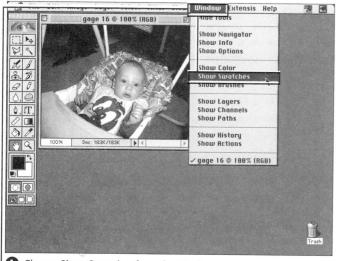

❶ *Choose Show Swatches from the Window menu.*

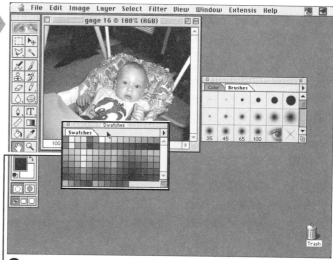

❷ *Click and drag the Swatches palette's tab away from the group. Release the mouse button to separate the palette.*

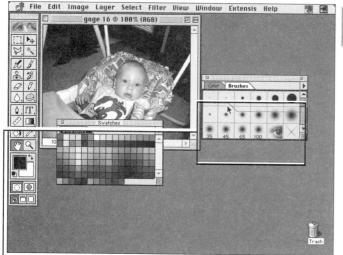

❸ *To rejoin the palette with the group or any other group, click and drag the tab to the other palette. You'll see a darker outline around the other palette when you are joining.*

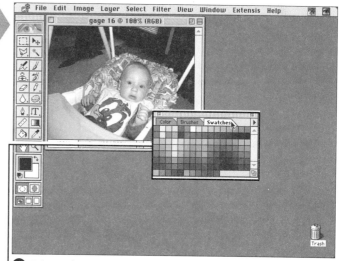

❹ *Release the mouse button, and they'll be grouped together.*

# What's in the Toolbox

That nifty-looking box on the left of your monitor is called a *toolbox*. Photoshop has grouped tools together and organized them to remain consistent with some of Adobe's other programs such as Illustrator and PageMaker. The lines between tool groupings separate the tools by function. At the very top of the toolbox is the Photoshop eye logo. If you click that logo, you activate the Adobe Online window, where you can choose from Update, Configure, or Close. You must be logged on to the Internet to access this feature.

The first four tools you see at the top of the toolbox are the Selection and Move tools. You can make selections using the Marquee, Lasso, or Magic Wand tools. With the Rectangular Marquee tool, you can access the Elliptical Marquee, Single Row Marquee, Single Column Marquee, and the Crop tools. With the Lasso tool, you'll find the Polygonal Lasso and the Magnetic Lasso tools.

The next grouping of tools are what we call the painting and editing tools. In this group you have the Airbrush, Paintbrush, Rubber Stamp, History Brush, Eraser, Pencil, Blur, and Toning tools. With the Rubber Stamp tool is the Pattern Stamp tool. The Pencil tool is grouped with the Line tool. The Blur tool has its partner Sharpen tool. Finally the three toning tools are the Dodge, Burn, and Sponge tools. The Dodge tool is by default the one you see in the toolbox.

The next grouping of tools is a mishmash of tools that just don't fit anywhere else. You have the Pen tool, which houses the Magnetic Pen, Freeform Pen, Add Anchor Point, Delete Anchor Point, Direct Selection, and Convert Point tools. The Type tool includes the Type Mask, Vertical Type, and Vertical Type Mask tools. The Measure tool stands alone. The Linear Gradient tool includes the Radial Gradient, Angle Gradient, Reflected Gradient, and the Diamond Gradient tools. The Paintbucket and Eyedropper tools round off that grouped section. The Eyedropper houses the Color Sampler tool. The bottom two tools are the Hand and the Zoom tools.

Underneath the main tools are the *swatches*. The default black swatch is the foreground swatch and the white one is the background swatch. The arrow in the upper right switches foreground and background colors. The small swatches in the lower left will return the main swatches to the default colors.

The next area is the Quick Mask area. The square on the left is the Edit in Standard Mode. The right square is Edit in Quick Mask Mode. The last area of the toolbox is viewing. The left square is for standard viewing with menus and palettes. The middle is for viewing full screen with a gray background (instead of your desktop) and a menu bar. The right square is for full screen with a black background and no menu bar. To hide your palettes and toolbox, press the Tab key. Press Tab again to view the palettes and toolbox.

## TAKE NOTE

### ▶ ACCESSING THE POP-UP TOOLS FROM THE TOOLBAR

You'll notice that on some of the tools you can see a small arrow in the lower-right corner. That indicates that there are more pop-up tools grouped with that particular tool. To access the other tools, click and hold the tool and then drag over to the tool you wish to use. That new tool will appear in the main toolbox.

**①** *Click and hold the Lasso tool to see the pop-up tools. Drag over to the Magnetic Lasso.*

**②** *Let up with your mouse to place the Magnetic Lasso in the toolbox.*

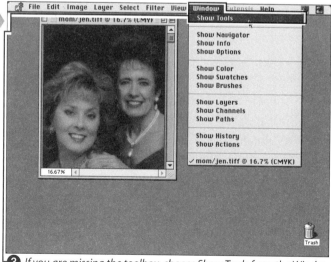

**③** *If you are missing the toolbox, choose Show Tools from the Window menu.*

# Making the Most of the Help Features

Every computer program out there has some sort of Help feature. Many users ignore this extremely useful feature. You can access the Help menu either from your keyboard (Help key on the Mac) or from the Help pull-down menu at the top of your screen.

If you press the Help button of your Mac keyboard, you'll access three tabbed areas: Contents, Index, and Find. The Contents area lets you view topics in terms of books. You can click a book and see more of the available subtopics inside. When using the Index tab, you'll find topics listed in detail and alphabetical order. The Find tab is our favorite. If you don't know exactly what you are looking for, you can type in the general idea, and the relevant topics are displayed below. To read the topic, you click it to highlight and then choose Display. You can not only look up stuff using different methods but also easily print out any information that you display.

If you access the Help pull-down menu, you'll find Balloon Help, Help Contents, Keyboard, How to Use Help, Export Transparent, and Resize Image. The Balloon Help only pops up descriptions of items over which you position your cursor . We don't find this particularly helpful, and it is a tad annoying after a while. With the Keyboard choice, you can either access a Quick Reference or type in a keyword to get information on a topic.

Let's say that you have questions about printing your Photoshop file. First, access the Help feature with your keyboard or the Help pull-down menu. Go to the Find tab, type in Print, and then choose Search. As you can see, you can choose from many topics. If this method is too daunting, you may want to check out the Contents topics and choose the Printing book. Here, you'll find fewer choices and more direct options from which to choose.

Another area you'll want to check out if you have Internet access is Adobe's Web site. You'll find not only useful information on all Adobe products but also tips, hints, art, and step-by-step help on many topics. At this Web site, you can access a trial version of Photoshop 5, read about its features, register Photoshop, check out tips, view the gallery, and read frequently asked questions and answers.

## TAKE NOTE

### WHEN HELP JUST ISN'T ENOUGH

If the Help features aren't enough, access Adobe's online help by clicking the Adobe icon. Of course, you must have Internet access to use this helpful feature. The Adobe Online help updates you with any new information and helpful Web sites when you click the Update button.

## CROSS-REFERENCE

For more on using the menus, see the later part of this chapter.

## FIND IT ONLINE

To access Photoshop tips, tricks, and more, visit http://www.adobe.com/prodindex/photoshop/main.html.

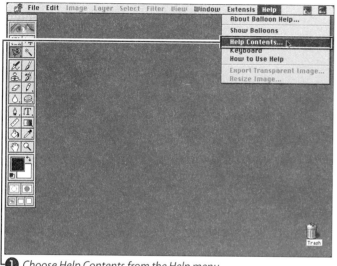

① Choose Help Contents from the Help menu.

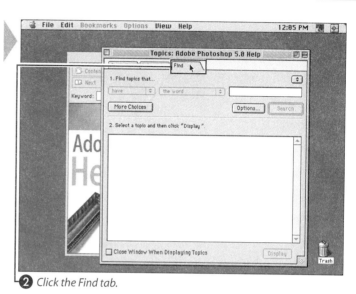

② Click the Find tab.

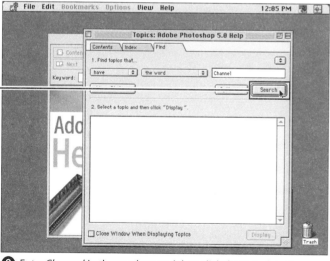

③ Enter Channel in the text box, and then click the Search button.

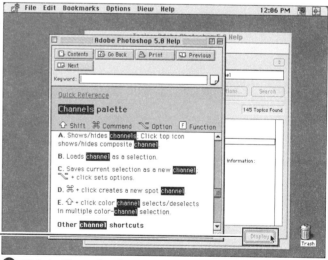

④ Click the Channels palette topic, and then click the Display button to read about the Channels palette.

# Managing with Color

Color is one of the more confusing topics in Photoshop. You will find multiple color modes from which to choose. Also, you should use certain color modes for different outcomes on your image. Whether you output to a printer or to a Web page, you need to know what is what when using Color.

Chapter 2 discusses color modes in full, but here we just introduce them. In order from the Image/Mode pull-down menu are Bitmap, Grayscale, Duotone, Indexed Color, RGB Color, CMYK Color, Lab Color, and Multichannel. Bitmapped mode displays only black and white pixels. Grayscale mode displays 256 tones of black. Duotone mode is used with a grayscale image and one other ink color. Indexed Color mode is used for Web images. RGB color displays 256 tones of red, 256 tones of green, and 256 tones of blue. CMYK mode displays 256 tones of cyan, 256 tones of magenta, 256 tones of yellow, and 256 tones of black. Lab Color mode is used for color separations, and Multichannel is used for grayscale images with 2 or more inks.

In addition to color modes, you have color that you use in your image, monitor, and printer color options. All monitors display colors in RGB mode, even if you have chosen CMYK as your image's mode, the monitor can only show colors in RGB. Printers print in CMYK or spot colors. In other words, what you see on your screen isn't what you'll actually get from the printer.

When applying color to your image you can use the Swatches palette or the Color Picker. Within the Color picker lies even more choices to apply color. You can enter a color by entering a number in the HSB, RGB, Lab, or CMYK areas. You can wing it by dragging the color slider bar to the approximate color then dragging the circle within the main swatch. Another option is to click the Custom button to access a slew of color tables. You can choose from ANPA Color, DIC Color Guide, FOCOLTONE, PANTONE Coated, PANTONE Process, PANTONE ProSim, PANTONE Uncoated, TOYO Color Finder, and TRUMATCH. Choosing the color is only the start. Once you choose a color or create your own, you can add that color to your Swatches palette and fill or paint with your chosen color.

## TAKE NOTE

### COPYING AND PASTING DIFFERENT MODES

When you copy and paste an RGB image into a CMYK image, the RGB image converts to CMYK. Whatever you are pasting into becomes the color mode regardless of what it was initially.

### GRAYSCALE MODE

When you copy a grayscale image into a color image, it won't miraculously get color. A grayscale image pasted into a color image remains grayscale.

### CROSS-REFERENCE

For more on managing your colors see Chapter 15.

### FIND IT ONLINE

For more on Digital images and color, see **http://www. electroimage.com/imgtut.htm.**

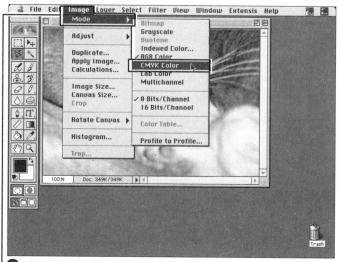

**1** *Choose Image ➪ Mode ➪ CMYK Color.*

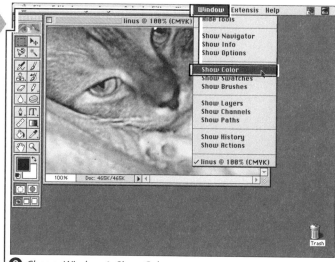

**2** *Choose Window ➪ Show Color.*

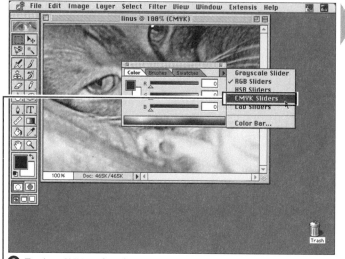

**3** *To view CMYK color, choose CMYK sliders from the Color palette's pop-up menu.*

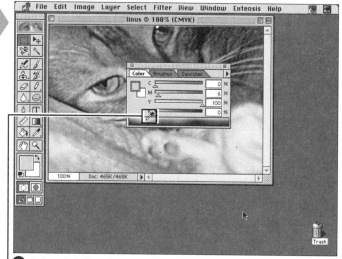

**4** *Either click the color you want at the bottom of the palette or enter the numbers.*

# Using the Menus

The pull-down menus are the source of everything in Photoshop. Below, we list only some of the menu commands to give you an idea of what is available. We suggest that you get familiar with what is where in the pull-down menus on your own and then learn the keyboard shortcuts. They will make your life much easier. Every task in Photoshop is found somewhere under the pull-down menus.

**File.** The File menu holds filing functions and basic commands in Photoshop. This is where you'll start and end in Photoshop. The File menu is where you'll first open a file, save a file, and possibly print a file.

**Edit.** The Edit menu is where you can use editing functions on your image.

**Image.** The Image menu lets you change and adjust the whole or just part of your image. This is where you clean up those crusty images and fine-tune your scanned images.

**Layer.** The Layer menu applies to layers in your file. Layers let you work with ease by making some parts of your image separate from other parts. This way you can apply filters or effects to certain sections of your image without having to make tedious selections.

**Select.** This menu is where you access different options for your selection. Use Select to enclose only small portions or a certain color so you can adjust or apply a filter or any effect to just that area.

**Filter.** The Filter menu holds the cool effects that you can apply to the whole or just part of your image. The filters used on a regular basis are Blur or Sharpen to clarify or soften your image.

**View.** The View menu is where you can choose how to view your image.

**Window.** The Window menu is where you find the palettes and tools.

**Help.** The Help menu includes the commands Hide/Show Balloons, Help Contents, Keyboard, How to Use Help, and so on.

**CROSS-REFERENCE**

For information on automating those tedious Photoshop tasks, see Chapter 13.

**FIND IT ONLINE**

To make those menus stay when you click them, see http://macworld.zdnet.com/cgi-bin/software.pl/ Utilities/Software.221.html.

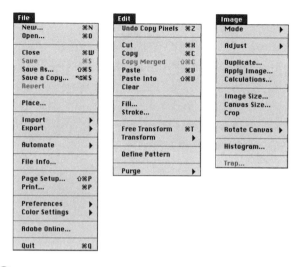

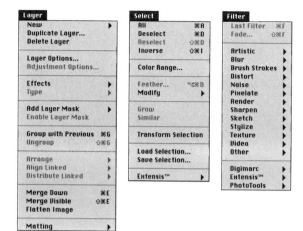

**①** *Open the File menu to view options.*
*Review the options in the other pull-down menus*

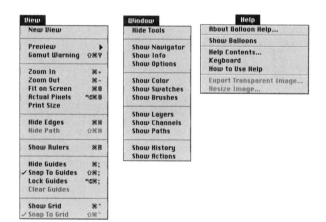

# Opening a Document

Now that you have installed Photoshop, you probably want to open an existing image to play with. You can open a document from the File menu by choosing Open. That seems pretty straightforward; there must be a catch. There's no catch; you just have to know how to get around your hard drive and where the image is that you want to open.

Photoshop will open many different file types from many different sources. You can open a file from Photoshop's samples, from a CD-ROM, from an external or internal hard drive, from the Web, and more. If you have a scanner attached, you can scan any image or photo.

Files saved in the following formats can be opened in Photoshop 5.0: Photoshop 4.0, Photoshop 3.0, Photoshop 2.5, Photoshop 2.0, Amiga IFF, BMP, EPS, Filmstrip, GIF, GIF89a, JPEG, MacPaint, PCX, PDF, PhotoCD, PICT File, PICT Resource, PIXAR, PixelPaint, PNG, Raw, Scitex CT, Targa, TIFF, and TWAIN-scanned files.

When you open a file using the File menu's Open command, you can see the file format by clicking a file you want to open. Some formats provide you a preview of the file to be opened.

Some scanners enable you to scan while running Photoshop, in which case the scanning software is reached using the Import command from the File menu. Import is also used to import files in other formats, including EPS files saved using JPEG compression, anti-aliased PICT files (created in programs such as MacDraw and Canvas), PICT Resources, and images to be scanned via the TWAIN interface. Video frame grabs are also brought into Photoshop using the Import command. To acquire a file using an import module:

▶ Select an Import module from the File menu.
▶ Depending upon your choice, you may be presented with a File Open box, a dialog box requesting additional information, or another screen specific to the module's manufacturer.

Files saved using Kodak's PhotoCD format can be opened using the Open command. A PhotoCD dialog box appears, giving you a choice of color mode and resolution. Select Lab Color if you plan to use the image for color separations. The RGB mode opens the file in RGB format, and the Grayscale mode removes the color information from the file.

## TAKE NOTE

### RAW FILES

Unless you are familiar with the file saved as Raw, don't use this as a choice to open an unfamiliar file. It may display the file as a bunch of static instead of your image.

**CROSS REFERENCE**

For more on file types, see Chapter 2.

**FIND IT ONLINE**

Visit http://www.metairieprinting.com/graphics.htm for information on importing images.

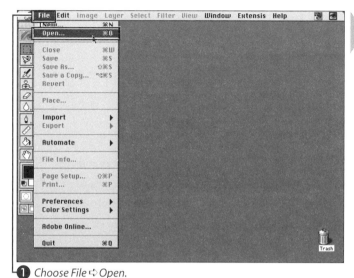

**1** Choose File ⇨ Open.

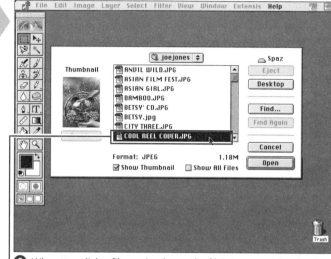

**2** When you click a file, you're shown the file's type as well as its size.

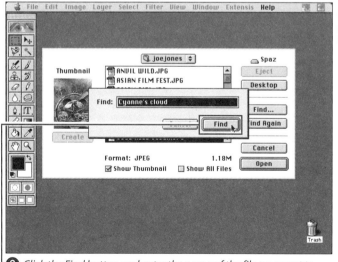

**3** Click the Find button and enter the name of the file you want to find.

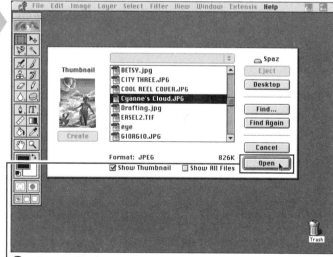

**4** When the file is located, click the Open button to open the file.

# Saving a Document

You can save a document using either the Save or the Save As command. The Save command saves a file in its existing format. In the case of a newly created file, the default is the native Photoshop format. Save As enables you to save a file in another format.

Photoshop's native format is not encoded, and it supports all the possible image modes listed under the Mode menu for the version of Photoshop you are using. You can also save *mask channels,* which are part of a document when you use this format. The disadvantage of this format is that many page layout and illustration programs do not support it, and it takes up a lot of space.

TIFF (Tagged-Image File Format) is a widely accepted format for desktop publishing. TIFF files can be reduced in size using *LZW (Lempel-Zif-Welch)* lossless compression, and they can be exported to many layout programs, including PageMaker and QuarkXPress. *Lossless* means that no data is lost when the file is compressed. TIFF enables you to save channels with the document.

Like TIFFs, PICT files can contain grayscale or full-color bitmapped images. PICTs can be exchanged between different programs and are perfect for many graphics applications, including drawing programs, multimedia, and video. Compressed PICT documents can be quite compact, especially when an image contains large areas filled with the same color. PICT files can be saved with mask channels when 32-bit/pixel resolution is selected, but not when JPEG compression is selected. PICT files won't print with the quality of resolution of a TIFF or EPS file.

Encapsulated PostScript files (EPS or EPSF) are a desktop publishing standard accepted by most illustration and layout programs. Many lines of coded commands create images saved in the EPS format. This is different from PICT and TIFF images, which are created in bitmapped form. An EPS file will be the largest file saved. You also need to include the actual EPS file with your page layout program file when sending your file to a printer. The EPS format lets you save each color as a file if you'd like. EPS files can be viewed in any layout program, it just makes the program run slower, so many opt to use a smaller, crustier preview with the EPS (JPEG preview).

## TAKE NOTE

### SAVING AS A TIFF
When saving your image as a TIFF, be sure to save on the appropriate platform. Or save as IBM/PC, which both the Mac and Windows platforms can open.

## CROSS-REFERENCE
For more on saving files for the Web, see Chapter 16.

## FIND IT ONLINE
Check out this printer's tips on sending files for output at http://www.donrayprinting.com/photoshop.htm.

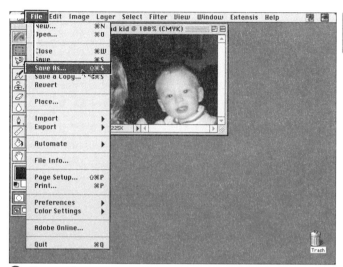

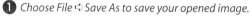

**1** Choose File ➪ Save As to save your opened image.

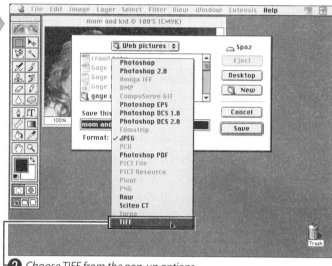

**2** Choose TIFF from the pop-up options.

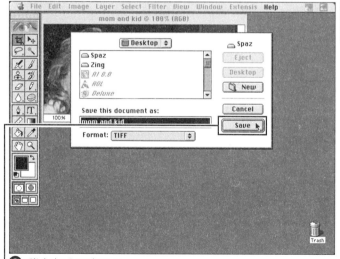

**3** Click the Save button.

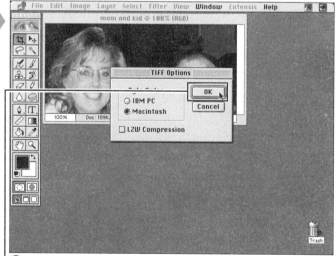

**4** Choose the platform on which you want to save your file (either IBM PC or Macintosh).

21

# Saving a Document

JPEG (Joint Photographic Experts Group) has become one of the most popular formats for use on the Web. In the JPEG format, undetectable amounts of data are dropped, resulting in a smaller file size. Although this is a sy method, the quantity of missing data is usually not noticeable and is actually less than the other popular hypertext format, GIF.

Grayscale, bitmapped, and indexed color images can be saved in the GIF (Graphics Interchange Format) format with resolution from 1 to 8 bits per pixel. GIF89a (found under File ➪ Export) lets you specify transparent areas in the file and enables you to save in RGB format. GIF89a also supports multi-frame images (GIF animation).

Windows system computers use PCX format. Many different Photoshop modes (including RGB, Grayscale, Bitmapped, Lab, and Indexed Color) can be saved in the PCX format.

The format for MacPaint files is used to transfer black-and-white (Bitmapped mode) images to other applications. Popular in the Macintosh world for moving graphics files between programs, this format can be especially useful for transferring files that have large areas of solid color. This can be helpful for archiving alpha channels stored in black and white.

The PNG format is a lossless compression method for use on the World Wide Web. Select Adam 7 for Interlace if you want the image to display gradual and increasing detail while being downloaded.

The raw files format is sometimes used when you want to save an image for use on a different computer platform. In this binary format, the file information consists of a stream of bytes. In each channel, pixel brightness is described on a scale of 0 to 255, with 0 as black and 255 as pure white.

## TAKE NOTE

### SAVING FOR THE WEB

When saving any file for Web use, first convert the mode to Indexed. If you choose Adaptive, your image adapts to the color options available on the computer displaying it.

### CHOOSING COMPRESSION IN JPEG

When JPEG is chosen, the dialog box asks you to decide the amount of image compression and the image quality. Notice that there is an inverse relationship between the two: the better the quality, the less the compression; the better the compression, the lower the quality. You can use JPEG files in layout programs, but the quality of the printout isn't as good as the TIFF or EPS.

**CROSS-REFERENCE**

For more on printing, see Chapter 15.

**FIND IT ONLINE**

For tips on getting your files ready for output, check out http://www.electric-pages.com/fenton/go2sb.htm.

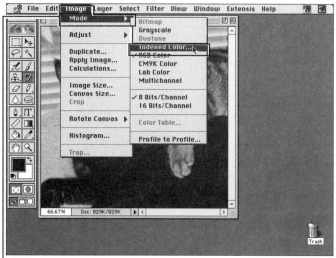

① Choose Image ➪ Mode ➪ Indexed Color.

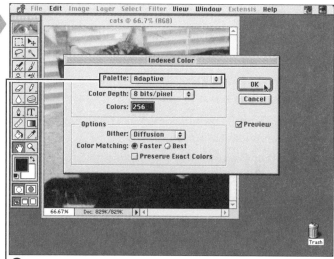

② Choose Adaptive from the pop-up menu and then click OK.

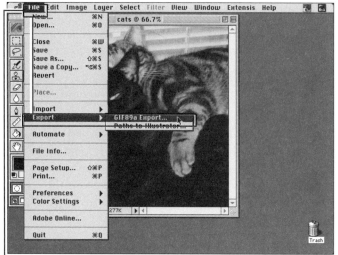

③ Choose File ➪ Export ➪ GIF89a Export.

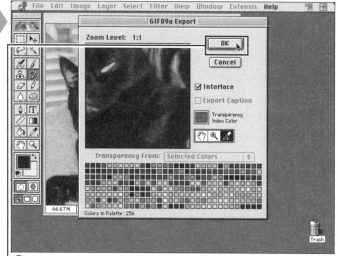

④ Click OK, then give the file another name and/or location if you wish, and then click Save.

# Navigating in Photoshop

The Navigator palette is one way to get around in Photoshop. You can click the Zoom In or Zoom Out button to move in or out from your image. You can also use the Zoom slider to drag in or out. In the numerical field in the lower left, you can enter your zoom number and then press Return (Enter) to activate it. When zoomed in close, you can drag the red rectangle to move yourself around your image without having to zoom out and in again.

By choosing Zoom In from the View menu, you can magnify your image at a predetermined amount. If you choose Fit On Screen, your image zooms out to fill your monitor's screen. The Actual Pixels option automatically takes you to 100% view. The Print Size option zooms out the image to the size at which it will print.

The Preview option found under the View menu lets you preview your RGB image in CMYK, or the individual Cyan, Magenta, Yellow, or Black channels. If your image is already CMYK, then this option isn't available.

The Rulers option lets you make accurate editing changes to your image in Photoshop. You set the ruler increments by choosing File ➪ Preferences ➪ Units & Rulers. You can change the Rulers origin by holding the upper-left corner between the horizontal and vertical rulers while dragging the origin to a new area. To reset the origin back to (0, 0), double-click in that same upper-left corner.

*Guides* are lines that you drag out to help you work with your image. These guide lines will not print. You can drag a guide from the Rulers. Click and hold either the horizontal or vertical ruler and drag down on your image to where you want a guide line. To change the color and style of the guide lines, choose File ➪ Preferences ➪ Guides & Grid. You also have the Snap to Guide and Clear Guides options .

The Grid option can be turned off or on from the View menu. The Grid, like the Guide, will not print. When you activate the Grid option, you also activate the Snap to Grid option. If you don't want your editing to snap to the grid, then simply uncheck this option under the View menu. You can change the color, style, and spacing of the grid in the File ➪ Preferences ➪ Guides & Grid.

## TAKE NOTE

### ▶ CHANGING GUIDE LINES ON THE FLY

To change a guide line from horizontal to vertical, press the Option (Alt) key while dragging your guide.

### ▶ HIDING EDGES AND PATHS

To see the results of a selection without seeing those annoying marching ants at the edges (the animated border), be sure to remember to Show Edges again or you can end up making adjustments to a selection and not know it. The Hide/Show Path will do the same thing as Hide/Show Edges except with paths. Turning off a path's edges makes working easier.

**CROSS REFERENCE**

For more on setting preferences for rulers and measuring, see Chapter 2.

**FIND IT ONLINE**

To check out using the Measure tool see http://designcafe.com.au/articles/11-6-98a/measure.htm.

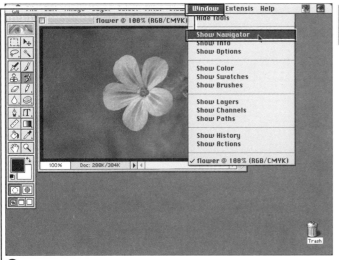

**1** *Choose Show Navigator from the Window menu.*

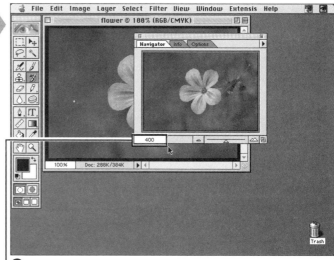

**2** *Enter the number 400 in the Zoom field.*

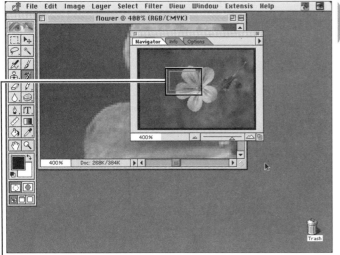

**3** *Press the Return (Enter) key to zoom in. Click and drag the rectangle in the Navigator palette to move around your image.*

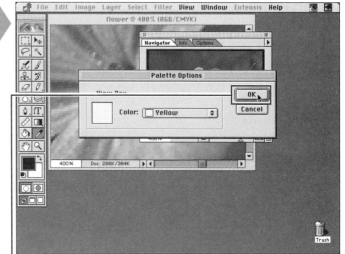

**4** *To change the color of the Navigator rectangle, choose Palette options from the Navigator pop-up menu. Choose a different color and then click OK.*

# Personal Workbook

## Q&A

**1** How do you separate a palette from its group?

_____

_____

_____

**2** How do you access the pop-up tools?

_____

_____

_____

**3** What color mode does a computer monitor display?

_____

_____

_____

**4** What is a quicker way to access some pull-down menu options?

_____

_____

_____

**5** What kind of files can Photoshop open?

_____

_____

_____

**6** How do you save a document for the Web?

_____

_____

_____

**7** What is the best way to save a document for a page-layout program?

_____

_____

_____

**8** How can you change the guide line color?

_____

_____

_____

ANSWERS: PAGE 333

## EXTRA PRACTICE

**1** Zoom in to your image 311.25% using the Zoom field at the bottom left of your image's window.

**2** Open all of the palettes and combine to create a palette of the palettes you use the most.

**3** Reset all of your tools and palettes back to their original places by choosing Reset Palette Locations to Default found in the General Preferences (Command+K [Ctrl+K in Windows]).

**4** Practice saving a file in different ways and compare the sizes.

**5** Open a file from the Open dialog box and use the Find button.

**6** Practice using Guides and Grids with the Snap feature on to move copied sections around your image.

## REAL-WORLD APPLICATIONS

✔ Use the Navigator to zoom in and move around your image easily. This greatly replaces the need to constantly zoom in and out to get around your image.

✔ You use certain palettes that aren't naturally grouped together. By dragging palettes from their groups, you create your ultimate palette that houses the main palettes you access.

✔ You need to save an image with multiple layers and also a flattened one for sending to the client. You save the original as a Photoshop file, and choose the Save a Copy option found under the File menu to save a flattened layered version for your client.

## Visual Quiz

How did we make this large all-encompassing palette, and how do we change it back?

_____

_____

_____

_____

_____

_____

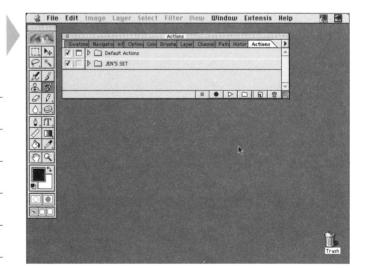

# CHAPTER 2

# Getting to Know the Photoshop Environment

This chapter addresses the nitty-gritty stuff. It may be a little harder to digest than other chapters, but it is crucial in order to get Photoshop to do what you want.

In this chapter, we cover the mystery of resolution and what it means to images. When you understand the basics of resolution, you'll be able to copy, paste, scan, resize, and more, and the printed image will turn out exactly as you want.

When you get familiar with Photoshop, you'll want to customize it to your own style. In the Preferences dialog box, you can set up Photoshop to be exactly the way you want it each time you launch the program.

Understanding basic Photoshop concepts and why the program does what it does helps in your use of the program. Here, you also learn to use Photoshop's pixel-based tools to manipulate your images and achieve amazing results.

You encounter three similar-sounding methods of measuring an image's density. The three work together to produce documents that display well onscreen and look good when printed: PPI is *pixels per inch,* the number of pixels in any given inch of a document. It also refers to the monitor's resolution and how the monitor represents he image onscreen. DPI is *dots per inch,* referring to the printer resolution. LPI refers to line frequency and stands for *lines per inch.* The numbers relate to the number of lines of cells in an inch of a halftone screen.

# Understanding Pixels

*ixel-based* programs (like Adobe Photoshop, Fractal Design's Painter, and Corel PhotoPaint) enable you to create pictures with minuscule dots called *pixels,* which are the smallest units of measurement on a computer screen. To transfer a photograph or drawing to the computer for image processing, it must first be digitized. That is, it must be turned into numerical data by a scanner. Only then can data be displayed as a large collection of pixels.

A pixel-based program lets you literally change an image one pixel at a time. This is great for retouching, creating natural textures, and representing the real objects in a photo-realistic manner.

*Vector-based* programs (such as Adobe Illustrator, Adobe FreeHand, and CorelDRAW) let you create images in a totally different manner. In vector-oriented/illustration programs, shapes and lines are made up of mathematical instructions rather than dots of color, so that they become solitary objects. In a sense, vector-oriented graphics are manipulated by changing the lines that make up the graphic. They are excellent for the creation of line illustrations and hard-edged text. A drawback of vector images is that they have a computer-drawn look and feel.

You can't properly retouch a photograph or create the same kind of subtle painterly effects using a vector-based program, like you can in Photoshop. Adobe's PostScript has become the universal language for the creation of these equation-drawn lines and shapes. For example, when you draw a shape in a vector-based program, you tell the computer its size, outline, and dimensions; whether or not it should have a border; and how thick the border should be, what color to use as a fill, and so on. Through PostScript, these instructions are coded into each object you create, so that you can move objects around on the screen, or copy and paste them into other documents without affecting them.

Each time you rotate or resize a selected Photoshop image (or portion of an image) you affect the picture quality on a pixel-by-pixel basis. For example, you add pixels when you enlarge an area and you take them away when you reduce. Repetitive enlarging and reducing has no effect on image quality in a vector-based program because there are no pixels to manipulate, just formulas. But it makes a big difference in Photoshop, and the cumulative results may not be what you desire.

## TAKE NOTE

### PIXEL OR VECTOR?

Both pixel programs and vector programs are excellent tools, each with specialized uses. You can use both programs together to achieve the best of both worlds. Use Illustrator to define the layout and determine the color, then use Photoshop to enhance, add light, texture, shadows, and more.

## CROSS-REFERENCE

For more on editing in Photoshop, see Chapter 6.

## FIND IT ONLINE

For neat design examples check out the firm at **http:// www.adobe.com/studio/artgallery/turntable/main. html**, which uses Adobe's programs in their work.

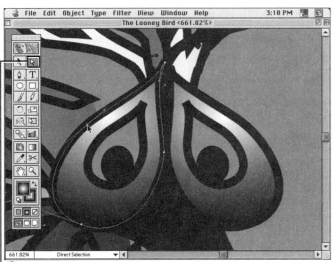

**①** *Open Adobe Illustrator. Open an Illustrator file, and then click the Zoom tool to see your image. When you choose the Arrow tool to edit the image you can see clearly that the image was created using points, lines, and direction handles rather than pixels.*

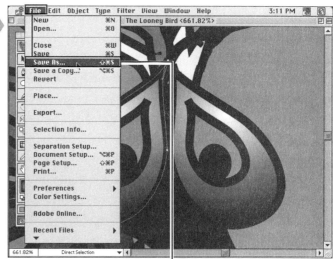

■ *We like to save the file with a different name so the original Illustrator file isn't altered.*

**②** *Save the Illustrator file by selecting File ⇨ Save As, and choosing a name.*

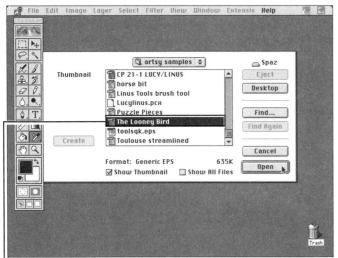

**③** *Open the Illustrator file in Photoshop by choosing File ⇨ Open and selecting its filename from the correct directory.*

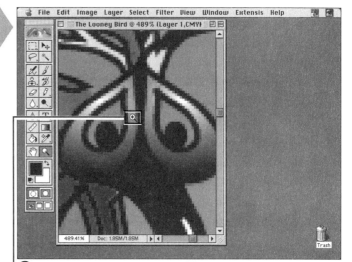

**④** *Select the Zoom tool from the palette, and then click the image to zoom in to see the individual pixels.*

■ *Notice the difference between the Illustrator file with its smooth lines and curves and the Photoshop file with its jagged edges.*

# Introduction to Color Modes

Photoshop supports a number of different color modes, some of which are covered in greater detail in later chapters. To take advantage of Photoshop's many tools, you must understand the program's four primary modes: Grayscale, RGB, CMYK, and Bitmapped.

In Photoshop's *Grayscale* mode, the picture is made up of 256 shades of gray, from pure white (255) to solid black (0). The median color in the grayscale spectrum has a value of 128. In the Grayscale mode, you can use all the painting and editing tools, including Photoshop's many plug-in filters.

Red, Green, and Blue, or *RGB*, is an additive color mode, which means that all colors of the spectrum can be created using red, green, and blue in varying degrees of brightness (*values*). Each of these component colors occupies its own channel. Typically you have 1-, 8-, or 24-bit color depths. Twenty-four-bit color lets you employ the most color information for each pixel. Because 24-bit color employs eight bits of information (256 possibilities) for each pixel component of red, green, and blue, 24-bit color gives you $256 \times 256 \times 256$ possibilities, or 16,772,216 colors, which should be enough for any one designer. Any of these 16.7 million colors can be represented with varying brightnesses of red, green, and blue in their respective channels. In each channel, 0 is the darkest value (black) and 255 is the lightest (white).

Just as the RGB mode has three channels, the *CMYK* mode has four channels: cyan, magenta, yellow, and black (K is the abbreviation for black in four-color printing, to avoid confusion with the B used to represent blue in the RGB model). CMYK colors represent the inks used in the four-color printing process; therefore, they are called *process colors*. Translating an image from the computer screen (RGB mode) to the printed page requires color separation, and RGB files must be converted into CMYK files before separations can be created.

In contrast to the grayscale and color modes, the *Bitmapped* mode offers only black and white pixels — no colors and no shades of gray. Although many wonderful effects can be obtained working in this mode, bitmapped files cannot be scaled, distorted, or treated with Photoshop's filters. To convert a color file to Bitmapped mode, it must first be converted to grayscale.

## TAKE NOTE

### COLOR AND NUMBERS

Two-hundred fifty-six is the number — you will see it repeatedly throughout Photoshop describing color and grayscale values. This is the maximum number of colors or grayscale pixels per channel. If you have more than one channel, as in RGB, you have $256 \times 3$ or 768 colors available in your image.

**CROSS-REFERENCE**

For more on changing color modes, see Chapter 7.

**FIND IT ONLINE**

Check out an artist at **http://www.adobe.com/studio/artgallery/smolan/main.html** who uses most of Adobe's products.

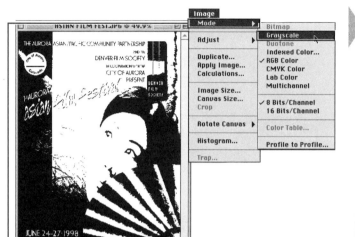

❶ Select Image ➪ Mode ➪ Grayscale to change it to Grayscale mode.

■ Open an RGB image.

❷ If you have layers, as this image does, you'll be asked if you want to flatten the layers or not. We chose to flatten. Flattening will put all layers on the background layer. Once you flatten an image, you can't put it back into the original layers.

❸ Select Image ➪ Mode ➪ Bitmap to change the grayscale image to bitmap.

■ Note that you can only convert a grayscale image to Bitmap mode.

❹ In the Bitmap dialog box, you have some choices. This figure shows the four available choices.

# Understanding Displayed versus Printed Color

Color is described differently on the computer than in print. On a computer, color is *additive*. In print, color is *subtractive*. This is an important distinction when designing on the computer, and we define these terms next.

Because the colors red, green, and blue (RGB) can be combined in different ways to make the colors we can see, they are called additive colors. When you watch TV or see lighting effects at a concert, you're experiencing the effects of additive color.

In elementary school you learned that red, yellow, and blue were primary colors, and when you combined them you got a muddy brown. But those were actually *primary pigments*, the components of paints or inks, which are completely different from the primary colors that make up the visible spectrum. When you describe light, which is how color is displayed onscreen, the primaries are red, green, and blue, as Isaac Newton discovered with a prism more than 300 years ago. Each visible color occupies a different position on the spectrum and has its own distinctive wavelength and frequency. When your eye sees all the colors of light together in equal intensity, the perception is white light. By the same token, when no light at all strikes the retina, we have the illusion that we're seeing black.

While additive colors deal with how colors display on your computer screen, subtractive colors form the basis of printing on paper. The pigments cyan, magenta, yellow, and black (CMYK) are combined in varying percentages to create the colors of the spectrum.

Back in elementary school, starting with a clean sheet of white paper, the more red, yellow, and blue paint you added, the darker and muddier the color became. Because combining these primary colors absorbs reflected light and creates the impression of black, they are called subtractive colors. Each additional color overlaid on paper subtracts from the amount of light that bounces back to your eye.

It's important to recognize the difference between these two color models, because here lies the challenge of converting what you see on your computer monitor (an additive model) to what you want to see on the printed page (a subtractive model). Photoshop gives you the techniques and tools to translate between these two basic color models, as you learn later in the chapter when you explore creating color separations for printing.

## TAKE NOTE

### TEST PAGE

Because what you see onscreen isn't exactly what prints, you should always print a test page from the printer that will print your final results. The test page may cost more than just printing from your Color LaserWriter, but in the end the results will be worthwhile. If you are printing a test page, combine a variety of images altered in different ways so that you can choose from many different options. Some software plug-ins like Extensis' Intellihance 4.0 even include what is called a "test strip."

## CROSS-REFERENCE

For more on filters, see Chapter 14.

## FIND IT ONLINE

Check out **http://www.adobe.com/studio/artgallery/ guip/guip.html** to learn how Photoshop helped "free" this artist's mind.

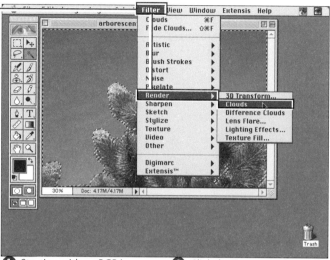

**1** *Starting with an RGB image and a selected sky, select Filter ⇨ Render ⇨ Clouds.*

**2** *Click the Foreground swatch. After you choose the color you want, click OK, and the new color will show up in the Foreground swatch. Repeat with the Background swatch.*

**3** *Click with your eyedropper on the blue part of the sky to see the intensity of the color.*

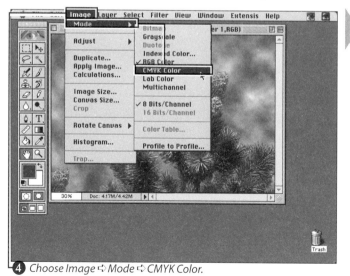

**4** *Choose Image ⇨ Mode ⇨ CMYK Color.*

**5** *Click with your eyedropper on the blue part of the sky to see how the color has changed since we changed modes. You'll notice that the sky color is more subdued when changed to CMYK. That is because by changing your mode to CMYK, Photoshop had to add 256 more pixels into the existing ones.*

# Getting File Information

Many times you'll need file-specific data while editing an image. Luckily, Photoshop makes finding that data easy. The lower left-hand corner of an open window provides the percentage of the file you're currently working on as well as its size in kilobytes (K). Also shown in the box is the size the file will be when saved in compressed format.

The pop-up menu at the File Size box lets you choose to view document size or scratch size. To access this pop-up information, hold down the Option (Alt) key while you click the File Size box.

You can view the measurements in many different increments. You can change the increments in the Units preferences found in the Preferences dialog box.

We utilize this pop-up menu daily. Any time that we get a file from an unknown source, we can quickly see what kind of file, including resolution, with which we are working. If you click the File Size box without holding anything down, you see how your image is laid out on your page. We like to use this to double-check that the file will print out on the specified page size. Many times you can make a file fit by changing the orientation from portrait (vertical) to landscape (horizontal). Sure, you can find out all of this information by accessing Page Setup and Image Size, but it is much quicker to find out all you need to know by clicking the File Size box.

Another area to get file information is the Image menu's Image Size submenu. This dialog box lets you see your image's pixel dimensions in pixels or percent. You can also get the print size in percent, inches, centimeters, points, picas, or columns. You can view the resolution in pixels per inch or centimeters per inch. The print area can tell you numerically whether the image is portrait or landscape. You can change the setup of portrait or landscape in the Page Setup dialog box found under the File menu. It is still much easier to get the information in one area.

If your image is way too large to print on your printer, you can change the scale of the image in the Page Setup dialog box. The default scale is set to 100%. You can change this number to reduce or enlarge the image before you print. If you choose to save after you change the scale, the new scale value is saved along with your file.

## TAKE NOTE

### CHANGING RULER UNITS
A quick way to activate the Ruler and Units preferences is to double-click the rulers. If the rulers aren't visible, press Command+R (Ctrl+R in Windows).

## CROSS-REFERENCE
For more on channels, see Chapter 12.

## FIND IT ONLINE
This gallery shows how photography can be enhanced with Photoshop: http://www.adobe.com/studio/artgallery/campbell/main.html

**1** The File Size box holds more information than just the size.

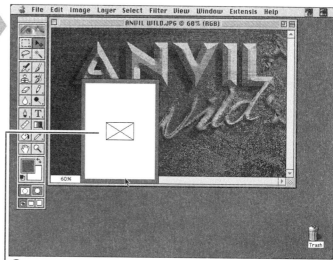

**2** Click and hold the File Size box to see how your image sits on the page.

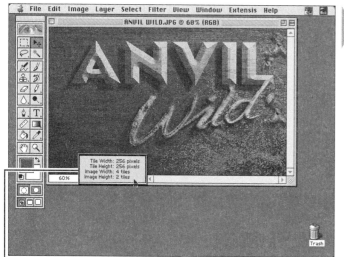

**3** Pressing the Command (Ctrl) key, click the File Size box to see the tile and image height and width.

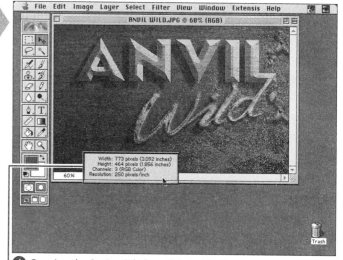

**4** Pressing the Option (Alt) key, click the File Size box to see the image's width, height, channels, and resolution.

# Setting Preferences

The Preferences menu enables you to customize Photoshop to suit your working style and your printing and color-separation requirements. The Preferences menu contains eight general-purpose dialog boxes:

**General.** Enables you to choose the type of Color Picker and to designate the way new pixels are created through the *interpolation* options when a file is resized or resampled. Interpolation is a method used to apply color to new pixels when they are derived from the image's original pixels. You can choose from an Apple Color Picker, a Windows Color Picker, or a Photoshop Color Picker.

**Saving Files.** Photoshop offers you the option of downward compatibility with earlier versions of Photoshop, as well as other specialized saving options.

**Displays & Cursors.** This box provides faster or smoother CMYK composites, dithering and diffusions options, as well as options for viewing some of the cursors in different ways. *Dithering* refers to the process of creating new colors by mixing existing pixel colors. *Diffusion* helps remove the patterns created when light and dark areas are close together.

**Transparency & Gamut.** This option enables you to set transparency and color for the Gamut Warning indicator as well as options for how the grid is viewed. *Gamut* refers to the color system you have chosen (RGB, CMYK, and so on).

**Units & Rulers.** You can select the way your document is measured: inches, pixels, centimeters, picas, or points. You can also set the Column Size Width and Gutter to correspond with dimensions in your desktop publishing program.

**Guides & Grid.** Select the color and measurement system for your grid and guides. You might try playing with some of these if any of the current colors bother you. Resetting the width of the grid might bring it more in line with a familiar publishing program.

**Plug-ins & Scratch Disk.** Use this option to select the folder in which your plug-ins will be kept. Plug-ins include the filters that appear under your Filter menu as well as Acquire and Export options (such as scanning and file-compression modules) that appear under your File menu. Select your choice of primary and secondary scratch disks in this dialog box. Your primary scratch disk should be your fastest and largest hard disk.

**Memory & Image Cache.** This option refers to the level of RAM memory desired for working images.

---

### TAKE NOTE

#### ▶ PREFERENCES FILE

The Preferences file (since Version 5) is now found in the Photoshop folder. You can trash this folder (when you aren't running the program) and all of the default preferences will return. It is a good practice to trash this file when things aren't running very smoothly or if you crash often.

---

### CROSS-REFERENCE

For more on plug-ins, see Chapter 14.

### FIND IT ONLINE

Tune into **http://www.adobe.com/studio/artgallery/adobeevents.html** for Adobe's upcoming events.

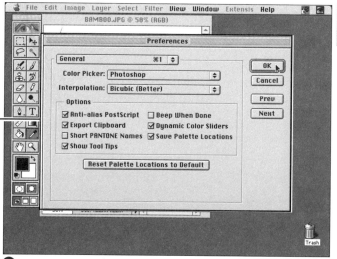

**1** To reset palettes to their original locations, you need to access the General Preferences dialog box. Press Command+K (Ctrl+K) and then click Reset Palette Locations to Default. Choose the Next button to access the next set of preferences in Photoshop (Saving Files). The Previous button takes you to the previous set of preferences (Image Cache).

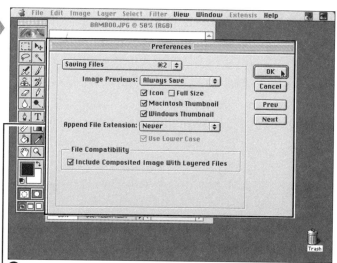

**2** If you use a Macintosh and you would like to save files with a file extension, you can choose Always from the Append File Extension drop-down list in the Saving Files preferences. Some of your other choices are to save with a Macintosh or Windows thumbnail. You can also choose to never save the image with a preview, always save with a preview, or ask when saving.

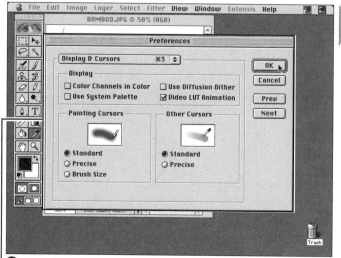

**3** One of our favorite preferences is the Display & Cursors preference. Access this dialog box by choosing File ➪ Preferences ➪ Display & Cursors. We like to set the Painting Cursors to Brush Size so we can see exactly the size of the brush as we are painting. This is also where you'd check the box to display channels in color rather than the default grayscale.

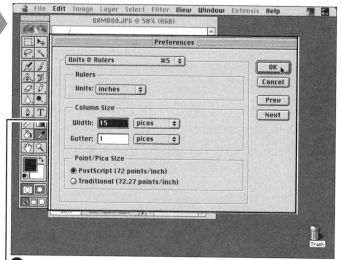

**4** By choosing File ➪ Preferences ➪ Units & Rulers, you can change the rulers to be pixels, inches, centimeters, points, picas, or percent. Change the Ruler units to points in the Units drop-down list within the Units & Rulers preferences. In this dialog box, you can also change the column width and gutters. To view the change, be sure to check Show Guides under the View menu.

# Understanding Resolution

Resolution is the key to successful printing. Whether you start with an existing image or are scanning one in from scratch, you need to understand resolution. When you copy and paste, resize, scale, or transform your image, you affect its resolution. If you scale an image up or down, Photoshop needs to fill in or remove pixels. Whenever you resize, resample, scale, skew, distort, change perspective, or rotate an image, the values of the new pixels are determined by interpolation. Photoshop offers three interpolation methods, which you can choose by selecting File ➪ Preferences ➪ General.

▶ *Bicubic* interpolation, the default choice, is recommended by Adobe as being the most precise, although the slowest, method.

▶ *Nearest Neighbor* interpolation is much faster than Bicubic because it simply divides each pixel into more of the same color. The lack of precision inherent in Nearest Neighbor, however, can cause a jagged appearance, especially if an image is transformed more than once.

▶ *Bilinear* interpolation is a compromise between the first two methods. It is not as precise or as slow as Bicubic, but it is more precise than the Nearest Neighbor method.

In most cases, Bicubic Interpolation is the method to choose.

Resolution is the key to great printed images. A common mistake is to scan or use only very high-resolution files. If you use too high a resolution, the image will print out too dark because the pixels are too close together. If you paste an object scanned at a high resolution into a low-resolution file, the pasted object will expand in size (and conversely, a low-resolution image pasted into a high-resolution file will contract).

To figure out the right resolution of an image, you need to know some basic rules. The resolution of your image should be 1 ½ to 2 times the line screen of your output device. We recommend calling your printer and asking them the line screen of their output device. A 300 dpi printer has a line screen of 53 lpi, which means that your resolution should be 106 ppi. A 600 dpi printer has a line screen of 85, giving you a resolution of 170 ppi. A 1,200 dpi printer has a line screen of 105 lpi, giving you a resolution of 210 ppi. The 2,400 dpi printer has a line screen of 133 lpi, giving you a resolution of 266 ppi. All of this is if your image stays at 100% and you don't size up or down. If you do, then take that into account when figuring out the resolution.

## TAKE NOTE

### ▶ DPI, PPI, LPI

DPI refers to dots per inch (refers to printer). PPI refers to pixels per inch (refers to monitor). LPI refers to lines per inch (refers to printer).

### ▶ MONITOR

Your monitor only displays 72 ppi, so if you are creating Web images, 72 ppi is as high as you need.

**CROSS-REFERENCE**

For more on printing, see Chapter 15.

**FIND IT ONLINE**

Check out **http://www.adobe.com/studio/ tipstechniques/phspaint/main.html** for creating a painterly effect.

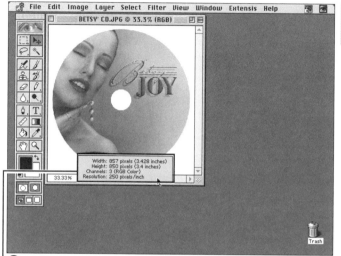

❶ Check the resolution of your file by choosing Image ➪ Image Size (or you can press the Option [Alt] key as you click the File Size box in the window).

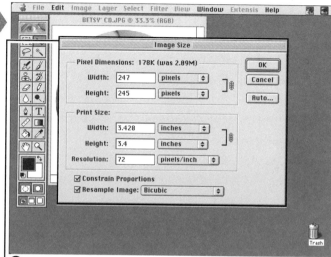

❷ Change the resolution from 250 to 72 in the Image Size dialog box.

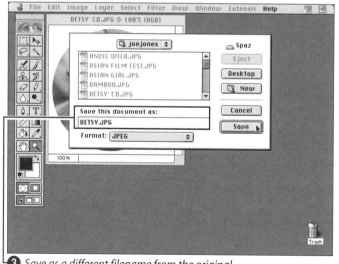

❸ Save as a different filename from the original.

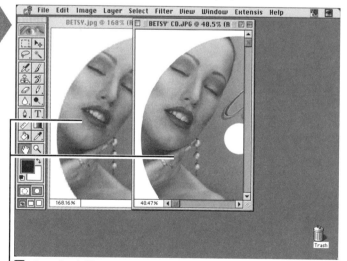

■ Open both files and view at 100% to see the resolution difference

41

# Changing Color in Photoshop

The Color Picker is easy to access by clicking on the foreground or background swatch in the toolbox or the swatches in the Color palette. You can change the color of the swatches by moving the circle in the color field, moving the color slider, or entering a color numerically. The numeric color fields you can enter are HSB, RGB, Lab, or CMYK.

Color has three different attributes that give its unique position in three-dimensional color "space." Each color can be described in terms of:

**Hue.** A description of the absolute place of the color on the spectrum according to its wavelength. In the visible spectrum from infrared to ultraviolet, orange-red has a long wavelength while indigo has a shorter wavelength. The slider bar for hue looks like a rainbow.

**Saturation.** The intensity of a color, or its purity. In video, saturation is also known as chroma level. The saturation of a color is inversely related to the amount of the opposite color that it contains. For example, a fully saturated red contains no green or blue. Add equal parts of green and blue to pure red, and you lower the saturation.

**Brightness.** A description of how bright or dark the color appears in terms of how much light is reflected to the eye. Another word for brightness is *value.* When you add black to a hue, you lower its value. Adding white raises or increases its value.

Although HSB is a viewing option on the Colors palette menu, it is not a true mode like RGB, CMYK, or Grayscale. It is merely a way of viewing and evaluating the color in an image.

The Swatches palette is the easiest way to change colors. Click on a color in the Swatches palette that you'd like, and it automatically replaces the current foreground color. To fill the current background color, hold down the Option (Alt) key before you click on the color.

Custom Colors are found in the Color Picker by clicking on the Custom button. You can access nine different custom color choices. If you know the number of the custom color, type in the number on your numeric keypad and Photoshop will quickly display that choice.

Grayscale Slider, HSB Slider, RGB Slider, CMYK Slider, Lab Slider, and Color Bar are your choices from the Color Palette pop-up menu. You can drag the sliders to create a color, or enter a color numerically. You can also click on the color bar below the sliders to pick a color.

## TAKE NOTE

### ▶ MOVING WINDOWS

When more than one window is open, clicking any place in a rear window makes it active and brings it to the front. If the other windows are smaller, they will be obscured. To see the smaller windows, either reshape the large window to reduce it, or select the other windows by name from the bottom of the Window menu.

**CROSS-REFERENCE**

For more on the Color Picker, see Chapter 7.

**FIND IT ONLINE**

For more on color palette see **http://www.adobe.com/ newsfeatures/palette/main.html.**

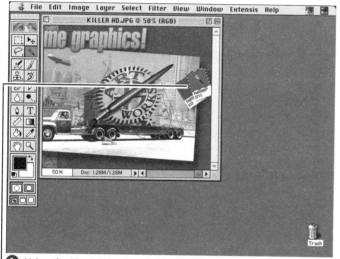

**①** Using the Magic Wand tool, select a solid area of an image that you want to fill.

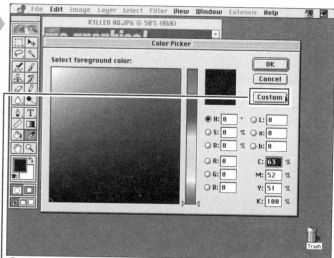

**②** After clicking the color swatch to access the Color Picker, click the Custom button to access the Custom Colors dialog box.

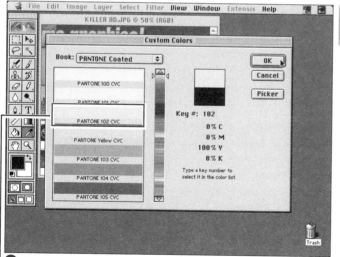

**③** Enter a number. We chose 102 Pantone Coated.

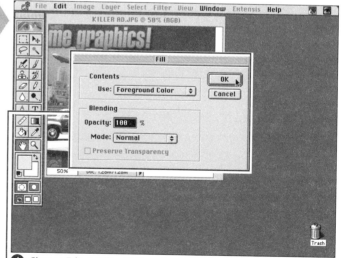

**④** Choose Edit ➪ Fill to fill the selection with 100% of the foreground color.

# Resizing an Image

Resizing stuff in Photoshop can be confusing until you understand what's going on and why. An image's dimensional size is governed by the file's resolution. The way a file looks onscreen is determined by the pixel dimensions that relate to the document itself as well as by the size of the monitor and its settings.

The higher the resolution of the file, the more pixels the file contains and the more room it takes up when saved to disk. A 1 × 1-inch portion of an image with a resolution of 72 ppi will contain just over 5,000 pixels. A 1 × 1-inch portion of the *same* file saved at 300 ppi would contain close to 100,000. Such a vast difference means a real difference in file size, but it also means a difference in the way the file is represented on the screen. In a very general way, the 300-ppi file will *look* better onscreen when viewed at 100% because more pieces contribute to making up the whole.

The 300 ppi file will also *print* much better than the 72 ppi file. Onscreen it can be hard to see the difference because both are viewed at 72 ppi. But you can see it if you view them at 100%. The ppi and dpi are essentially the same thing, except dpi refers to a printed document and ppi refers to your screen.

The amount of disk space a file takes is directly proportionate to these other measurements. For instance, a 1 × 1-inch file saved at 600 ppi takes up about 1.38 megabytes (MB) on your hard drive. The same file saved at 72 ppi demands a much more modest 21K. However, sometimes factors other than disk space are involved. As much as possible, it's important to know precisely what the final purpose of your file will be *before* you start to work.

You can use the Image menu's Image Size command to increase the size of an image while keeping the resolution the same or increasing it. *Resampling* an image actually alters the dimensions of an image's pixels and, along with that, the file size. Resampling must be done only with the utmost care. When you sample an image down, decreasing the number of pixels, information is deleted along with the pixels. When you resample up, Photoshop must add pixels where there were none before. Photoshop adds information based on the color values of the pixels that were already there. Understandably, this can degrade image quality because all of those extra pixels can make the image appear blurry and out of focus.

## TAKE NOTE

### ▶ STARTING OUT RIGHT

It is far better to start with the right size rather than force the size later. If you know beforehand that the image you are scanning is going to be used double the size it is, then scan it in at 200%, letting the scanner do the work. When possible, let the scanner scale up or down your image before going into Photoshop.

**CROSS-REFERENCE**

For more on scanning, see the section on scanning later in this chapter.

**FIND IT ONLINE**

Check out **http://www.adobe.com/studio/ tipstechniques/phssurfgif/main.html** for more on creating GIF images.

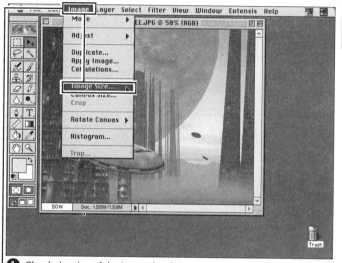

① *Check the size of the image by choosing Image ⇨ Image Size.*

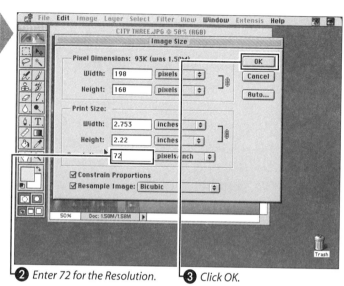

② *Enter 72 for the Resolution.*　③ *Click OK.*

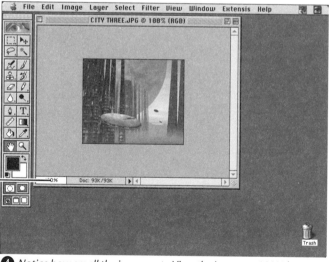

④ *Notice how small the image gets. View the image at 100% by changing the number in the Zoom box at the bottom left of the window.*

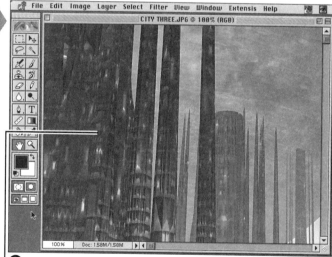

⑤ *Repeat steps 2 and 3, but this time uncheck the resample box and see the difference.*

# Adding More Canvas

When you use the Image Size command from the Image menu, you alter the size of the image. Sometimes you just need a bit more space to work in and don't actually want to change the size of the image onscreen. For this, use the Canvas Size command. Like the name says, this command changes the size of the canvas you're working on, *not* the image itself.

In the Canvas Size dialog box, you have a few choices. Three, to be exact: Width, Height, and Anchor. The Width and Height fields let you enter a number in percent, pixels, inches, centimeters, points, picas, or columns. Add how much canvas you want to the existing numbers. The existing number is the size of the image. If you know you want 2 inches added to the sides, then add 2 to the Width field number. The Anchor box is pretty cool. It defaults to center, assuming that you want to add canvas on the sides, top, and bottom with your image centered in the middle. If you want to add Canvas to just the right side of the image, click the left center square.

For example, we had to make a portrait-size image into a landscape-size image. To fill up the space, we first added canvas to one side. Then we copied and pasted the original, flipped it, and used the Rubber Stamp tool to fill in and make the areas look different. In the end, the image looked like it was photographed that way from the start.

The canvas added to your image will be the color of the Background Color swatch in the toolbox. If you want the canvas to be a certain color, change it in the background color before accessing the Canvas Size option.

Another useful feature of Photoshop is cropping an image. If you have added more canvas than you need (not a bad habit), you'll need to cut the image down to size. Photoshop offers to crop an image: You can use the Crop command from the Edit menu, or you can use the Cropping tool from the toolbox.

When you crop using the Cropping tool, you can rotate, scale, move, and crop the image in one shot. You can also use the Crop command, but it is very limited. First of all, you have to use the Rectangular Marquee and it must be a rectangle shape to crop. You can't create a bunch of rectangles and crop with them, it can only be one perfect rectangular shape. The Cropping tool is by far the better tool to use. You can adjust in one area and do more than just crop. To quickly access the Crop tool, press C.

## TAKE NOTE

### ▶ TEXT HEADING

Use the Canvas Size command to add a space to the top of your image for a text heading for an article.

### CROSS-REFERENCE

See Chapter 1 for more on the Crop tool.

## FIND IT ONLINE

This Web site shows you the system requirements for Photoshop: **http://www.adobe.com/prodindex/ photoshop/prodinfo.html#requirements**.

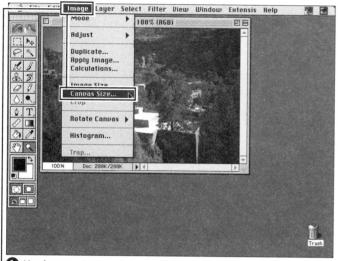

**1** *You have an image and you need to add more canvas on the right. Choose Image ⇨ Canvas Size.*

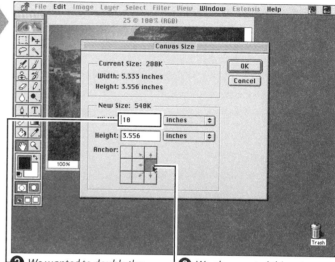

**2** *We wanted to double the length of this image, so we doubled the Width field.*

**3** *We also wanted this extra canvas added to the left side, so we clicked the left center box in the Anchor area.*

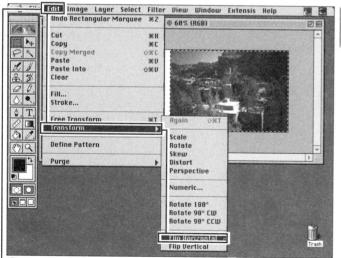

**4** *After selecting the image, copying, and pasting it, we chose Edit ⇨ Transform ⇨ Flip Horizontal.*

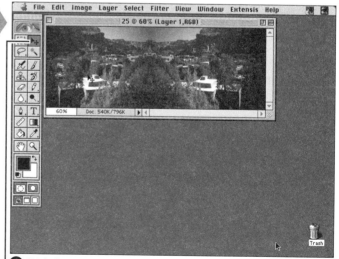

**5** *With the Move tool, move the copied image to the left side. If it looks too mirrored, you can use the Rubber Stamp tool to change the center area.*

# Saving Files in Formats Other Than Photoshop

If you are looking to save your image in a format other than the native Photoshop format, you need to choose Save As from the File menu. There are stipulations on saving in certain formats. For example, if you want to save a file as an EPS file, you cannot have any layers or extra channels in the file. For more on layers, see Chapter 11. For more on channels, see Chapter 12. If you want to save a file as a GIF 89a Export for the Web, you must first convert the file to Indexed color (select Image ⇨ Mode). For more on modes, see the section "Introduction to Color Modes" earlier in this chapter.

Photoshop supports all the modes listed under the Mode menu for the respective version of Photoshop you are using (Photoshop 5.0, 4.0, 3.0, 2.5, and 2.0 Files). Saving as a Photoshop file also enables support for multiple layers and channels. While this may sound great to you, your limitation is that you cannot open this file or place it in any program other than Photoshop.

The following are the formats and requirements on saving them in these formats. For more information on what each format is, see Chapter 1.

TIFF files can be placed, opened, or imported in other programs like Adobe Illustrator and Adobe PageMaker. To save a file as a TIFF image, the layers must be compressed to one layer. With a TIFF image, you can have multiple channels.

PICT documents can be small files, especially when an image contains large areas filled with the same color. PICT files can be saved with multiple channels when saved as 32 bit/pixel resolution. A PICT file can be saved in either RGB or Grayscale mode. You cannot save a PICT as a CMYK mode file. However, there is disagreement about the usefulness of PICTs in page layout applications. PICT files don't print at a quality resolution as other saved file types.

The EPS file is probably the most common way to save a file. It is also the largest way to save a file. To save a file as EPS you cannot have any extra channels or multiple layers. You can save the EPS in any color mode. With the EPS format, you can choose a JPEG preview so the image doesn't take as long to preview, but still prints clearly. This tends to be the largest file size when you save, because it retains the most information and can be used by many other programs.

The standard way to save a file is the bitmap image. If you opt to specify Run Length-Encoding compression (RLE) you will add lossless compression. You will

*Continued*

---

**TAKE NOTE**

### CAN'T SAVE AS AN EPS

You can't save as an EPS if you have saved any selections as channels. If you can't save in a format that you want, you need to check some areas like Layers or Channels. You'll need to flatten layers and remove extra channels to save as any file type other than Photoshop.

---

**CROSS-REFERENCE**

For more on saving see Chapter 1.

**FIND IT ONLINE**

If you are upgrading from Version 4 or earlier see http://www.adobe.com/prodindex/photoshop/prodinfo.html for 5.0's new features.

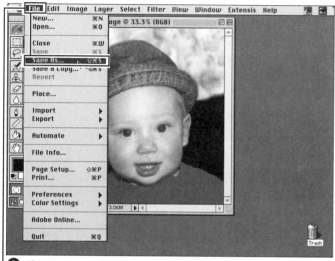

**①** *Choose Save As from the Edit menu.*

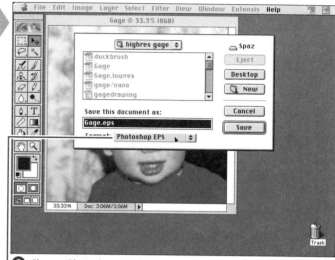

**②** *Choose Photoshop EPS from the Format drop-down list.*

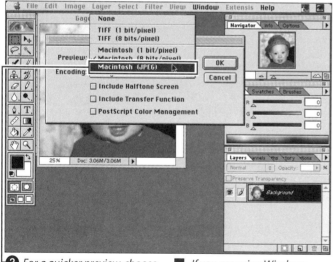

**③** *For a quicker preview, choose Macintosh (JPEG) if you are using a Macintosh.*

■ *If you are using Windows, choose TIFF (8 bits/pixel).*

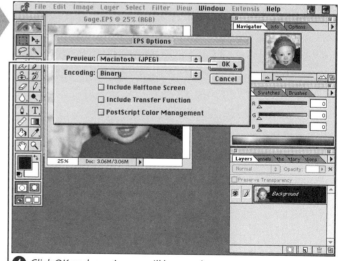

**④** *Click OK and your image will be saved.*

# Saving Files in Formats Other Than Photoshop

*Continued*

need to specify the operating system format (Windows or OS/2), as well as the bit–depth, in the BMP Options dialog box.

In the JPEG format, undetectable amounts of data are dropped, resulting in a smaller file size. Although this is a lossy method, the quantity of missing data is usually not noticeable, and is actually less than with GIF.

When you open a Filmstrip file created in Adobe Premiere, you can save it again in the same format. This option is not available with other files.

Grayscale, bitmapped, and indexed color images can be saved in GIF format, with resolution from 1 to 8 bits per pixel. GIF89a (found under File ⇨ Export) lets you specify transparent areas in the file and enables you to save in RGB format. GIF89a also supports multiframe images (GIF animation).

Windows systems use PCX format. Many different Photoshop modes can be saved in the PCX format.

The PICT Resource File format for Macintosh can be especially useful for transferring files that have large areas of solid color. This can be helpful for archiving alpha channels that are stored in black and white.

Images can be saved in the PIXAR format for export to high-end PIXAR workstations.

The PNG format employs a lossless compression method.

Only CMYK and Grayscale images can be saved in the Scitex CT format, which is used for very sophisticated image processing.

Use the Targa (TGA) format to save a file to be used on a system with a Truevision video input/output board. You do not have to save files in TGA format to use them with Truevision's NuVista video boards for the Macintosh.

DSC stands for Desktop Color Separations and is Quark's version of the standard EPS format. DCS supports CMYK and multichannel files.

Choose Amiga IFF (Interchange File Format) when you are using Video Toaster with transferring files to/from a Commodore Amiga computer. It is also used with DeluxePaint by Electronic Arts.

Photoshop PDF (Portable Document Format) can be viewed in Adobe Acrobat. Acrobat is usually included with many programs you purchase, including Photoshop.

## TAKE NOTE

### SAVING CHOICES

If you're not sure which file type to choose, sometimes it's best to save a couple of different versions of your file, especially true when sending files to be read by another computer. Giving others several files to work with can increase their chances of getting what they need and your chances of making your deadlines!

**CROSS-REFERENCE**

For more on Web creation, see Chapter 16.

**FIND IT ONLINE**

To join a great Photoshop alliance called the National Association of Photoshop Professionals see **http://www.photoshopuser.com/**.

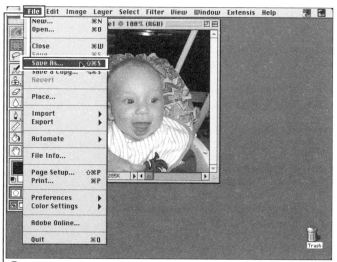

❶ *Choose Save As from the Edit menu.*

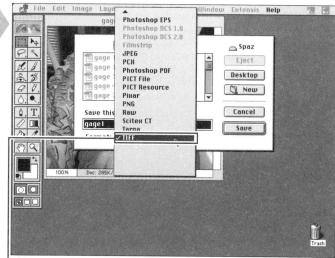

❷ *Choose TIFF from the pop-up options.*

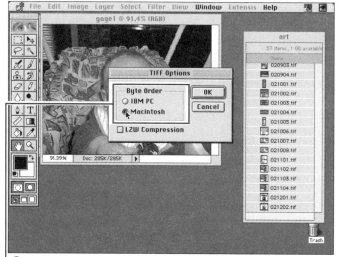

❸ *Choose IBM PC or Macintosh depending on which platform your image will be viewed on. (Note: If you choose IBM PC, a Macintosh can still view it, but if you choose Mac, your Windows system can't view it.)*

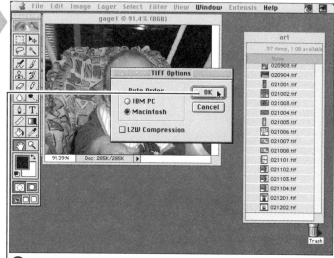

❹ *Click OK to save your image.*

# Scanning with Photoshop

Just a few years ago, it was impossible to find any type of scanner for under several hundred dollars. At the time of this writing, you can own a flatbed scanner for under a hundred bucks. Anyone can have their own scanner.

Purchasing a scanner and scanning an image are alike in one very important way: before you either make a scan or buy the peripheral to make them, determine what your final output will be. Do you want to be able to scan photos for your Web page? That inexpensive scanner will do nicely. Are the scanned images going to be printed on a magazine cover? If so, you're going to need a scanner that is capable of higher resolution.

Again, when you make a scan, what is your goal? Determine this before you begin. You want to be able to scan it in as close as possible to the size that you'll be using it.

These days, most scanners ship with a Photoshop-compatible plug-in. If you don't have one, contact the manufacturer of your scanner to see if they can help. It's good to have because it lets you scan images directly into Photoshop.

The plug-in module must be placed in the plug-ins folder that you created on your hard drive when you installed Photoshop. You must restart Photoshop for the module to appear under the Import command under the File menu. Most scanner-provided software enables you to crop images, adjust image brightness and contrast, and do some basic color correction as the image is scanned, as shown at right.

To help you make good scans, remember to

▶ Make sure both the scanner's glass surface and the image you wish to scan are clean, free of dirt, dust, fingerprints, and pet hair. (Trust us on this, you don't want Aunt Gertrude to have a more noticeable beard than she already does.)

▶ Warm up the scanner in advance of your first scan.

▶ Place the print in the middle of the scanning area. If you place it too close to the top, it might become overexposed because the light tube takes a moment to begin moving.

▶ Prescan the image so that you can limit the area you'll want to scan, thereby reducing file size.

▶ Set the resolution and dimensions of the scan.

---

**TAKE NOTE**

### MY SCANNER DOESN'T HAVE A PHOTOSHOP DRIVER. HELP!

If your scanner doesn't ship with a Photoshop-compatible driver, you can still scan your images in the software provided with the scanner. Save the images as TIFF, BMP, or PICT files and then open them in Photoshop. When using stand-alone scanning software, the scanned images need to be saved to disk and then opened in Photoshop using the File ⇨ Open command.

---

**CROSS-REFERENCE**

See Chapter 8 for more on Image Adjusting.

**FIND IT ONLINE**

For a great scanning resource see
http://www.scanshop.com/.

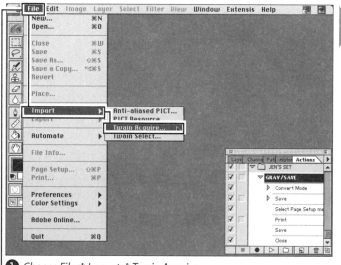

**1** *Choose File ➪ Import ➪ Twain Acquire.*

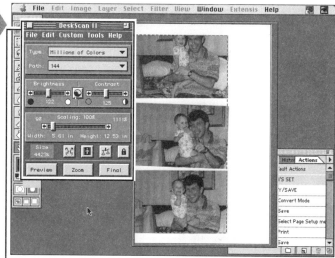

**2** *If your scanner has been hooked up and the proper software loaded, this should take you right into your scanning software dialog box.*

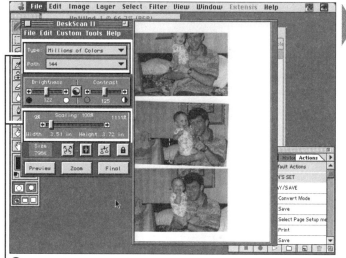

**3** *We set the Type to Millions of colors, the Path to 144 (resolution), and scaled the image up 100%.*

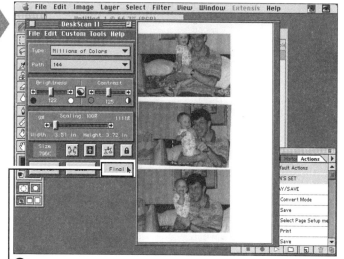

**4** *Press the Final or Scan button to have the image scanned into Photoshop for further adjustments and enhancements.*

# Getting an Image from the Web

Most of us have started exploring the Internet by now, and if you haven't yet, you will. As you are viewing cool Web sites and images, you are naturally wondering how you can snag an image from the Web. It is fairly easy, but don't be fooled into thinking you'll grab this image and reprint it for a high quality advertisement. First of all, it just isn't right to "steal" art without getting permission. Second, any image you download from the Web will have a resolution of 72 dpi, meaning that it isn't a high-quality image and won't print out nicely. It is meant for viewing onscreen.

On a Mac system you can click and hold your mouse button down to access a pull-down menu on a Web page. This menu lets you open, save, copy the image, and copy the image's location. On a Windows system, right-click with the mouse to get this menu.

If you want an image, choose the Save option so you can save it to your hard drive. Throughout this book, in every task, we include Web site references. Check them out for cool images, tips, and more. GIF, JPEG, and PNG are the three basic file formats for Web pages.

**GIF.** GIF (Graphics Interchange Format) enables 1-bit transparency and a palette of a maximum of 256 colors. When you save an image as a GIF file, you can specify how the image will load. If you select Interlace from the file options, the image will download gradually in ever-increasing detail.

**JPEG.** When you save a file as JPEG (Joint Photographic Experts Group), you retain all of the color information of an RGB image. The downside is that JPEG compression works by tossing out information deemed not necessary to rendering the image. This makes for an imperfect compression because data that is lost can't be recovered. So the file you save will be inferior to the one with which you started.

**PNG.** PNG (Portable Network Graphics) file format is being developed as an alternative to the GIF format for displaying images on the Web. PNG is exactly like GIF but is more powerful. PNG not only retains all color information of the original file, it also retains the alpha channels. PNG is a lossless compression method, so none of your valuable bits of data get dropped in the translation.

## TAKE NOTE

### ▶ GETTING A FILE

If you are really excited about an image you saw on the Web, contact the person or company that owns that page. I am sure they would be delighted in your feedback and you might even score a better copy of the image.

## CROSS-REFERENCE

For more on Web stuff, see Chapter 16.

## FIND IT ONLINE

This Web site at **http://www.nwlink.com/~theman/ index.html** warns you ahead of time not to copy images without written permission.

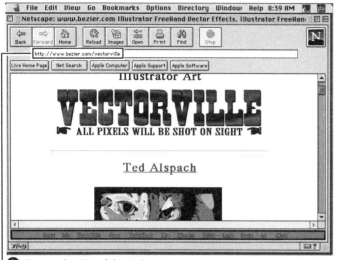

① *Type in the URL of the Web site you want to access. We chose http://www.bezier.com/vectorville.*

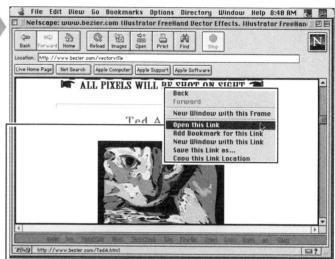

② *On a Mac system, click and hold the image to access the pop-up menu. On a PC, right-click to bring up the pop-up menu.*

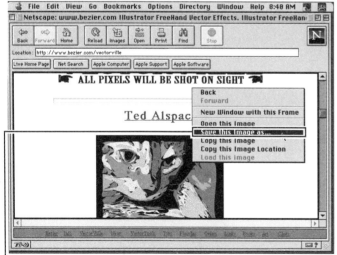

③ *Choose Save this Image as so you can save it to your hard drive.*

④ *Give the image a name or keep it the same, and click Save.*

# Getting an Image into and out of Photoshop

Files saved in the following formats can be opened in Photoshop 5.0: Photoshop 4.0, Photoshop 3.0, Photoshop 2.5, Photoshop 2.0, Amiga IFF, BMP, EPS, Filmstrip, GIF, GIF89a, JPEG, MacPaint, PCX, PDF, PhotoCD, PICT File, PICT Resource, PIXAR, PixelPaint, PNG, Raw, Scitex CT, Targa, TIFF, and TWAIN-scanned files.

Many scanners enable you to scan right into Photoshop, in which case the scanning software is reached using the File ⇨ Import menu. The Import command is also used to import files in other formats, including EPS files saved using JPEG compression, anti-aliased PICT files (created in programs such as MacDraw and Canvas), PICT Resources, and images to be scanned via the TWAIN interface. Video frame grabs are also brought into Photoshop by using the Import command.

You can open any Illustrator document in Photoshop either by choosing File ⇨ Open, or dragging and dropping the Illustrator file into a Photoshop document.

Photoshop also offers several export modes, which can be found under the Export . . . submenu under the File menu. Images can be exported to Adobe Illustrator with the Paths to Illustrator command under Edit . . . Export.

You can export files using the special plug-in modules available under Export (File menu). These options include GIF89a for viewing on the Web, compressing EPS files with JPEG, and exporting paths to Adobe Illustrator. To use an Export module, simply select Export from the File menu and choose one of the formats. When the corresponding dialog box appears, enter the appropriate data and click OK.

At times you may want to export a path created with the Pen Paths tool so that it can be modified in Adobe Illustrator. For example, you might want to add some Illustrator-modified text to a Photoshop image.

## TAKE NOTE

### OPEN AS

In Windows, you can use the Open As command to open a file with a missing or incorrect file extension, or if the file doesn't appear in the Open dialog box.

**CROSS-REFERENCE**

For more on the Pen tool in Photoshop see Chapter 10.

**FIND IT ONLINE**

Check out **http://www.cooltype.com/** for tons of Photoshop stuff:

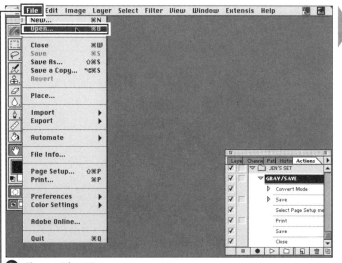

**①** *Choose File ➪ Open.*

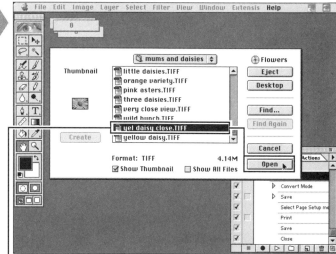

**②** *Find the file you want and click Open. Notice the dialog box tells you the type of file and the size of the file.*

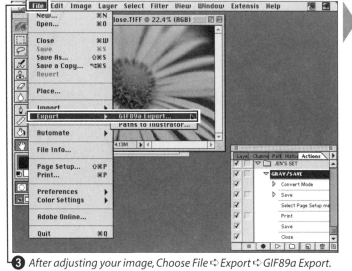

**③** *After adjusting your image, Choose File ➪ Export ➪ GIF89a Export.*

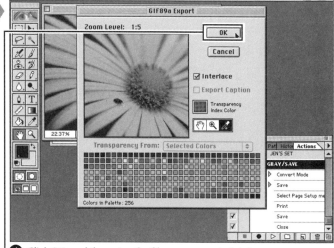

**④** *Click OK, and then give the file a name and click Save.*

# Personal Workbook

## Q&A

**1** What does *ppi* abbreviate?

_____

_____

_____

**2** Why is it important to start with an image close to the size you need it?

_____

_____

_____

**3** What is *resampling*?

_____

_____

_____

**4** When would you use the Image Size command?

_____

_____

_____

**5** Can you scan straight into Photoshop?

_____

_____

**6** Where does the scanner plug-in module go?

_____

_____

**7** How would you get Photoshop paths into an Illustrator file?

_____

_____

_____

**8** When would you use File Information?

_____

_____

**9** How are Preferences accessed?

_____

_____

ANSWERS: PAGE 333

## EXTRA PRACTICE

1. Open an image file. Resize it up and down, with and without changing the dimensions of the image.

2. Open an image file. Resize the file up drastically, first with resampling on, then Undo and do with resampling off. Both times, zoom the file up with the Navigator tool and check what it's done to your image.

3. Open an image file in Photoshop. Enlarge it as big as it will go using the Navigator tool. Examine the rough, pointy-looking edges. These are pixels and — at this enlargement — you could manifest pixel by pixel changes if you desired.

## REAL-WORLD APPLICATIONS

✔ You want to design a logo to have printed on a brochure and also grace your Web page. You create the logo in Photoshop and then save three versions. An EPS version will go on a disk to your printer, and a GIF version will be uploaded to your Web page. But you don't save copies of those two. Instead, you opt to keep only the final Photoshop version on your hard drive.

✔ Someone sends you an image file that you've asked for. When it arrives, it's as big as the disk it came on — over 20MB — and it sprawls gracelessly off your screen. You use the Image ⇨ Image Size command to bring it down to a real-world size with a real-world PPI.

## Visual Quiz

How did this image become blurry and pixelized without using any filters?

_____

_____

_____

_____

_____

# PART

# II

Contents of 'Desktop'

Name

My Computer

Network Neigh

Internet Explore

Microsoft Outloo

Recycle Bin

My Briefcase

3252-9

3259-6

3261-8

3262-6

3281-2

3286-3

DE Phone List

Device Manager

In

Iomega Tools

# Selections and Editing

CHAPTER **3**

MASTER
THESE
SKILLS

▶ **Using the Rectangular Marquee Tool**
▶ **Making Elliptical Selections**
▶ **Using the Lasso and Polygon Lasso Tools**
▶ **Using the Magnetic Lasso Tool**
▶ **Using the Magic Wand Tool**
▶ **Adding, Subtracting, and Intersecting Selections**
▶ **Inverting and Modifying Selections**
▶ **Moving and Copying Selections**
▶ **Using Select All, Select None, and Cropping**
▶ **Fine-Tuning Your Selection with Quick Mask**

# Making Selections

**M**aking selections is *the* most important thing to learn in Photoshop. As the name suggests, a *selection* is a portion of an image that has been selected through one of various ways, usually by dragging one of the Selection tools over the area with which you want to work.

The selection is actually the portion of the image inside the *selection border* that you define with one of the Selection tools. When you create a selection in Photoshop, you are defining an area in which a process can take place. The area outside the selection border won't be affected by changes that you apply to the selected area. Photoshop allows you to make selections with three kinds of edges: *anti-aliased, feathered,* and *aliased* (jagged edged).

The following actions are among those you can perform on selected areas:

▶ Paint or fill selected areas with color or pattern.

▶ Edit a selected area using any of the editing tools in the available modes.

▶ Fill selections with the contents of other selected areas.

▶ Mask selected areas to prevent them from being changed.

▶ Apply a filter to a selected area.

▶ Alter a selection by scaling its size, skewing or distorting its shape, combining it with another selection, and so on.

▶ Save selections in channels or layers for later use.

▶ Convert selections to PostScript-defined paths.

The Select menu gives you access to many Selection commands, especially those that help you prepare a selection to become a path. Or you can convert any type of selection to a path with the New Path command accessed through the Path palette. *Paths* are more precise selections that can be generated with the Pen tool. For more on using the Pen tool to create paths, see Chapter 10. The tools you can use to make selections are Marquee, Lasso, Magic Wand, and Pen. The tool you select depends on the nature of the job at hand.

# Using the Rectangular Marquee Tool

The easiest way to make rectangular and square selections is with the Marquee tools. The Marquee tool comes in four flavors, accessible from the Marquee icon in the main toolbar:

▶ The *Rectangular* Marquee tool makes square and rectangular selections.

▶ The *Elliptical* Marquee tool makes circular and oval selections.

▶ The *Single Row* Marquee tool selects an area one pixel wide along a horizontal line.

▶ The *Single Column* Marquee tool selects an area one pixel wide along a vertical line.

Of the four, you're likely to use the Rectangular Marquee tool most often. However, you can use all of the Marquee tools to quickly define areas for manipulation or cropping.

There are three styles available for both the Rectangular and Elliptical Marquee. These styles are available from the pop-up menu of the Marquee Options palette. *Normal* allows you to create a square or rectangular Marquee in a freehand fashion. This is the default setting. *Constrained Aspect Ratio* limits the dimensions of the marquee and enables you to specify the height-to-width ratio of the rectangle or oval you're going to draw. *Fixed Size* enables you to specify the exact shape of the rectangle or oval you're going to draw before you draw it.

The Single Row and Single Column Marquees are good for when you want to designate a very specific area. This is useful in creating spacer graphics for Web pages, which aren't intended to be seen but rather to hold the place of something. In that case, you'd fill the Marquee with the background color of your Web page. The Single Row and Single Column Marquees have no style options and are always *aliased*. Aliased means that the edges are jagged. Anti-aliased will add one pixel that is a combination of the foreground and background colors.

## TAKE NOTE

### ▶ KEYBOARD SHORTCUTS

To create a square while using the default (Normal) Marquee setting, press Shift as you click and drag.

To create a rectangular selection around a central point, press the Option (Alt) key as you drag the mouse. Press Option (Alt)+Shift as you click and drag to make a square around a central point. (You can press just the Option [Alt] key if you have constrained the aspect ratio to square proportions in the Marquee Options box.) The square will grow symmetrically from your origin point. In these examples, the cross hairs are centered on the X to begin with. This centering technique also works with the Elliptical Marquee.

## CROSS-REFERENCE
For more on the Toolbox, see Chapter 1.

## FIND IT ONLINE
This Web site at
**http://myhouse.com/rupert/images1.htm**
is a gallery for Photoshop art.

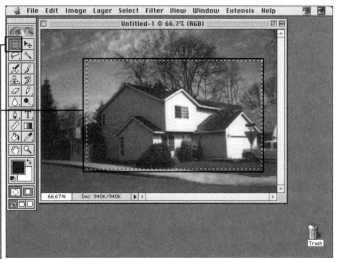

❶ To create an instant frame, first choose the Rectangular Marquee in the toolbox by clicking on it. Click and drag out a rectangle, holding down the Option (Alt) key so you are drawing out from the middle of your image.

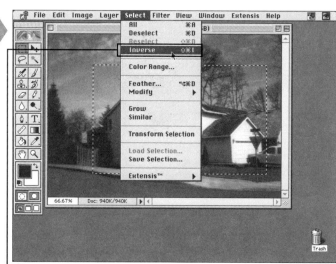

❷ Choose Select ➪ Inverse.

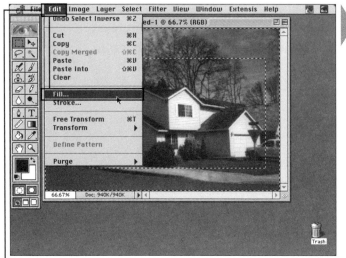

❸ Choose Edit ➪ Fill.

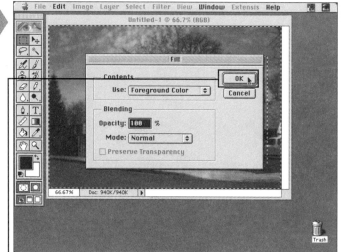

❹ Choose Black from the Contents drop-down list, 100% for the Opacity, Normal mode, and then press OK in the Fill dialog box for an instant frame.

# Making Elliptical Selections

The Elliptical Marquee tool is used for creating oval and circular selections. These selections can also create an oval or circular "frame" for your images. Or you can use them to create any circular selection on your image. The Marquee options are the same as and work in precisely the same way as those of the Rectangular Marquee tool and the Lasso tools. Marquee options are

▶ Double-click the Elliptical Marquee icon in the toolbox with your mouse to open the Marquee Options palette.

▶ Choose Normal to create an oval of any size and shape.

▶ Choose Constrained Aspect Ratio and type in a ratio in the Width and Height boxes to designate a proportional width and height for the shape, such as 2:1, 1:2, or 3:4. Use this option to create an oval with fixed proportions, although you may draw it as large or small as you prefer. When you set the aspect ratio at 1:1 you will be drawing a circle.

▶ Choose Fixed Size to designate a circle or oval of a specific height and width.

▶ Enter a number in the Feather box to specify the amount in pixels of feathering to apply to the selection. Feathering is explained below.

The Keyboard shortcuts you'll use with the Marquee tools are

▶ Use the Shift key to select a circular shape, even if you're in the Normal mode.

▶ Press the Option (Alt) key to draw a circle or an oval outward from a central point.

▶ Press Shift + Option (Alt) to draw a circle outward from a central point.

*Feathering* is a change that can be applied to a selection border to soften the transition between the inside of the border and the background. You can specify feathering with all of the Selection tools.

Feathering builds a transition between the selection and the pixels that surround it. This build creates a slight blur in the transitional area and can cause a loss of detail. This loss is part of the plan. It duplicates the transitions we see in real life when we look at an object against another object. Try it now by looking at something in your environment: our eyes seldom see hard edges. Feathering can be specified from the Marquees and Lassos and work in the same way in both instances.

### TAKE NOTE

▶ **TRANSFORMING THE MARCHING ANTS**

If you need your marquee larger, smaller, or altered, choose Selection ⇨ Transform Selection. It works the same as your regular transformations work on objects, but this only works on the marching ants or selection borders.

**CROSS-REFERENCE**

For more on selection options, see Chapter 4.

**FIND IT ONLINE**

This Web site shows you a feathering sample:
**http://library.tamu.edu/edms/feather.htm.**

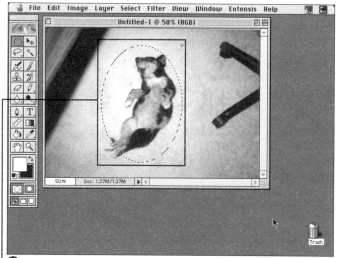

❶ *Click the Rectangular Marquee and hold so you can drag over to the Elliptical Marquee. Make an elliptical selection by holding the Option (Alt) key while dragging from the center of your image.*

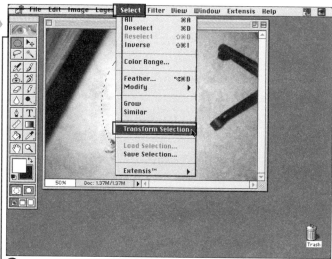

❷ *If you want to make your selection larger or smaller, choose Select ⬄ Transform Selection.*

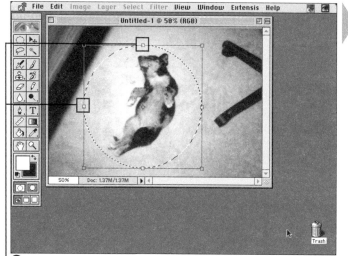

❸ *Drag the side sliders out to make the selection wider. Click Return to accept the new selection size. You can drag the sliders in to make the selection smaller or larger. By dragging from a corner, you can evenly enlarge or reduce the size of the selection.*

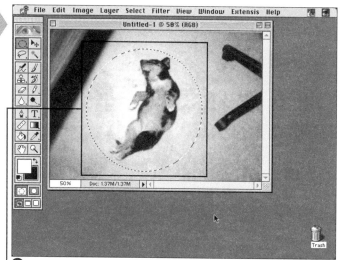

❹ *To move your elliptical selection place your Marquee cursor on the inside of your selection and click and drag. You can also use the arrow keys on your keyboard to "nudge" your selection.*

# Using the Lasso and Polygon Lasso Tools

The Lasso tools let you manually select part of an image. This duplicates the type of cutout you make on a halftone image in traditional graphic arts, cutting away the bits you don't want or need.

There are three tools accessible from the Lasso icon on the main toolbar: Lasso, Polygon Lasso, and Magnetic Lasso (this tool is discussed in the next task). The Lasso tool enables you to make loose, irregular selections by hand. The Polygon Lasso tool makes straight line segment selections. The Magnetic Lasso tool snaps to the edges of any area you define.

To make a freeform selection border, use the Lasso tool. Drag the Lasso tool around the part of the image you want while holding down the mouse button. You must hold the mouse button down the entire time you're dragging. As soon as you release the button, the beginning and ending points of the line connect, closing the selection. Use this tool for selecting any kind of irregularly shaped area.

To draw a selection border with straight lines use the Lasso tool. Hold down the Option (Alt) key and the mouse button as you drag along key points of the perimeter of the object you're selecting. The selection border Lasso stretches and contracts like a rubber band, enabling you to create a selection border with straight lines.

Release the Option (Alt) key (but not the mouse button) to continue drawing a border in the freehand mode. Press the Option (Alt) key when you want to draw a straight line again. You can go back and forth like this, pressing and releasing the Option (Alt) key all around an object.

When you release the Option (Alt) key and the mouse button, the selection will close, and the marching ants will appear. If you have not completed drawing the shape and have released the mouse button by accident, the beginning point and the ending point of the lasso line will self-connect. You cannot undo this operation. You have to start over again.

Lasso Options include feathering. Enter a number in pixels for the feather radius as you did with the Rectangular and Elliptical Marquees. If you don't want to feather the selection and prefer a smooth edge, click the Anti-aliased checkbox. In a 6:1 enlargement, you'll see that anti-aliasing lightens some of the pixels along the outer edge of the selection, but it doesn't blur the image as feathering does. If neither anti-aliasing nor feathering are applied, the border will have a jagged appearance. The selection border has been hidden in these images so that you can see the edge more clearly.

## TAKE NOTE

### HIDING THE SELECTION BORDER

To hide the selection border at any time (while allowing it to remain active), press Command (Ctrl) +H. Pressing this command a second time makes the border reappear.

## CROSS-REFERENCE

For more information on copying, cutting, and pasting, see Chapter 5.

## FIND IT ONLINE

This Web site at **http://www.hol.gr/gallery/artzone/zon_lpho.htm** shows you photographic art sources.

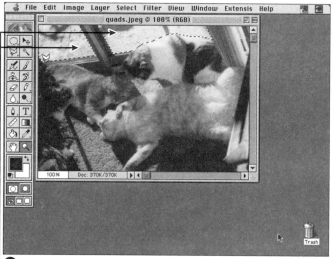

**1** Using the Polygon Lasso tool, select the window as shown in the image. To add to your selection, press and hold the Shift key until all parts are selected.

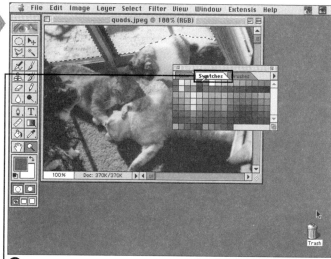

**2** Choose a blue color to replace the black foreground color from the Swatches palette.

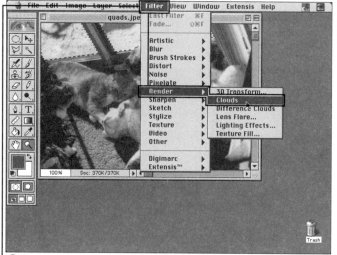

**3** Choose Filter ➪ Render ➪ Clouds to fill in the selected area with clouds.

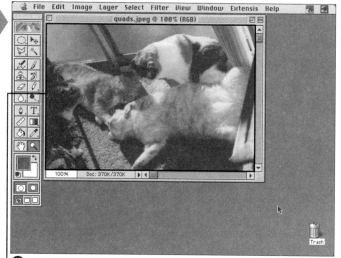

**4** Press Command+D (Ctrl+D) to deselect the active selection.

# Using the Magnetic Lasso Tool

The Magnetic Lasso is a wonderful new tool in Photoshop 5. This intuitive tool reads the difference between pixel colors and creates a selection based on the difference in the area you drag. You can drag the Magnetic Lasso with the mouse button up or down. The Magnetic Lasso creates a line determined by the edge it reads between the pixel colors. The closeness to pixels is set by entering a percentage for the Edge Contrast option found in the Magnetic Lasso Options palette. You access the palette by double-clicking the Magnetic Lasso tool. It also creates anchor points along the path. You can manually set an anchor point by clicking with your mouse.

In many ways, the more you work with and learn about Selections, the more you'll be able to do in Photoshop. Selection skills are called for in almost every chapter in this book, in everything you read about Photoshop, as well as in every cool Photoshop project you admire.

If you've been using computers for a while, you've probably noticed that there is seldom one correct way to do anything, difficult *or* simple. There always seems to be half a dozen ways to get the result you want. Selecting the *right* way is often as much a matter of personal preference as it is of taking the correct path. Using selections is like that. On the surface of things, several of the Selection tools seem to be doing much the same thing, it is just that some tools work for certain selections better than other tools.

If you want to select the outline of a particular shape in a photograph, you can use the Lasso to draw around the shape or the Magnetic Lasso, which snaps to the edges of the shape. You could also use the Magic Wand tool to select the pixels or the Color Range command for a document with distinctively colored areas. Or you could draw the shape to create a path with one of the pen tools. None of these ways is more correct than another, though some of them are better in particular instances. Part of what determines your choice is your own proficiency with a particular tool. That's one of the reasons why you should spend some time playing with *all* of the Selection tools: knowing each of them really well will help you pick the one that's best for a particular job when the time comes. And picking the best one can be the difference between artwork that has that professional snap and stuff that looks sort of okay and good enough.

## TAKE NOTE

### STARTING WITH THE MAGNETIC LASSO

This great new tool is a good start to creating a selection. If you use this first, then in Quick Mask mode you can clean up any edges that may have been missed. For more on Quick Mask mode, see later in this chapter.

### CROSS-REFERENCE

For more on filters, see Chapter 14.

### FIND IT ONLINE

For images created in Painter and Photoshop, visit
http://www.nashville.net/~hartc/.

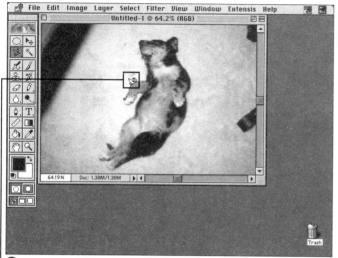

❶ With the Magnetic Lasso tool, click the edge of the area you want to select and release your mouse.

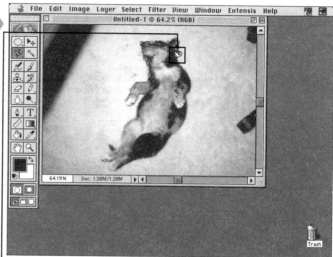

❷ Start moving your mouse along the edge of the area you want to select.

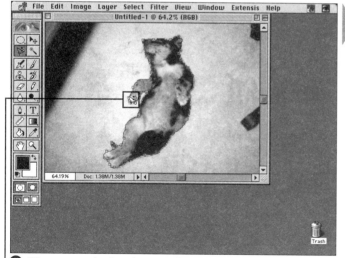

❸ When you get back to the start of your path, the Magnetic Lasso displays a small circle to let you know it is connecting.

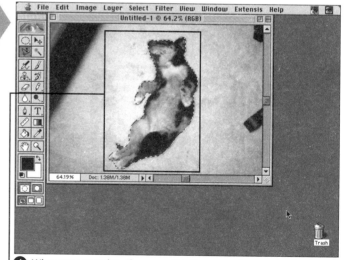

❹ When you complete the area, click the mouse button. A selection border will surround your selection.

# Using the Magic Wand Tool

The Magic Wand selects all touching or adjacent pixels that are similar in hue and value to the pixel you first click. You tell the wand how choosy to be by setting its tolerance in the Magic Wand Options palette. Based on the tolerance you set, the wand extends the selection outward until it finds no more pixels with the color values you want. If the tolerance is set to 40 and you click with the wand on a pixel that has a color value of 100, the Magic Wand would select all pixels with values between 60 and 140. (Both hue and luminance are figured into a special equation as the wand decides which pixels it can select.) A high tolerance selects a wider range of pixels. A low tolerance selects a very narrow range of pixels.

If you want to select a wide range of a color, from bright to dark, set the tolerance higher than the default (32) and click the wand in the middle of the range of color values. If you click in an area of the color that is very dark or very light, you are giving the wand less latitude. (Remember, color component values can range from 0 to 255.)

Using the Magic Wand effectively requires some trial and error, as the tolerance required depends very much on which object you're using the Magic Wand. You'll probably need a couple of tries before you click the pixel that gives you the Selection you want.

As with all of the selection tools, you can always add and subtract from selections. You can combine the selection tools to create the perfect selection. A popular method is to use the Color Range selection option (found in the Selection menu) to make the initial selection and then use the Magic Wand tool to remove parts of the selection that you don't want.

The Magic Wand tool is one you'd want to use if you wanted to select out a certain range of colors. If you want to select the blue sky to replace it with a different sky, the Magic Wand is perfect for making the selection. The only catch is that you probably shouldn't use this tool if the same color range is throughout your image. For example, if you want to make a selection of a blue sky, and the same range of blue is used throughout the foreground, the Magic Wand isn't your best choice. When making any selection, first look at your image and determine which tool or tools would work best.

## TAKE NOTE

### ▶ DESELECTING AN IMAGE

To deselect any selection at any time, press Command (Ctrl)+D or click anywhere on the screen (with a selection tool) outside of the selection border. If you click outside the border with another tool, this shortcut will not work.

## CROSS-REFERENCE
For more on Color Range selections, see Chapter 4.

## FIND IT ONLINE
Examine great Web designs that use Photoshop at
http://www.forcefx.com/netscape/nav.html

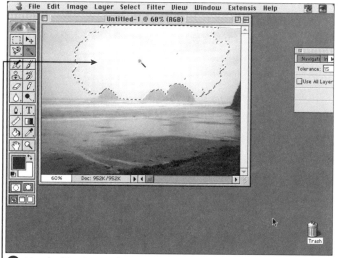

**1** Use the Magic Wand to copy a selection from one image and paste it onto another. Click the sky in the image. If the default tolerance (32) isn't high enough, set it higher.

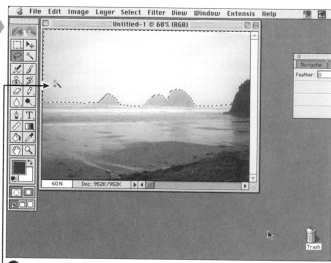

**2** Hold the Shift key and click the rest of the sky to add to your selection.

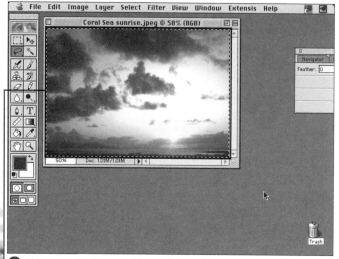

**3** Open another image with a different sky. Select the sky of this other image and press Command (Ctrl)+C.

**4** Go back to the original image and press Command+Shift+V (Ctrl+Shift+V). (We went back to the original layer and adjusted Levels to blend the images better.)

# Adding, Subtracting, and Intersecting Selections

I t's the subtle things you do with Selections that can make all the difference and turn your work from pedestrian into something really special.

Sometimes, in the process of selecting a portion of an image, you or one of the tools might select too little or too much. In these instances, it's useful to be able to add and subtract from a Selection. By using the Add and Subtract commands, you can easily remove or add the portions you desire.

To add to any Selection or to add multiple Selections, first select either the Lasso, Marquee, or Magic Wand tool and then hold down the Shift key and click in the area to be added.

If you are using the Magic Wand, adjust the tolerance to limit or expand its range before doing this. You can adjust the tolerance as many times as you wish. Just remember to hold down Shift before each additional click.

When using the Lasso tool, drag to encompass the additional area to be added. You can release the mouse button and move the mouse to encompass multiple noncontiguous areas, as long as you hold down the Shift key while making the selections.

If you are using a Rectangular or Elliptical Marquee tool, drag around the area to be added.

As long as you remember to press the Shift key before making each additional selection, you can even switch Selection tools.

To subtract from any Selection or from multiple Selections hold down the Option [Alt] key. Again, remember to hold the key down before each additional click.

If you are using the Magic Wand tool, click in the area to be subtracted. (Reset the tolerance if necessary.) If using the Lasso tool, drag to encompass the area to be subtracted. If you are using the Rectangular or Elliptical Marquee tool, drag a marquee around the area to be subtracted.

## TAKE NOTE

### ▶ KEYBOARD SHORTCUTS

Remember that pressing Shift adds to a selection and Option [Alt] subtracts from a selection.

### ▶ SELECTING WITH EASE

Selecting All (Command [Ctrl]+A) selects everything in the document window right out to the edge.

Selecting None (Command [Ctrl]+D) deselects all selections, as does clicking with the Selection tool anywhere outside a selection border or borders, if there are multiple noncontiguous active selections.

When you want to preview a selection without those pesky "marching ants," you can choose to Hide the selection. You can toggle the Hide and Show Edges command by using Command [Ctrl]+H.

## CROSS-REFERENCE

For more on editing in Photoshop, see Chapter 6.

## FIND IT ONLINE

This Web site (http://www.ams-lab.demon.co.uk/new.htm) shows you some darker images created with Bryce and Photoshop.

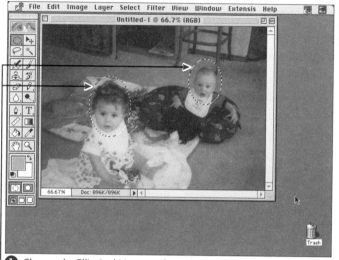

**1** Choose the Elliptical Marquee from the toolbox. Make an initial oval selection, then hold the Shift key to add another oval to the original selection.

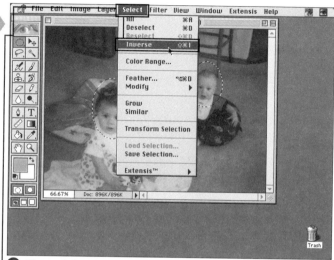

**2** Choose Select ⇨ Inverse.

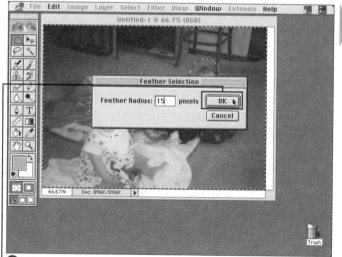

**3** Choose Feather from the Select menu, and enter a value of 15. Click OK.

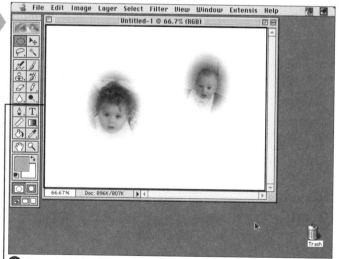

**4** Press the Delete key to fill the background area in white. Press Command (Ctrl)+D to deselect your selection.

# Inverting and Modifying Selections

You'll find the Inverse command under the Select menu. The Inverse command reverses what is selected and not selected in the document window. This is an extremely handy technique for drawing on both the inside and outside of a selection border or for applying Filters to areas outside of the selection you're working on. For more on filters, see Chapter 14.

When you look at an image, you should decide whether it's easier to select the object or the background. If you select the easier of the two, you can always use Inverse to select the other.

Inverse isn't the only option found under the Select menu. The Select menu offers several other ways of modifying selections.

The Feather command is used to feather the edges of any selection, even if the selection was not feathered when it was created. The Magic Wand tool, for example, does not have a Feathered Radius option, but you can feather a selection made with the Magic Wand using this command.

The Border command enables you to select a bordering area around a selection border.

The Modify command will let you alter the selection border in various ways. The Select ⇨ Modify ⇨ Contract command enables you to remove edge pixels from the border of a selection. Sometimes when you cut an anti-aliased image from one background

and paste it into another, you'll see traces of the old background around the very edge of the selection. With Contract those offensive pixels are replaced with pixels that don't contain the background color.

The Select ⇨ Modify submenu also includes Smooth and Expand commands. Smooth gets rid of the rough edges of a selection, while Expand, which is the opposite of Contract, adds pixels to the edge of a selection.

The Grow command (Command [Ctrl]+G) enlarges the extent of a selection based on pixel color. It takes its instructions from the Magic Wand's tolerance setting.

The Similar command enlarges the selection to find all colors that are the same as the Magic Wand's target color, no matter where they may be in the image.

Experiment with these modifications on different images and with different tools. As you grow more proficient with Photoshop, you'll find yourself using them more and more.

---

## TAKE NOTE

### ▶ CAUTION FOR BITMAPS

The Grow and Similar commands do not work on bitmapped images because the Magic Wand does not work with those files.

## CROSS-REFERENCE
See Chapter 15 for more information on printing.

## FIND IT ONLINE
While this Web site at **http://www.mindspring.com/~seanrox/images/** is not initially attractive, the images are

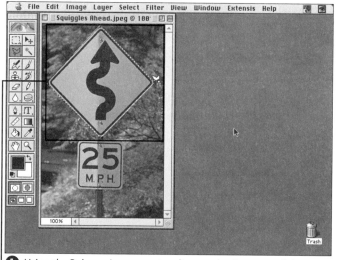

**1** Using the Polygon Lasso, create a linear selection around the yellow sign.

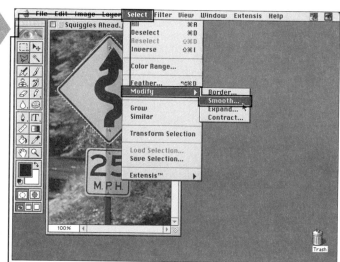

**2** Choose Select ⇨ Modify ⇨ Smooth.

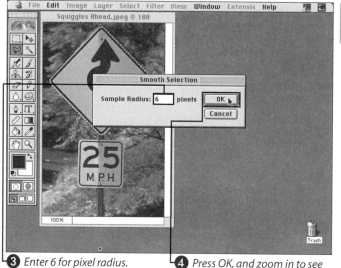

**3** Enter 6 for pixel radius.

**4** Press OK, and zoom in to see the beautiful smooth edge created.

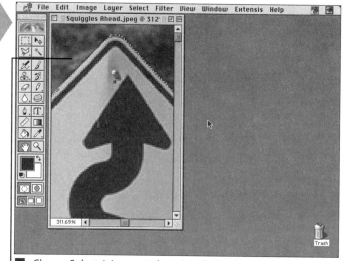

Choose Select ⇨ Inverse to have just the background selected so you can apply any effect to just the background.

# Moving and Copying Selections

All of this discussion about Selections is no good to you at all if you don't know how to move the selection from one file to the next. After all, a lot of the time, what you're doing when you're making a selection is preparing something that will ultimately be used somewhere else.

You can copy a selection in several ways. The simplest way is just to press Command (Ctrl)+C (Copy) and Command (Ctrl)+V (Paste). In that case the copy of the image would be pasted directly on top of the original image, but in a new layer. You can also copy within the same file by pressing the Option (Alt) key while dragging the selection with the Move tool. The Move tool is found in the upper right of the toolbox.

You can use the Edit ➪ Copy and Edit ➪ Paste commands or the equivalent keyboard commands to move selections between Photoshop documents. It's easier on both system resources and your own time to simply drag a selection from one open file and drop it into another. Photoshop creates a new layer for the dropped selection.

You'll want to remember that there are really two copy commands: the Copy command we've mostly used throughout this book, and the Copy Merged which is accessible from the Edit menu. If you select Copy or use the equivalent keyboard commands, the stuff that goes into your Clipboard is from the highlighted layer only. If you Select Copy Merged, the Selection that gets placed on the Clipboard will contain information from all layers.

Sometimes when you look at a Photoshop document, the cool effects of superimposition are ruined by a halo effect between foreground and background images that have been merged. This halo comes from the pixels that surround the Selection border getting moved or pasted with an anti-aliased selection. The Layer ➪ Matting commands can help reduce that haloed effect.

▶ The Defringe command replaces the fringe pixels with the pure colors of nearby pixels.
▶ The Remove Black Matte command is for pasting an anti-aliased selection against a white background.
▶ The Remove White Matte command is for pasting an anti-aliased selection against a black background.

---

### TAKE NOTE

▶ **REMEMBERING RESOLUTION**

It's important to remember that when you copy a selection from one file to another, the pasted portion of the image remembers where it came from and retains its pixel dimensions. This can result in some strange-looking files. Before you move the selection, use the Image ➪ Image Size command in both files old *and* new to make sure that both files have the same resolution. If they don't, change one so that both are the same.

---

**CROSS-REFERENCE**

For more on resolution, see Chapter 2.

**FIND IT ONLINE**

If you are looking for schools to learn Photoshop, check out **http://www.fullsail.com/**.

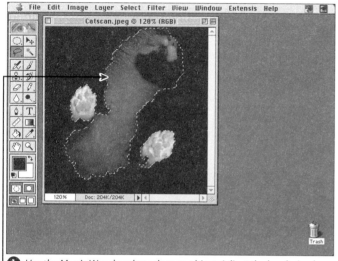

① Use the Magic Wand tool to select an object. Adjust the border's edge as needed.

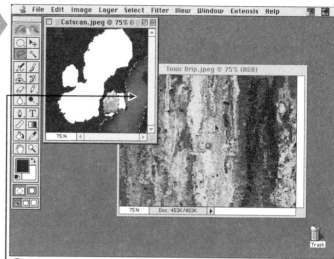

② Using the Move tool, drag and drop the selection into another document. This results in the selection being copied and then pasted into your new file. It is a much quicker way to get parts of one image into another.

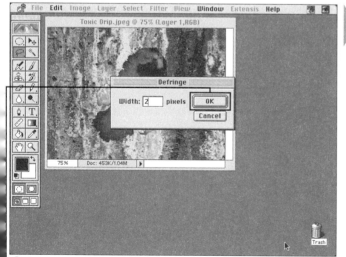

③ Choose Layer ➪ Matting ➪ Defringe. Enter 2 for the pixel Width.

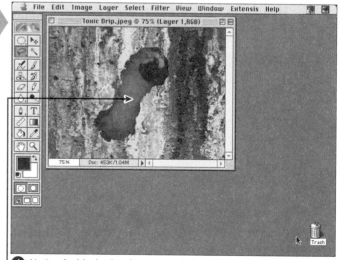

④ Notice the black edge that was copied over is removed by the Defringe command.

# Using Select All, Select None, and Cropping

ow that you are selecting right and left, you may wonder how to select everything or get rid of your selections. Under the Select menu you'll find Select All (Command [Ctrl]+A) and Select None (Command [Ctrl]+D). These two functions are best used with keyboard commands. Most programs use the same keyboard command for Select All. You may remember the Select None by thinking, "Deselect."

There may be times when you want to apply effects to your whole image or make a copy of everything on a layer. Use Select All to apply effects to your whole image. Or use it to make a copy of everything on that layer. If you have a transparent layer and want to copy an object that is on that layer, an easy way to do that is to use Select All. The "marching ants" appear around the edges of the window, and if you want to see them only around your object, select the Move tool, press the left-arrow key, and then the right-arrow key.

The Crop tool is on the same toolbox icon bar as the Marquee tools. You can choose it if you're cropping an image and want to do it very quickly and accurately. To use it, simply select the area to be cropped just as you would with the Rectangular Marquee tool. You can move the border at the corners until you have the area defined. When you are happy with the Selection area, press Return or Enter to complete the crop. You can also crop with the Rectangular Marquee, but it isn't nearly as accurate.

The Crop tool has one check box in the Options. You can specify a Fixed Target Size by entering a Width, Height, and Resolution. If you choose the Front Image button, the image's width and height will automatically be entered.

The Fixed Target Size is great if you have a bunch of images that need to be exactly the same size. If you don't check that box, you'll get a box around your image that you can move in proportion, horizontally, vertically, and rotate. The Crop tool can rotate, but keep in mind it doesn't scale your image, rather it cuts it off.

Be flexible. Photoshop supplies you with a wealth of tools so that you can have more image-editing flexibility. Don't become dependent on one tool to do everything. Experiment with different combinations until you become skilled with all of them.

## TAKE NOTE

### ACCESSING THE CROP TOOL
To quickly access the Crop tool, press the C key.

## CROSS-REFERENCE
For more on making selections see http://www-pac.adobe.com/studio/tipstechniques/phsselections/main.html.

## FIND IT ONLINE
Kick back, relax, and check out cool 3D art at http://www.3dcafe.com.

**①** Drag a box across your image using the Crop tool.

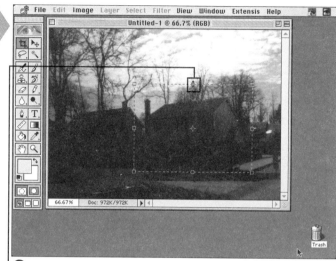

**②** Resize the box using the handles.

**③** Rotate the image by placing your cursor outside of one of the four corners and dragging.

**④** Press the Return or enter button to see the newly cropped and rotated image.

# Fine-Tuning Your Selection with Quick Mask

If you want to make changes to only a small part of a file or image, you have several ways in which to select only this area. Use the Lasso tool to select the area to work on. Drag around all of it, using the Shift and Command keys to add to and subtract from the selection. Or use the Magic Wand tool to select the area by color. Use the Pen tool to click points around the edge of the item to be changed and then convert that path to a selection. For more on using the Pen tool see Chapter 10.

Use the Quick Mask option to paint an area that will be converted to a selection. The Quick Mask is the right button found under the Foreground and Background Swatches in the Toolbox. In the Quick Mask mode, you draw a mask in a transparent mask channel that lays on top of the color or grayscale image. For more on Channels see Chapter 12. A Quick Mask is just like other mask channels in that it contains only eight-bit grayscale information: the pixels can be only black, white, or one of 254 levels of gray.

Just as with other channels, you can use white, black, and gray paint to edit a mask. However, neither the black or white paint appears when you're in the Quick Mask mode. By default, the mask appears as a transparent red color and indicates the area to be protected. Painting with black adds to the colored overlay and painting with white erases the colored overlay. This overlay can represent either the masked area or the selected area, depending upon what you

indicate in the Mask Options dialog box. When you select the Quick Mask button, the foreground and background swatches found in the toolbox appear as their default values (black is foreground, white is background).

You change these options in the Mask Options dialog box. This dialog box is accessed by double-clicking the Quick Mask button. And you can also change the Quick Mask color by clicking Swatch in the Quick Mask Options dialog box to activate the Color Picker. You can also set the Opacity (but you should try to keep the Opacity at 50%).

You exit Quick Mask mode by clicking the Normal Mode icon, which converts the mask into a selection border. You can now save this selection in a mask channel using Select ⇨ Save Selection.

## TAKE NOTE

### ADDING A SELECTION TO AN EXISTING CHANNEL

You can save a selection to an existing channel by dragging the Selection icon to the channel on the Channels palette. Holding down the Shift key adds this new selection to the current selection in the channel; holding down the Command key subtracts the new selection from the current selection; and holding down Shift+Command selects only the portion that intersects the old and new selections in that channel.

## CROSS-REFERENCE

For more on making perfect selections, see Chapter 4.

## FIND IT ONLINE

For more exercises on making selections, browse http://www.nobledesktop.com/ex07craw.html.

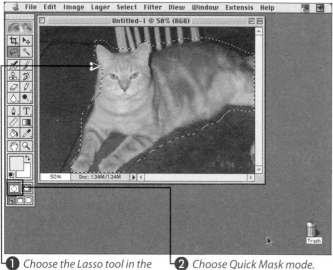

**1** Choose the Lasso tool in the toolbox. Make a rough selection with the Lasso tool.

**2** Choose Quick Mask mode.

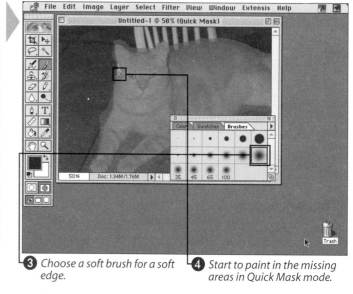

**3** Choose a soft brush for a soft edge.

**4** Start to paint in the missing areas in Quick Mask mode.

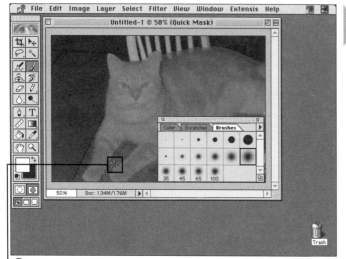

**5** To erase the mistakes where you went over the edge that you wanted to create, press the X key to switch foreground and background colors. Then paint out the overflow areas.

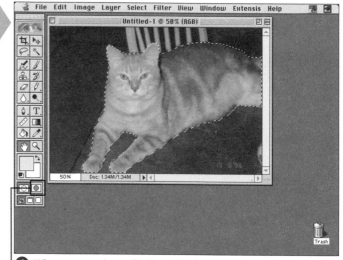

**6** When you are done painting, click the Standard Mode button to see your active selection.

# Personal Workbook

## Q&A

**1** Name the *Selection tools.*

_____

_____

_____

**2** How are *selections* and *paths* related?

_____

_____

_____

**3** What's the easiest way to make a square selection?

_____

_____

_____

**4** How does the Magic Wand work?

_____

_____

_____

**5** What tool would be the correct one to use to outline a specific shape from a Photograph?

_____

_____

_____

**6** What are the keyboard shortcuts for adding to a selection?

_____

_____

_____

**7** What are the keyboard shortcuts for subtracting from a selection?

_____

_____

_____

**8** Which is more accurate, the Rectangular Marquee or the Crop tool, for cropping an image?

_____

_____

_____

ANSWERS: PAGE 334

## EXTRA PRACTICE

**1** Experiment with all the Marquee tools by making a selection border with each of them and then filling the selection with color.

**2** Use the various Lasso tools to make manual selections in various images. Practice using all three lasso tools on the same part of the same image to get a feel for the differences.

**3** Use the Magic Wand tool in a strong-colored image. Practice selecting various elements. Then, copy them to the Clipboard and paste them into a new document to see your results.

**4** With the Elliptical Marquee tool, make a selection around the focal part of an image. Select Inverse. Apply a feather of 15, then press delete to see a soft feathered edge background.

## REAL-WORLD APPLICATIONS

✔ You're creating a piece of art that will include bits of multiple images. You use the Rectangular Marquee tool to select a square bit of one photo; the Magic Wand to select the bright colored parts of another; and you draw with the Pen tool to create original and interwoven bits of the image.

## Visual Quiz

Look at the before and after of this image. How was the black line edge removed?

_____

_____

_____

_____

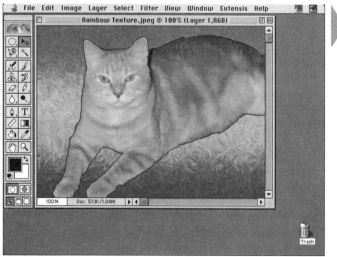 

CHAPTER **4**

**MASTER THESE SKILLS**

# Using Selection Features and Creating Text

Now that you have learned the basics of making selections, we can take the next step. The first group of topics in this chapter deals with fine-tuning selections for better manipulations and saving them for later use. The second group addresses type and some of the fun things you can create with type in Photoshop.

This chapter also covers some of the third-party plug-ins you can use to create a selection or to mask an image, including Extensis' Mask Pro 2.0, Chroma Graphics' Magic Mask/Edge Wizard combo, and Ultimatte KnockOut. Many third-party developers come up with plug-ins that extend the abilities of Photoshop. While Photoshop can make selections and masks, selecting things such as wispy hair and similar backgrounds can be next to impossible or very time consuming without these plug-ins.

Type in Photoshop has come a long way from previous versions. Before Version 5, many Photoshop users would use another program like Adobe Illustrator to create type and then copy and paste it into Photoshop. Type in earlier versions of Photoshop was not editable and had many limitations. Now, you can use Photoshop to create any cool effect with type to finish off your images.

# Selecting with Color Range

Color Range is found under the Select menu. Color Range goes beyond the Magic Wand tool in that you have more options. There is a pull-down menu within Color Range that enables you to make a selection from Sampled Colors, Reds, Yellows, Greens, Cyans, Blues, Magentas, Highlights, Midtones, Shadows, or Out of Gamut colors. You don't have that kind of versatility with the Magic Wand tool. If you are looking to select a certain color, choose that color from the pop-up menu. Then you can use the Color Range feature multiple times until you have the exact color you want. Each time you use the Color Range on the image you have open, it will pick only pixels within the last Color Range selection.

The Fuzziness setting is like the tolerance setting of the Magic Wand tool. You can determine the range of colors the tool selects by adjusting this setting. The lower the setting, the closer the range is to the original pick. The buttons below the image preview are Selection and Image. If you choose Selection, then you'll preview only the selection. The preview pane allows you to see the effects of your choices on the selection or the entire image. You can also choose to see None, Grayscale, Black Matte, White Matte, or Quick Mask.

The Eyedroppers let you make your samplings to create your selection. You'll use the first Eyedropper to make your initial selection. To add to the selection, use the Eyedropper with the plus (+). To remove a color from your selection, use the Eyedropper with the minus (–). The Invert command will select everything other than your original selection.

Finally, you can load or save any Color Range settings. This is helpful if you have many images that need a certain color selected repeatedly. The Color Range option is a great way to select colors that are scattered all over your image and would be difficult to select using the Magic Wand. We like using it because you can make your entire selection in one area and not have to shift and click multiple times to get a complete selection.

Keep in mind that the Color Range command works only on the active layer. To select on more than one layer, use Color Range, then save the selection under the Select menu. Click the next layer and do the same thing. You'll find the saved selections in the Channels palette. You can load multiple selections and add them together, as you'll see later in this chapter.

## TAKE NOTE

### UNDO AND COLOR RANGE

While you are in the Color Range dialog box, notice that the Edit menu is still active. This enables you to use the Undo command to undo the last area you selected. This is sometimes much easier than using the Eyedropper with the minus because it is hard to click the exact same pixel.

## CROSS-REFERENCE
Saving selections is discussed again later in this chapter.

## FIND IT ONLINE
Check **http://www.iserv.net/~rtideas/** for ticks on Photoshop (yes, ticks, you'll see).

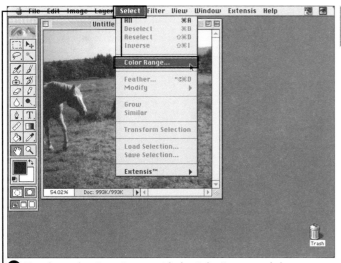

**①** To select colors in an image with the Color Range tool choose Select ➪ Color Range.

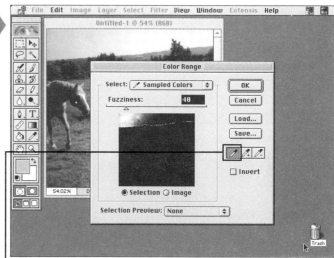

**②** Click the Eyedropper tool found in the Color Range dialog box to choose it. Click the sky to make your initial sampling.

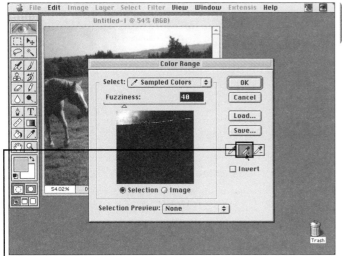

**③** Click the Eyedropper with the plus (+) sign to add to the initial selection. If you want to remove a color from your selection, choose the Eyedropper with the minus (−) sign and click the offending color. Click OK.

**④** Open another image with a different sky and select the new sky. Choose Edit ➪ Copy. Go back to the first image and paste the new sky into your selection by choosing Edit ➪ Paste Into. You may have to use the Move tool to adjust the sky in the selection.

# Feathering an Image

Feathering, or vignetting, creates a softened edge to a selection. A feathered edge is actually a blur. It is a transition created between the active selection and what is around the selection. Many users add a feathered effect when copying and pasting objects so that the edge of the copied object isn't harsh against its new background.

You can use the Feather command with any selection, whether your selection was created with the Lasso, Marquee, Magic Wand, or Color Range. The Lasso, Polygon Lasso, and Magnetic Lasso all have a feather option in their Options palette. If you don't choose a feather value there, you can always choose it later with the Feather command found under the Select menu.

You can even use a Feather with the Quick Mask option. As explained in Chapter 3, the regular Quick Mask creates an edge depending on your painting tool. If you use a Pencil, then the edge will be harsh. If you choose the Paintbrush, you can choose a hard or soft-edged brush. The soft-edged brush will create a small feather. You can also paint with a gray tone rather than 100% black to partially select pixels to create a feathered effect.

If you are compiling many images together, it is wise to use some sort of feather to blend them. We prefer to use a small feather of one to three pixels so there is no outlined edge to objects. If you use a Rectangular Marquee and set your feather to a high value like 25 pixels, then note that the Marquee's corners will become rounded along with your feather whether you want it to or not. More blending will occur between the selection and the background at the high setting. The lower the setting, the smaller the blend between the selection and the background.

The Feather command can be used to create a vignette appearance to a photograph. By creating a selection, entering a value for the Feather between 15 and 25, and selecting Inverse and Delete, you can give your images a soft effect much like those you see in wedding photographs.

When using the Feather command, you can only enter a value one time. If you enter a value of 20 pixels and change your mind, you should use Undo. If you choose Feather to change the number to 2 pixels from 20 pixels, your image won't change to reflect the 2 pixels. If you can't undo, fear not, you can always go to the History palette and drag the previous choices into the trash can.

## TAKE NOTE

### FEATHER TO ROUND CORNERS

If you use the Feather command to round the - corners of a Rectangular selection, you'll also get the blurred and blended pixels. If you really only want to round the corners, use Select ⇨ Modify ⇨ Smooth command.

CROSS-REFERENCE
See Chapter 3 for more on selecting.

FIND IT ONLINE
For a good Photoshop resource see http://www.i-us.com/.

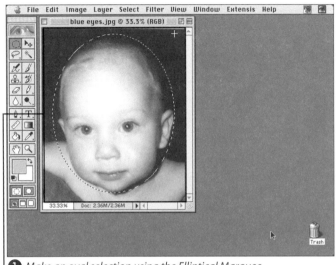

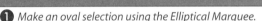

**1** *Make an oval selection using the Elliptical Marquee.*

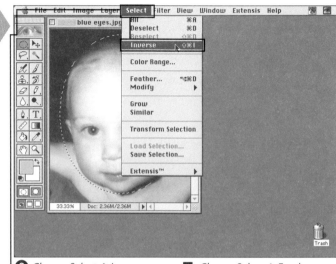

**2** *Choose Select ➪ Inverse.* ■ *Choose Select ➪ Feather.*

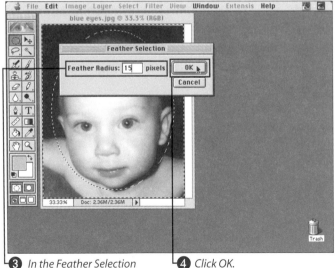

**3** *In the Feather Selection dialog box, enter 15 for the Feather Radius for a wide soft feather. For less or more of a feather enter a number between .2 and 250.*

**4** *Click OK.*

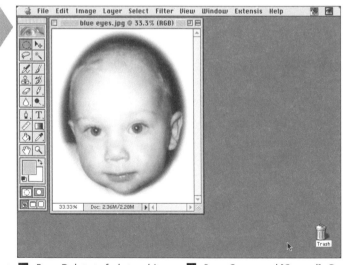

■ *Press Delete to fade to white or Option (Alt)+Delete to fade to black.*

■ *Press Command [Control]+D to deselect the image.*

# Modifying Selections and Touching Up with Matting

After spending minutes or hours making the perfect selection, you may find that you need to modify it after all. You may find that the selection is a tad too small, large, or jaggy. Maybe you have decided to add a frame around your selection. The Modify menu is found under the Select menu. The Modify menu is handy in fixing any selections you have made. To create a bordered edge like a frame around your selection, choose Border and enter a value for the frame width. The Smooth option rounds the corners of any selection, but works best on rectangular selections or selections made with the Polygonal Lasso. The Contract and Expand commands shrink or enlarge a selection based on the value you enter in pixels.

Use the Matting command to touch up the edges of a selection. The Matting command is for use after selection for touching up the edges between a newly pasted image and its background. Many masking techniques for soft wispy edges end up pulling in some of the original background and creating a haloed effect. By using one of the Matting commands you can totally remove the edge and make your object look like it has always been on the current background. For instance, many video and film editors shoot on a blue screen so the background can be added on a computer later. They select the people in the shots and when they are put on a background the blue edge shows up. The Defringe option removes the edge based on the pixel value that you enter.

The Matting commands are Defringe, Remove Black Matte, and Remove White Matte. Defringe replaces the edge pixels with the color of pixels close by. This works great on an edge that is neither black nor white. When you choose Defringe you'll get a dialog box in which you can enter the number of pixels you want to blend.

The Remove Black Matte or Remove White Matte commands remove the black or white edge within a 1 pixel width. For instance, if you copy an object from a black background, it will have a gray edge. The Remove Black Matte deletes the black pixels on the edge so the object blends better with its new background.

## TAKE NOTE

### ▶ ENTERING DEFRINGE VALUES

When entering a value for Defringe, the higher the value, the more banded the edge becomes. The default value of 1 is plenty. If you need more, then you should go back to your original selection and make it closer to the edge before copying and pasting.

### ▶ DEFRINGING DIFFERENT BACKGROUNDS

The Defringe command works best when you have copied an image from a black or dark background to a white or light background. It removes that "edge" without taking away from your selection.

### CROSS-REFERENCE
See Chapter 3 for more information on making accurate selections.

### FIND IT ONLINE
For a listing of digital artists, see
http://www.digitalthread.com/.

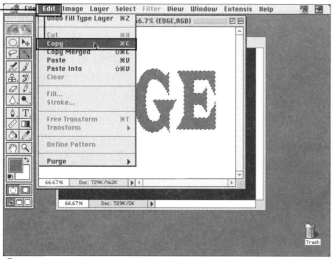

**1** *Copy rendered flattened type from a white background.*

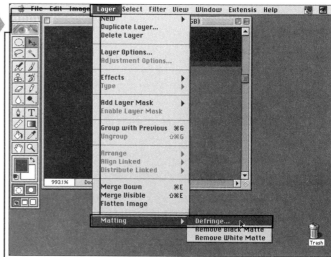

**2** *Paste the type onto a black background, and then choose Layer ⇨ Matting ⇨ Defringe.*

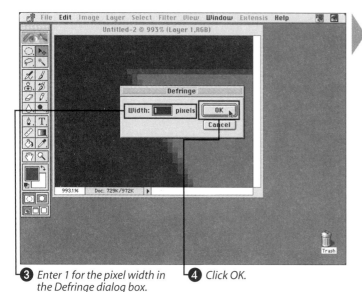

**3** *Enter 1 for the pixel width in the Defringe dialog box.*

**4** *Click OK.*

**6** *Press Command (Ctrl)+Z to see the before and after. The white background is removed from the edge of the letters, as shown in the image on the top.*

■ *The bottom is what your image would look like if you didn't smooth out the edges.*

# Saving and Loading Selections

Now that you have learned many different ways to create a selection, you also need to know how to save and load selections. A selection is actually saved as a black and white channel in the Channels palette. You can apply effects to the channels that ultimately affect the selection.

Saving a selection is so very important. If you have ever made a selection that seemed to take an eternity then accidentally clicked a few times (usually a hand cramp causes this) and your image became deselected, you know. Undo is not available because you clicked more than once. So then you have to start again.

A good method for determining when you should save a selection is to ask yourself how much of the selecting you'd like to redo. If you are working on a project that involves selecting 15 persons from various backgrounds to be combined on the same background, would you want to have to reselect all the people, three of them, or none? In this instance, you may choose to save each person as a selection. Doing so also gives you the flexibility to delete all but one selection and then you can save the file as a Photoshop file in case you need it later.

When you save a selection, you can give the selection a name. Saving selections is pretty easy, loading them is where it gets a little more complex. When you choose Select ⇨ Save Selection, you can save the selection to your existing document or to a new document. You also can make the selection a layer mask or a channel. A *layer mask* is a mask created on a specific layer that enables you to apply special effects to a portion of a layer. A *channel* is essentially a saved selection. If you choose Layer Mask, then you don't enter a name. If you choose Channel, you can choose from submenu options including New Channel, Add to Channel, Subtract from Channel, or Intersect with Channel. If you choose New, then you can enter a name for this new channel.

Use Load Selection when you want to bring a channel into your image as a selection. The Load Selection dialog box is similar to the Save Selection dialog box. You can choose which selection you want to load. The Invert box will load the opposite of your saved selection.

In the Save Selection dialog box, you can choose from several options. New Selection will create a totally new selection based on the channel. Add to Selection will add the chosen channel to the existing selection. Subtract from Selection will subtract the chosen channel from the existing selection. Intersect with Selection will create an intersection from the chosen channel and the existing selection.

## TAKE NOTE

### ▶ ALTERING CHANNELS

If you choose to apply effects such as blur or sharpen to saved channels, keep in mind that those changes affect the entire selection. If you want to keep the original selection intact, make a copy of that channel first so the original isn't changed.

## CROSS-REFERENCE

See Chapter 12 for more information on channels.

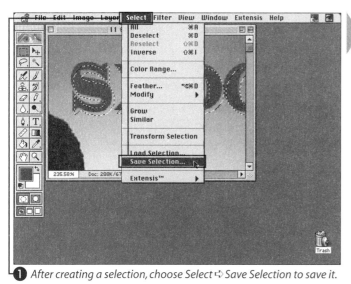

**1** *After creating a selection, choose Select ⇨ Save Selection to save it.*

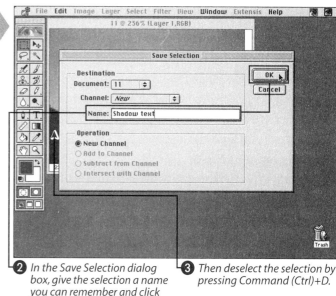

**2** *In the Save Selection dialog box, give the selection a name you can remember and click OK.*

**3** *Then deselect the selection by pressing Command (Ctrl)+D.*

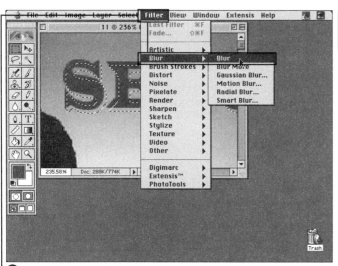

**4** *Apply a blur to the channel by first clicking the channel in the Channels palette and then choosing Filter ⇨ Blur ⇨ Blur.*

**5** *Click back on the RGB channel.*

**6** *Choose Select ⇨ Load Selection to load the new altered selection.*

**7** *Press Option (Alt)+Delete to make a blurred shadow.*

# Using Extensis' Mask Pro to Make Perfect Selections

**M**ask Pro 2.0 from Extensis is the de facto standard of masking software and for good reason. It gives users dozens of tools, functions, and features designed specifically for masking and creating selections. It's the perfect complement to Photoshop's selection tools and capabilities. Mask Pro is a plug-in for Photoshop 4 and 5.

Mask Pro works primarily by keeping and dropping different portions of an image based on Keep colors and Drop colors. You can define these colors by sampling them directly from the image or you can let Mask Pro do it automatically using the IntelliBrush tool. For many images, a professional, complex mask can be created in just minutes compared to hours using Photoshop (usually with lower quality results).

In addition to innovative color matching technology, Mask Pro also provides you with several other tools and functions designed to help make the most professional mask possible. Use the Magic Pen tool to create specific selections, or *paths*, that automatically snap to edges of varying contrast. You can specify the search area (how far the Magic Pen is allowed to look for an edge) by adjusting the Brush Size slider: the ring around the Magic Pen tool shows you graphically how far the tool can search for an edge. Press the Command (Ctrl) key to change the tool into a Magic Arrow, which can be used to adjust the path after it's drawn. Control the amount of contrast required for the path to snap to the background by adjusting the Threshold slider: drag it to the right to require edges to have more contrast, and drag it to the left to require less contrast.

Use the standard Mask Pro Pen tool to draw Bézier curves and straight line segments. The Pen tool works just like Photoshop's Pen tool; use the same keyboard commands to access the different Pen functions. You can combine Mask Pro's magic paths with regular paths simply by changing tools as you're creating a path. To drop out the contents of the path, close it and click inside the path.

You can make global adjustments to your mask by choosing Edit ⇨ Choke. The Choke dialog box enables you to adjust choke (path position) in fractions of a pixel. Enter the percentage amount of a pixel by which you'd like to adjust the mask. A negative value "spreads" the masked object, adding area to the nonmasked portion of the image.

---

**TAKE NOTE**

▶ **FIXING THE EDGE**

After you've created your mask, you may want to run EdgeBlender (part of Mask Pro) on it. EdgeBlender enables you to remove background colors from the edge pixels of your masked objects, while preserving the transparency of those same edge pixels. In the EdgeBlender dialog box, move the sliders to determine how far into the background you want to search for the background color (in pixels), and the amount of pixels you want to change (in pixels). Typically, most masks require from one to three pixels of change.

---

**CROSS-REFERENCE**

See Chapter 3 for more information on using Quick Mask.

**FIND IT ONLINE**

The Web site at **http://www.extensis.com** offers frequently asked questions about Mask Pro.

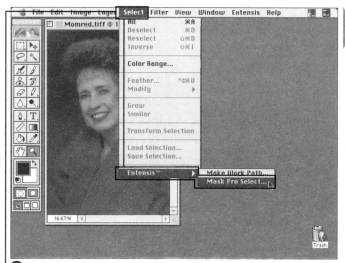

**1** To create a mask using Mask Pro choose Select ➪ Extensis ➪ Mask Pro Select.

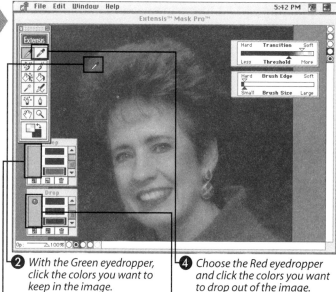

**2** With the Green eyedropper, click the colors you want to keep in the image.

**3** To add colors, hold the Shift key and click. You'll see the colors in the Keep window.

**4** Choose the Red eyedropper and click the colors you want to drop out of the image.

**5** Repeat Step 3 to add more colors. You'll see the colors in the Drop window.

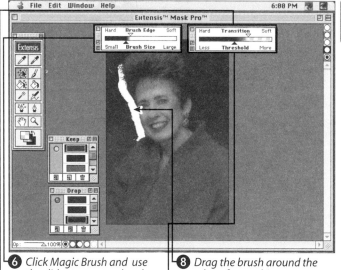

**6** Click Magic Brush and use the slider to create a brush.

**7** Set the Transition and Threshold to determine how much of the original is kept or dropped when you brush.

**8** Drag the brush around the edge of your object.

**9** If too much of the object is removed, reset the Transition/Threshold slider.

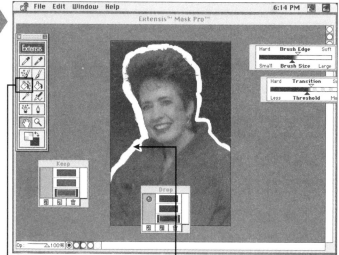

**10** Continue dragging around your image until you get a border around your object.

**11** Double-click the Magic Bucket tool to clean up specks in the brushed area.

# Using Extensis' Mask Pro to Create Pixel-Perfect Clipping Paths

You can use Mask Pro 2.0 to create clipping paths that are better than those created by using just Photoshop. A *clipping path* is used to define an irregularly shaped border, such as the shape of a person, or any other object or objects. Clipping paths are needed when you place a Photoshop image in another application, such as PageMaker, QuarkXPress, or Illustrator, and you don't want the image you've placed to have a rectangular border. When the image is saved in Photoshop as an EPS file and the clipping path is attached to the image, only areas within the clipping path can be seen (and will print) in other applications.

Mask Pro creates clipping paths that enable you to adjust the tolerance (accuracy) and choke (position) of the path when it is created; Photoshop only allows you to adjust the tolerance. Mask Pro 2.0 gives you a proxy preview so you can see what is affected by adjusting the tolerance and choke of the path before it is applied.

The higher the tolerance, the less accurate the path. You can think of it as how tolerant the path is of the actual shape: the more tolerant it is, the greater chance it will stray from the original shape. If you use a tolerance of 0, you'll have the most accurate path possible. In all but exceedingly complex images, a set-ting of 0 will be your best bet for a good, accurate path. Photoshop only enables you to set the tolerance as low as .5, which results in several areas of the clipping path that are inaccurate.

The Choke setting of the path controls the position of the path by enabling you to determine how opaque a pixel must be in order for it to be selected by the clipping path. With a high value, fewer pixels will be selected. A high value avoids selecting very transparent pixels, which will appear different than the solid colored pixels. Photoshop doesn't have this control and places all paths at a choke of 50%, which mean all pixels that are 50% opaque or darker are selected.

---

## TAKE NOTE

### ▶ NO PRINTING PROBLEMS HERE

One other feature of Mask Pro's clipping paths differentiates it from Photoshop's: no Bézier curves are created with Mask Pro. This ensures that the clipping path will print without imagesetter or laser printer errors, and can dramatically reduce printing times. Of course, in using only straight line segments, the accuracy and end result of the clipping path is also drastically better.

---

## CROSS-REFERENCE

See Chapter 14 for more information on other Extensis plug-ins.

## FIND IT ONLINE

Discover tips and tricks on using Mask Pro at **http://www.extensis.com/products/MaskPro/Mac/tips.html**.

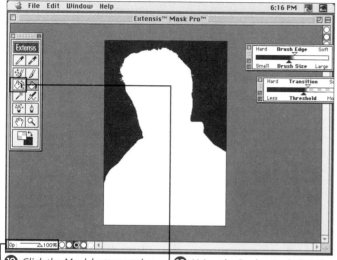

**12** Click the Mask button at the bottom of the screen to see just the created mask channel.

**13** Using the Bucket tool, click the background to fill it in with black.

**14** Click the Image button to see your image without the background (it gets filled in with white or a color that you choose; white is the default).

**15** Choose Save/Apply to see your selection.

**16** If you want to create a path of this selection, choose Select ⇨ Extensis ⇨ Make Work Path.

■ In the Make Work Path dialog box, set the Choke (position) and Tolerance (accuracy) of the path.

■ Then click OK.

# Using Other Third-Party Masking Tools

You can choose from two other major masking solutions besides Mask Pro (three if you count Photoshop itself): Chroma Graphics' Magic Mask/Edge Wizard combo and Ultimatte's KnockOut. Neither package is as useful as Mask Pro, but each has its own merits.

ChromaGraphics' products are consumer-level masking packages; that is, they're designed for the Photoshop user who does not need a high-quality end result. You need both the Magic Mask and the Edge Wizard in order to get anything close to an acceptable result. Magic Mask is the software that creates the initial selection, while Edge Wizard makes the edges soft. The two products can be accessed directly from each other's dialog boxes (in Magic Mask, click the unlabeled feather to access the Edge Wizard tools).

Magic Mask was created before Photoshop 5, so its Magic Lasso tool has a function similar to Photoshop's Magnetic Lasso. It also has a Color Wand, the most useful of all the tools, that enables you to select large areas similar in color and brightness with a single click. It works very much like Photoshop's Magic Wand.

Ultimatte's KnockOut is the yin to Chroma Graphics' yang. KnockOut is a tool only for very high end users. Unfortunately, instead of working as a plug-in to Photoshop, it is a standalone application (the Remove Black Matte function *must* be used in the KnockOut masking process). Make sure you have installed eight times the RAM of your image plus 3MB to use KnockOut or certain features of the masking software will be turned off (for a 30MB image, install 243MB of physical RAM). Keep in mind that you also have to have 5 times as much RAM as the size of the image you are working with to run Photoshop and KnockOut. You'll need 393MB of RAM to run both programs.

Masking in Knockout is done by slowly and carefully drawing a precise lasso-like marquee around each area of the image you wish to keep. Never go outside or inside the lines while drawing or the entire path will have to be redrawn if you try to undo. After you've created marquees inside and outside the areas to be selected, you can activate individual marquees by clicking the tool in the toolbox. You can then turn your selection into a mask by choosing Process from the Edit menu. Ultimatte automatically makes a blurry transition between the edges of the marquees you've drawn. KnockOut works best on images with perfectly solid backgrounds. Complex background details are typically picked up by KnockOut as part of the mask, requiring additional editing in Photoshop.

## TAKE NOTE

### ALERTING WINDOWS USERS

Windows users will have to find a Macintosh in order to use Ultimatte KnockOut. It is only for the Macintosh as of this writing.

## CROSS-REFERENCE

For more on using the Remove Black Fringe see this chapter's section "Modifying Selections and Touching Up with Matting."

## FIND IT ONLINE

This Web site shows you more information about Ultimatte KnockOut: **http://www.ultimatte.com**.

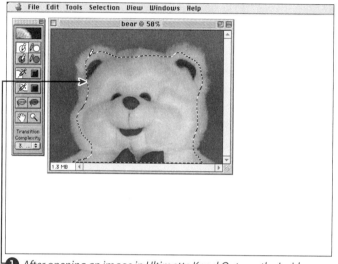

**①** *After opening an image in Ultimatte KnockOut, use the Inside Selection pencil to draw inside your object.*

**②** *Use the Outside selection pencil to draw around the outside of the object.*

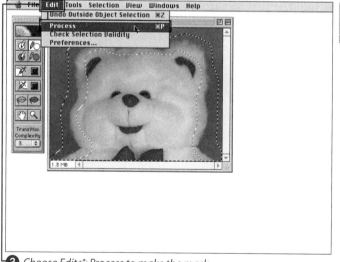

**③** *Choose Edit ⇨ Process to make the mask.*

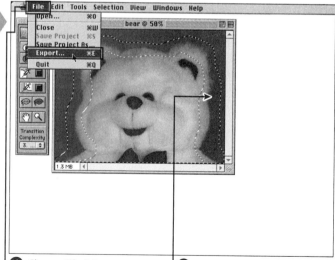

**④** *Choose File ⇨ Export to export the image into a Photoshop file.*

**⑤** *Once in Photoshop, you need to choose Layer ⇨ Matting ⇨ Remove Black Matte to get rid of any edge pixels.*

# Setting Type in Photoshop

Some of the coolest new stuff in Photoshop 5.0 is the program's improved type handling abilities. While Photoshop still isn't a typographer's dream, it adds many features that will delight most designers. One of the best improvements is a Preview check box in the Type Tool dialog box. It allows you to see what you're doing before you do it. Also new in version 5 is the ability to specify whether you want vertical or horizontal type.

In Photoshop 5, you do have some control over kerning, leading, and tracking, but the controls are not as precise as those that would satisfy the sharpest -eyed typographer. Photoshop works with type in a very different way than a program like QuarkXPress or Adobe Illustrator. Illustrator and QuarkXPress create type in a vector-based format. Photoshop creates the type in pixels.

The choices in the Type Tool dialog box include

- ▶ The *font* is the name of type you use, such as Times, Garamond, or Arial.
- ▶ The font size is expressed in points or picas, either of which you can choose from the pop-up menu. A point (pt) is a typographic unit of measurement, equivalent to $\frac{1}{72}$ inch. A pica (p) is six times the size of a point. There are 12 points to a pica, and 6 picas to the inch.
- ▶ *Leading* is the distance from the base of one line of type to the base of the adjacent line. The term comes from the old days of typography

when lines of type were spaced by inserting rows of lead between them. Most fonts have leading automatically built into them.

- ▶ *Anti-aliasing* changes the values of some of the pixels at the very edges of the selection so that type blends into its background. You must have Adobe Type Manager (ATM) installed or you must use TrueType fonts to take advantage of this.
- ▶ *Style* refers to whether your font is normal, bold, italic, or bold italic, among other things.
- ▶ *Kerning* is the spacing between the letters. You have to deselect Auto Kern to do your own kerning. To kern your type, place the cursor between letters and enter a value in the Kerning box.
- ▶ You can also choose from left-, center-, or right-aligned type. The type aligns from where you first clicked your mouse to activate the type.

## TAKE NOTE

### ▶ POSITIONING TYPE

Unlike other dialog boxes, the Type Tool dialog box lets you reach beyond it. When the Preview box in the Type Tool dialog box is checked, you can watch as your type specs unfold on the screen. You can even reach out and move type into position while you set it.

### CROSS-REFERENCE
See Chapter 5 for more on editing.

### FIND IT ONLINE
Check out **http://www.ccse.net/~harris/ FONTFUSION/main.html** for some free fonts.

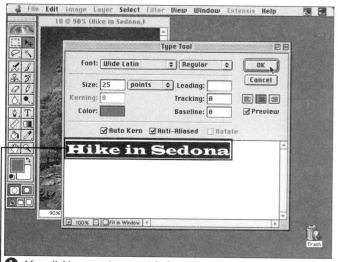

**1** *After clicking your image with the Type tool, enter your text.*

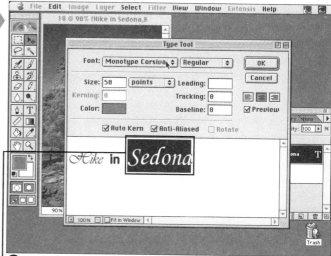

**2** *Highlight any letters or words and change the font from the Font pop-up menu. You can change the size, kerning, leading, tracking, and baseline. The Color will change for all of the text.*

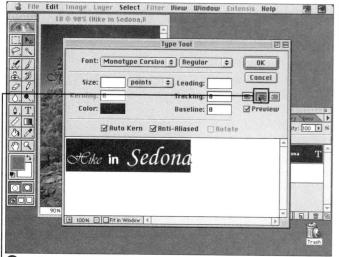

**3** *Highlight all of the text and choose the justification. You can choose flush left, center, or flush right.*

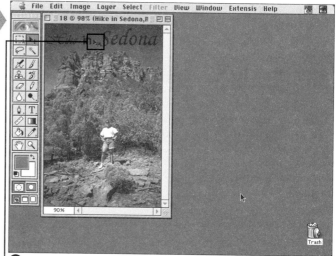

**4** *After clicking OK, move the type where you'd like using the Move tool (press V to access the Move tool).*

# Pasting into Type

Photoshop 5.0 gives you four Type options from the main toolbar: Type, Vertical Type, Type Mask, and Vertical Type Mask.

▶ Type and Vertical Type allow you to specify conventional bitmapped type; which shows up in your document just as you specified it, in whatever color you designated.

▶ Type Mask and Vertical Type Mask create active selection borders in the shape of the font you designated. This allows you to fill, copy, or otherwise manipulate the Type Mask as you would any kind of selection.

Another nice new plus is that it's very easy to change a line of type from Vertical orientation to Horizontal or vice versa. You simply select the alternate orientation from the Layer ⇨ Type menu. While this works like a snap with a single line of type, it does funny things with whole blocks of type. Maybe changing a block of text's orientation will be something for the next version.

One of the coolest features of using Photoshop with type is the ability to use the Paste Into function. Paste Into pastes a copied image into an existing selection. You can use type for that shape and create some interesting results.

While Photoshop still isn't a typographer's dream, it adds many features that will delight most designers. If the type you want to set requires special kerning or if you have a lot of it to set, you'll still want to actually set the type in a program like Adobe Illustrator and copy it into Photoshop. On the other hand, if you're setting a headline or creating icons for a Web site, give Photoshop 5 a close look before heading off in other directions. There are some great new features here.

## TAKE NOTE

▶ **PASTING QUICKLY**

The keyboard shortcut for Paste Into is Command (Ctrl)+Shift+V.

**CROSS-REFERENCE**

See Chapter 5 for more on copying and pasting.

**FIND IT ONLINE**

For Photoshop questions and answers see
http://www.graphic- design.com/letters/
questions/default.html.

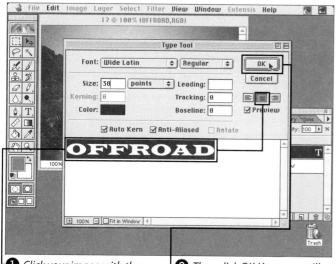

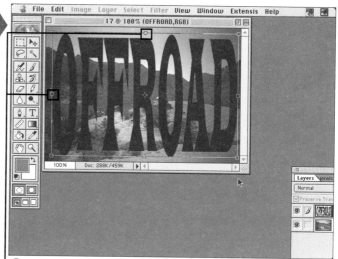

**①** Click your image with the Type tool. Enter the type in the type field, choose the justification.

**②** Then click OK. Your type will appear on its own layer on top of your image.

**③** Press Command (Ctrl)+T to access the Transform command. Drag the Resize handles to resize your type to fill the image and then press Return or Enter to accept the transformation.

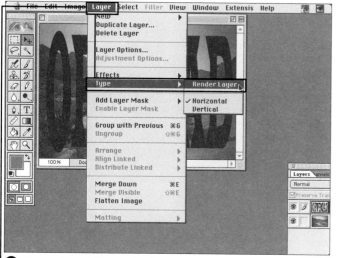

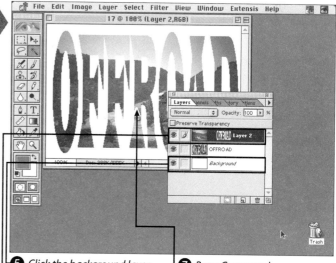

**④** Choose Layer ➪ Type ➪ Render Layer. When you render the type is changed to be pixels and not editable.

**⑤** Click the background layer and press Command (Ctrl)+X to cut the image.

**⑥** Click the type layer and select each letter using the Magic Wand tool.

**⑦** Press Command (Ctrl)+Shift+V to paste the image into the type.

■ Press V to access the Move tool to shift the image within the type.

# Working with Layer Effects on Type

Another new feature in Photoshop 5 is the ability to add Layer Effects to type. While this is not restricted to use on type, most designers will find it most useful when working with type. Accessed from the Layer menu, Layer Effects enable you to easily add Drop Shadows, Glows, Bevels and other effects to your type. This can be especially useful for the creation of graphics for the Web, where type that seems to bounce off the page is especially attractive and in demand.

Every time you set type in Photoshop, a Type Layer is created. The Type Layer can be viewed on the Layer's Palette. It contains all of the information regarding the specifications of that particular bit of type. This is a great new feature! It means that you can go back and change things you don't like and you can also go back much later to see just how you created that special effect or what font you used for a certain file. Just like other Layers, you need to flatten them, or in the case of type, render them to save the file as something other than a Photoshop file. A Layer Effect on type is an effect you choose from the Layer menu to apply to your type.

In addition to the Type Layer, a Layer is created each time you apply Layer Effects to a piece of type. That means that each effect can be changed or even deleted if you decide to change your mind about something you did earlier.

## TAKE NOTE

### ▶ THE ENTER OR RETURN KEY IN THE TYPE TOOL DIALOG BOX

Unlike other dialog boxes, you cannot activate the OK button with the Enter or Return key because that is used for text entry.

### ▶ ADDING TYPE TO A PHOTOSHOP DOCUMENT

You must keep in mind some essential points when considering adding type to a Photoshop document. The type that you create in Photoshop will not print as cleanly as the type created in an illustration program or in a layout, even though both work with the same PostScript Type 1 or TrueType fonts. Also keep in mind that once you render the type, it is no longer editable.

## CROSS-REFERENCE

For more on Pasting Into, see Chapter 5.

## FIND IT ONLINE

More tips and information on Photoshop are found at http://www.webpedia.com/cooltype/?.

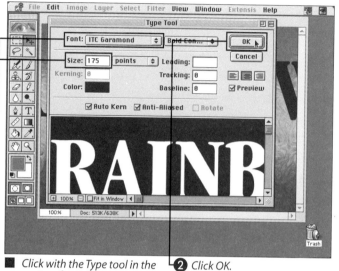

■ Click with the Type tool in the center of your image.

➊ Select your type font, size, and justification.

➋ Click OK.

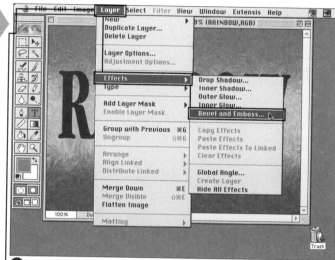

➌ Choose Layer ⇨ Effects ⇨ Bevel and Emboss.

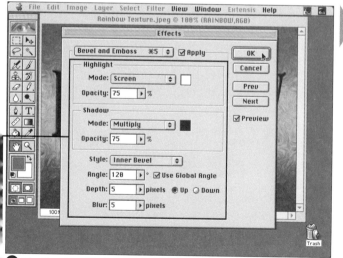

➍ The Bevel and Emboss dialog box lists many choices. If you have the Preview box checked you can see each change as you enter it. We chose a Screen Highlight Mode at 75% Opacity, a Multiply Shadow at 75% opacity, and an Inner Bevel style with an Angle of 120, Depth and Blur of 5 pixels.

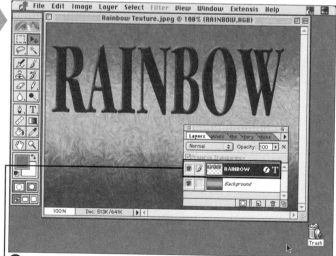

➎ After you click OK, the layer effect is added to the Layers palette.

# Working with Type Layers

Type layers can achieve a multitude of effects. Once the Type layer has been rendered in the Layers Palette, set the Magic Wand tool to a high tolerance (such as 250) and click inside a single letter's selection border. Then by holding down the Command (Ctrl) key you can move that individual letter. This can be much tidier than trying to drag the letter around with a Lasso. In this way, you can color and move single letters individually, even causing them to overlap or be out of line. Some interesting effects can be achieved with this technique.

You can create mixed fonts of white type in a black (mask) channel and then load all the type as one selection to be manipulated any way you'd like.

In most cases, when you create type in Photoshop it is because you want to apply some cool filter effect that only Photoshop can offer. Creating type while working on an image file in Photoshop adds the type to a new layer, so that you can work with the type independently of the various layers that might be involved with the image.

The type you create in an illustration program is sent directly to the imagesetter where the PostScript type instructions are interpreted and printed as smooth curves. The type you create in Photoshop comes into your document as a floating selection based on the PostScript outlines but is rasterized (turned into pixels) in order to be integrated into the image. If you want razor-sharp type overlaid on an image (such as a title on a magazine cover) you need to export the image to a layout or illustration program and add the type there to finish.

On the other hand, if your finished document will be displayed on a Web page, the reverse is true. The type can be set in an object-oriented program, and then exported as a graphic. You can then import it into Photoshop where it will behave like any other graphic created in another source.

## TAKE NOTE

### FIXING TYPE THAT OVERFLOWS

If you've accidentally specified type that overflows your canvas, don't worry. Photoshop makes sure that the edges of your type (or other data) won't get clipped. Simply manipulate the type into position using the Move tool or arrow keys, or choose Command (Ctrl)+T to transform the type and scale it down.

**CROSS-REFERENCE**

For more on Layers, see Chapter 11.

**FIND IT ONLINE**

For Photoshop techniques see **http://www.ludd.luth.se/ ~eagle/main.html.**

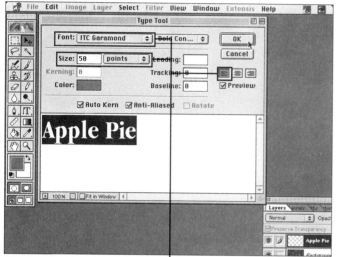

Click the center of your image with the Type tool.

❶ Enter the type font, size, and justification.

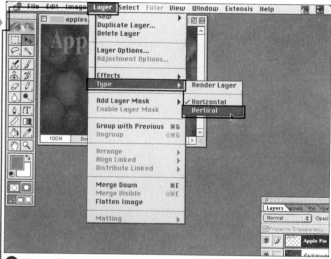

❷ Choose Layer ➪ Type ➪ Vertical to change the type's orientation.

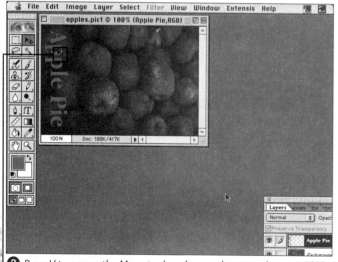

❸ Press V to access the Move tool, and move the type where you'd like.

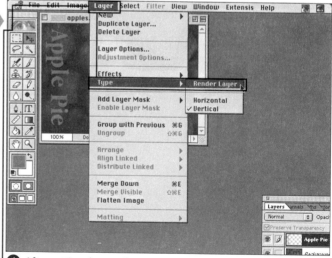

❹ After getting the type how you want it, you can choose Layer ➪ Type ➪ Render Layer to create a type layer. Only do this if you are done editing the type, because once you do this, you can't edit the type later.

# Personal Workbook

## Q&A

**1** When should you use Color Range?

_____

_____

_____

**2** How do you remove a black edge from your selection?

_____

_____

_____

**3** What Photoshop plug-in creates a great mask selection even with an image of a person with wispy hair?

_____

_____

_____

**4** What is a font?

_____

_____

_____

**5** What is the difference between _Type_ and _Vertical Type?_

_____

_____

_____

**6** How do you change Type orientation?

_____

_____

_____

**7** Why are type layers a good thing?

_____

_____

_____

**8** Can Photoshop type be edited?

_____

_____

_____

**ANSWERS: PAGE 335**

## EXTRA PRACTICE

**1** Use the Color Range tool to select a blue sky with white clouds and replace it with a stormy one using Paste Into.

**2** Copy and paste an object from a black background to a white background. Use Defringe set to 1 pixel to remove the edge.

**3** Create a dream shot of a favorite photo using the Feather option set to a high value, selecting Inverse and then pressing Delete.

**4** Create a new document and explore all of the options in the Type Dialog box. Practice changing colors and fonts, as well as experimenting with different kerning, leading, tracking, and baseline values. Remember to have the Preview box checked so you can see what's going on.

## REAL-WORLD APPLICATIONS

✔ You might use the Color Range tool to select the red pixels out of an image that has been overprocessed and has a tint of red. This makes the image clearer.

✔ You wish to create a Web graphic that incorporates a lot of carefully set type. You create the type in Illustrator, and import it into Photoshop to complete the graphic.

✔ You've done the pre-production work in Photoshop of a photo that will appear in a magazine. You have access to the fonts you need in Photoshop, but you export the graphic to an illustration program for the typographic portion of the program because you know Photoshop's type is bitmapped.

## Visual Quiz

How was this lion's fine wispy hair selected from the original background and put so effortlessly on the new background?

_____

_____

_____

_____

_____

CHAPTER **5**

MASTER
THESE
SKILLS

▶ **Copying, Cutting, and Pasting a Selection**

▶ **Masking with Paste Into**

▶ **Dragging and Dropping between Documents**

▶ **Transforming a Selection**

▶ **Using Numeric and Free Transformations**

# Copying, Cutting, and Pasting

Selecting is the most important skill to learn in Photoshop, but learning the gist of copy, cut, and paste are pretty crucial things to learn as well. Transformations — as well as copying, cutting, and pasting techniques — are at the basis of many other things you'll want to do in Photoshop. Not merely moving parts of an image from one file to another, but even very simple things like coloring a specific area or applying a filter to only one part of an image: to do much of anything in Photoshop requires one or more of these skills.

The good news is that these skills are not particularly difficult to learn: even to learn really well. In fact, if you're already familiar with either the Macintosh or Windows environment, you've probably had to do things very similar to what you'll be doing here before. As you learn, try to keep that in mind. Though some of the techniques can seem complicated, they're really little more than slightly more sophisticated versions of some of the things you probably already do in other programs every day with your computer: copying text in a word-processing program, for example. Or pasting URLs in your e-mail client.

The principals are the same, what we do with the Clipboard information is really all that's different.

To create some electrifying images, you'll definitely want to copy and paste parts from other images. You will find Cut, Copy, and Paste in many software programs. The concept is the same from program to program. When you copy or cut a section or a whole image, Photoshop places the removed or copied area to a Clipboard. More accurately, the Clipboard is a portion of *RAM (random access memory)* allocated as a holding area for whatever you choose to put there. This holding area is not a function of Photoshop. It is instead how your computer is set up to store copied or cut images/text. The Clipboard is a holding area for the purpose of transferring data between different files and applications.

Making selections are an important skill for making use of the Clipboard. If you haven't yet learned how to make a selection, you'll be unable to select the things you want to copy, cut, and paste. For more on making selections, see Chapter 3. For more advanced features of selecting, see Chapter 4.

# Copying, Cutting, and Pasting

There are essentially two types of selections in Photoshop: nonfloating and floating. When you make a selection using a selection tool, you have created a non-floating selection. If you move or delete a non-floating selection, you are essentially changing the pixels in the selection to the background color of that layer.

The floating selection is one that has been moved or transformed, but not deselected. A floating selection shows up on the Layers palette, but is actually a temporary layer. You can move and adjust the selection in any way, provided you don't deselect it. A floating selection "floats" above the pixels of the image. If a floating selection is cut, copied, or deleted, it disappears.

When taking these selections to more advanced stages, like applying filters or adjusting options, it's best to convert your floating selection into a layer. On a layer of its own, you'll be able to manipulate the floating selection without wreaking havoc on the other pixels on that layer.

When you copy or cut an image, the copy gets placed in the Clipboard. From there, it can be pasted into the same document or into another document. The Copy function is found in almost every program. Once you master it, you can use it everywhere.

Cutting a floating selection removes the selection border and the pixels within it. Cutting a non-floating selection removes the selection and replaces the pixels with the background color. Once you cut a selection, the "marching ants" or border disappears. When you Delete or Clear a selection, it is not copied to the Clipboard and therefore cannot be pasted elsewhere.

When pasting an image where there is a selection border or "marching ants" in the destination window, the image will be pasted automatically into that selection area. This replaces the pixels underneath with the copied pixels from the Clipboard. When there is no selection in the destination window, the cut or copied image will be pasted in the exact center of the document window. When you choose Paste, the pasted pixels will appear on their own layer.

## TAKE NOTE

### COPYING MULTIPLE TIMES

Once you copy an item, whether from Photoshop or any other program, you can choose Edit ⇨ Paste and paste the item into Photoshop or any other program. Once that item is copied to the Clipboard, you can paste it into any other programs that you are using.

### CROSS-REFERENCE
For more on selections, see Chapter 3.

### FIND IT ONLINE
To see more on Adobe's products see their Web site at http://www.adobe.com.

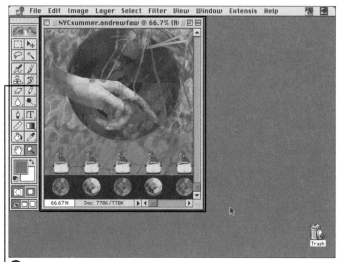

**①** Open a Photoshop file to copy a piece from.

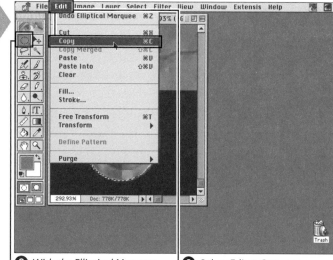

**②** With the Elliptical Marquee, make a circular selection from the center by holding down the Option (Alt) and Shift keys.

**③** Select Edit ➪ Copy or press Command+C (Ctrl+C).

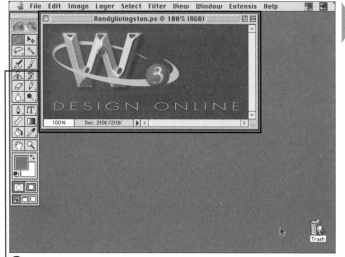

**④** Open another Photoshop file that into which you want to paste your copied object.

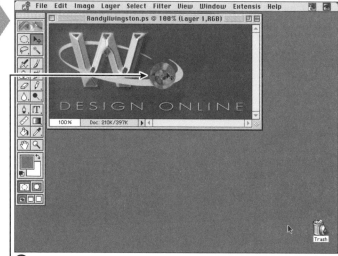

**⑤** Select Edit ➪ Paste to paste the Clipboard item into the document.

# Masking with Paste Into

You can paste copied pixels into a selection, giving you further control of pasting possibilities. Rather than just the typical paste of an image into another document, you can actually set the boundaries of where that pasted image will go. By creating a selection boundary, you can paste an image exactly within that selection with Paste Into.

What makes this feature so cool is that you can use this function as a mask. You use the active selection as the mask for the image you are pasting into. Think of masking as you do for Halloween. You wear a mask that only shows your eyes. A mask in this case is like using a cookie cutter, keeping only the parts you want in a certain shape.

Paste Into can be used between documents or within the same document. I like using it in the same document with type, then changing the color so it really stands out. This feature really comes in handy when you need an image to fit in a certain area, and creating a selection would take eons. You can paste this image into your active selection letting the active selection cut away the parts you don't want to see. The possibilities are endless with the Paste Into function. You can jazz up type, change a skyline, or create your own kaleidoscope with the Paste Into command. Another name for this function is masking.

If you're only going to use a portion of the image you have copied, you can use the Pointer tool or the arrow keys to move the pasted item into precise position. The Arrow keys are great for slight "nudging". The arrow keys move your image in increments of 1 pixel. If you want to move farther in 10 pixel increments, hold down your Shift key then press the arrow keys. If you've used Paste Into, you can only move the image within the borders of the selection.

If the image that is being copied is of a lower - resolution than the document you are pasting into, then the image may not fill up the active selection. To fix this, simply use Free Transform (Command+T [Ctrl+T]) and scale the image.

## TAKE NOTE

### PASTING RESOLUTION DILEMMAS

Before you paste anything in a Photoshop document, you must have copied or cut the item you want to paste so that it is in your Clipboard.

Keep in mind when you are pasting images with different resolutions, the copied item will take on the resolution of the document you are pasting into.

When you copy an image with a higher resolution than the file you are copying into, the image will be pasted very large. The same goes for a lower-resolution image into a higher-resolution file, the image will be pasted in small. If you scale up a small pasted image, the resolution will get grainier and not look as good.

## CROSS-REFERENCE

For more on advanced selection techniques, see Chapter 4

## FIND IT ONLINE

If you are on America Online, you can access the Photoshop forum by typing in the keyword: **Photoshop**.

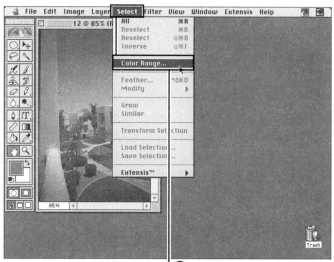

■ *Here is a photo I took from the balcony of my apartment, but the sky is so very dull.*

**①** *Choose Select ⇨ Color Range to select the background sky.*

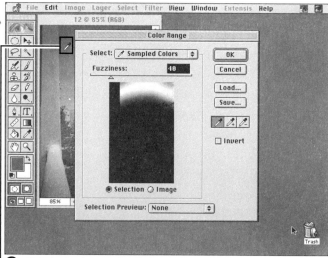

**②** *Click the background with the eyedropper to make your initial color range selection.*

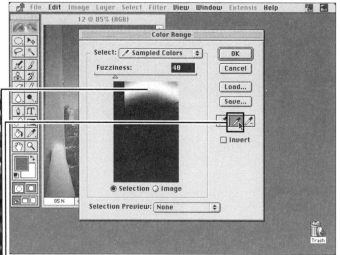

**③** *Choose the eyedropper with the plus (+) sign to add to the color selection.*

**④** *Click the other parts of the sky until the whole area shows up white in the dialog box.*

**⑤** *Open a different image to replace the original sky.*

**⑥** *Choose Select ⇨ All. Then choose Edit ⇨ Copy or Command+C (Ctrl+C).*

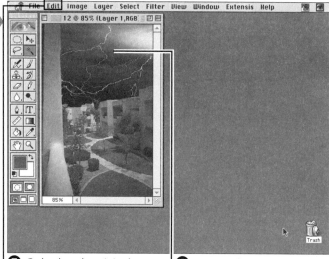

**⑦** *Go back to the original image by choosing it from the Window menu. With the selection still active, choose Edit ⇨ Paste Into.*

**⑧** *To move the pasted image, use the Move tool to get it exactly where you want.*

# Drag and Drop between Documents

You can use the Edit ➪ Copy and Edit ➪ Paste commands (Command+C [Ctrl+C] and Command+V [Ctrl+V]) to move selections between Photoshop documents. An even quicker way to get a selection from one document to another is to drag the selection from one open document and drop it into another open document. Photoshop creates a new layer for the dropped selection.

When something is pasted or dragged and dropped to another document, the selection you are copying takes on the characteristics of the file into which something is being copied. If you copy something from a CMYK file into an RGB file, the copied item is converted to RGB in the process. The same goes for resolution. If you are copying a selection with a resolution of 300 dpi into a file with a resolution of 72 dpi, then the pasted selection will have a resolution of 72 dpi. The pasted image will also be quite large because of the resolution conversion.

When Adobe came up with the Drag and Drop it was initially for using in between their programs. They came up with this for the ease of working between documents and programs. Instead of the copy and pasting, which can be time consuming for large files, you drag and drop. As with most things, there is a good and a bad side to this. The good side is that it is so quick and easy. The bad side is that

when you drag and drop Photoshop images into another program (other than Photoshop) the image's resolution is converted to 72 dpi. Why is that a big deal? Well, let's say you want to print out this file that you dragged into your PageMaker document. The text will look great, but the image will look pixelized and grainy because it isn't a high-quality resolution used for printing. If you are creating Web pages, then you'll be fine because you only need a resolution of 72 dpi. The reason for that is that a computer screen only displays at 72 ppi (pixels per inch), which is the same as 72 dpi.

---

**TAKE NOTE**

**REASONING WITH RESOLUTIONS**

Making decisions about image resolution is important because it affects both file size and quality of output. The higher the resolution, the more pixels it consists of, the better the output, the more disk space the file will take, and the longer it will take for the computer to perform operations on the file. Therefore, making a decision about image resolution will usually factor in several of these things. This doesn't mean that you should pick a high number and feel confident. If you use too high of a resolution your image will print out too dark because the pixels are too close together.

---

**CROSS-REFERENCE**

Learn more about Image Resolution in Chapter 2, "Getting to Know the Photoshop Environment."

**FIND IT ONLINE**

There is a special interest group (SIG) found on America Online. You can access the Photoshop SIG on America Online by entering the keyword: **Photoshop**.

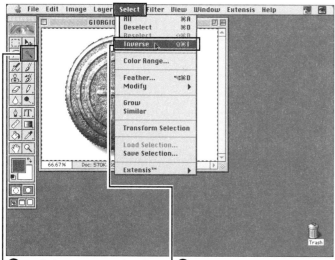

**❶** With the Magic Wand tool tolerance set to 60 select the background shadow of this logo piece.

**❷** Choose Select ➪ Inverse so just the logo is selected.

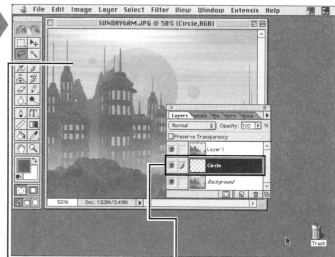

**❸** Open another Photoshop document that you want to drag and drop into.

**❹** In the city image I created a new layer between two layers so the dropped image will be in between two layers. Move the two document windows so you can see both easily.

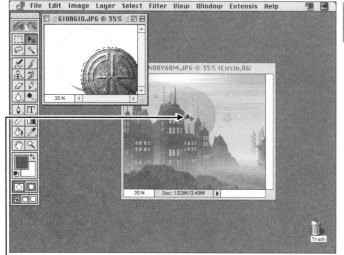

**❺** Drag the selected object and drop it over the new document.

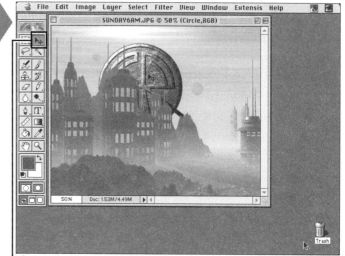

**❻** Use the Move tool to put the dropped image exactly where you want it.

# Transforming a Selection

Transform and Free Transform are two basic Photoshop functions that you'll find yourself using again and again. Both offer you varying degrees of control in terms of your image's dimension and perspective. In this task, you learn how to change the size, shape, and orientation of a selected area or areas and to gain an understanding of how those changes affect image quality.

Under the Transform menu you'll find Scale, Rotate, Skew, Distort, Perspective, Numeric, Rotate 180°, Rotate 90° CW, Rotate 90° CCW, Flip Horizontal, and Flip Vertical. You can rotate the entire image by choosing the Rotate Canvas options from the Image menu. When you apply any of these individual transformations, you can undo them by using the Undo command (Command+Z [Ctrl+Z]). Keep in mind that this Undo command only works with computer programs, you won't find that Undo button in real life. Believe me, I have felt pretty silly desperately looking for that Command+Z (Ctrl+Z) in those embarrassing situations. The Distort and Perspective options give you a box around your selected image and you can drag the handles to distort or create a perspective. Flip Horizontal and Flip Vertical let you flip the image around a vertical or horizontal axis.

Photoshop gives you the flexibility to rotate, scale, skew, distort, and alter the perspective of a selection or an entire layer using the Transform function. Free Transform lets you do all or any of these things in one operation. If you are a number person, you can enter a number exactly in the amount you'd like to move, scale, skew, and rotate. To do this, choose Edit ⇨ Transform ⇨ Numeric. Under the Transform submenu, you can also flip an image horizontally or vertically.

Transformations are a great way to add or enhance your image. For example, let's say you have this great image of a hotel garden and you need it to be longer to fill up a postcard. You can copy the image and then use the Flip Vertical to flip the copied image. After using the Rubberstamp tool, you can make that garden "grow" and no one can tell the difference.

## TAKE NOTE

### ▶ VIEWING FREE TRANSFORMATIONS

While using Free Transform to apply a number of transformations, you'll note that not all of the transformations show up onscreen right away. If you'd like to see your progress at any time, press Enter or Return. Remember, though, that doing this ends your transformations and you'd have to Undo or use the History palette to change back. As always, saving frequently is a good idea.

### ▶ USING THE NUMERIC COMMAND

When you do several operations in a single move by using the Numeric command, it is possible to Undo all of the effects at once.

## CROSS-REFERENCE
Learn more about the History palette in Chapter 12.

## FIND IT ONLINE
To check out some great tips on Photoshop check out Adobe's solutions Web site at **http://www.adobe.com/ prodindex/photoshop/solution1.html**.

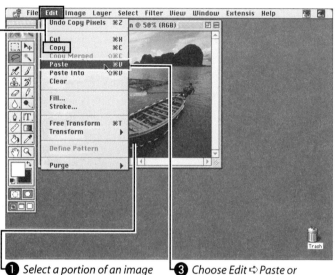

**①** *Select a portion of an image to copy and paste. I chose a boat from this image.*

**②** *Choose Edit ➪ Copy or Command+C (Ctrl+C).*

**③** *Choose Edit ➪ Paste or Command+V (Ctrl+V).*

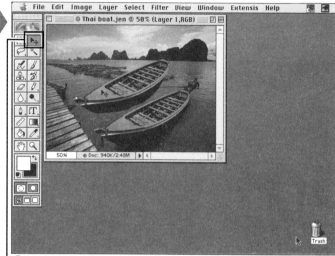

**④** *Move the boat along the dock using the Move tool (press V to access the Move tool).*

**⑤** *Resize the boat by choosing Edit ➪ Free Transform or Command+T (Ctrl+T). Drag one of the corners inward to scale the boat down, then press Enter.*

**⑥** *To add a shadow so the boat really looks like it's there, click the background layer in the Layers palette.*

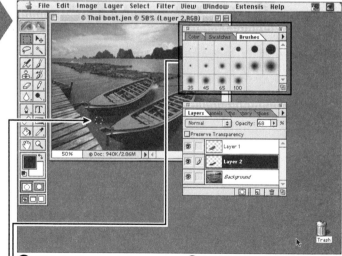

**⑦** *With the Burn tool, choose a large soft edged brush.*

**⑧** *Drag the brush at the base of the boat to create a shadow in the water.*

**⑨** *Repeat steps 2–7 to add a small fleet of boats to the dock.*

# Using Numeric and Free Transformations

Free Transform lets you scale, rotate, skew, distort and adjust perspective in a freehand way. This makes placement of the transformation easier. Also, because the data is resampled in one pass, you can expect better image quality. While you're transforming your image, you may need to move the object on the page. With the Free Transformation function, you can move, rotate, or scale in one shot as well as undo all of these transformations in one shot with Command+Z (Ctrl+Z). I like using the Free Transformations to tweak and move the center point exactly where I want. For example if you wanted to rotate a triangle from the right edge, you just move the center point in the Free Transform box to the right edge. This really makes using Free Transformations flexible.

Sometimes that "devil may care" transformation attitude just won't cut it and you need stability. That is where the Numeric function comes in. Not all of us are freeform artists; some want to rotate something exactly 32 degrees, not one degree less or one degree more.

If you are a number cruncher, you can be easily satisfied using the Numeric function. The options in the Numeric dialog box are Position, Scale, Skew, and Rotate. All of these transformations can be applied in one fell swoop. For consistency, you may want to use the Numeric so you get an exact 15-degree rotation on each selected area. The Numeric dialog box will retain the last entered information when you access it again, unless you quit Photoshop and relaunch it.

If Free Transformation or Numeric Transformations aren't enough, you can apply transformations one at a time under the Transform submenu. At the top of the Transformation submenu is the option Again (Command+T [Ctrl+T]). This handy feature enables you to apply the previous transformation again. It is best to apply transformations to an image on a separate layer. That way, you can remove or do more transformations without affecting the image underneath.

## TAKE NOTE

### INTERPOLATION

Whenever you resize, resample, scale, skew, distort, change perspective, or rotate an image, the values of the new pixels are determined by interpolation. Photoshop offers three interpolation methods, which you can choose by selecting Preferences ⇨ General from the File menu.

*Bicubic interpolation,* the default choice, is recommended by Adobe as the most precise method, although it's the slowest.

*Nearest Neighbor interpolation* is much faster than Bicubic because it simply divides each pixel into more of the same color. But the lack of precision in Nearest Neighbor can cause a jagged appearance, especially if an image is transformed more than once.

*Bilinear interpolation* is a compromise between the first two methods. It is not as precise nor as slow as Bicubic, but it is more precise than the Nearest Neighbor method.

**CROSS-REFERENCE**
To learn more about Layers see Chapter 11.

**FIND IT ONLINE**
Check out this ultimate Photoshop Web site for ultimate tips at **http://www.ultimate-photoshop.com/tips/**.

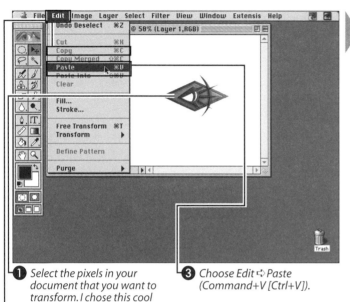

**1** Select the pixels in your document that you want to transform. I chose this cool eye logo.

**2** Choose Edit ➪ Copy (Command+C [Ctrl+C]).

**3** Choose Edit ➪ Paste (Command+V [Ctrl+V]).

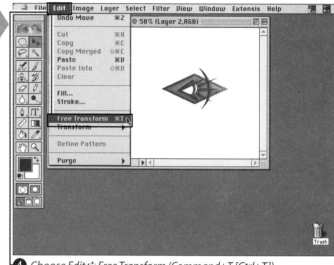

**4** Choose Edit ➪ Free Transform (Command+T [Ctrl+T])

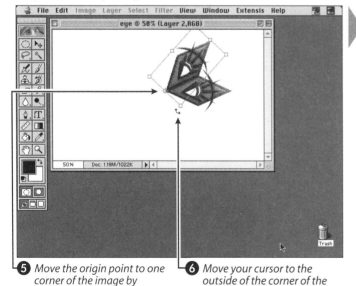

**5** Move the origin point to one corner of the image by dragging it.

**6** Move your cursor to the outside of the corner of the transform rectangle and drag to rotate the object.

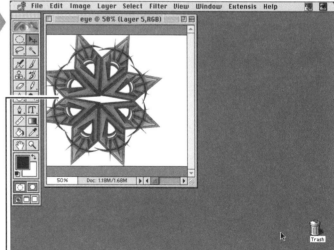

**7** Repeat steps 2–7 to create a cool pattern.

# Personal Workbook

## Q&A

**1** Where does a copied or cut object go?

_____

_____

_____

_____

**2** How many items can the Clipboard hold?

_____

_____

_____

_____

**3** What is a "floating" selection?

_____

_____

_____

_____

**4** What can happen when you drag and drop between documents?

_____

_____

_____

_____

**5** When would be a good time to use the Paste Into?

_____

_____

_____

_____

**6** What are the differences between the _transform_ and the _free transform_?

_____

_____

_____

_____

**ANSWERS: PAGE 336**

## EXTRA PRACTICE

**1** With something Cut from an RGB file in your Clipboard, paste the item into a file saved in a different color mode like CMYK. See what happens to the color of the added piece.

**2** Copy a large image to the Clipboard, set some type with the Type Mask tool. Use the Paste Into command to fill the type with your image on the Clipboard. Choose the background layer from the Layers palette. Choose Image ⇨ Adjust ⇨ Levels and drag the Output levels black slider (at the bottom of the dialog box) and drag the slider to the middle. See the background lighten and your text remain darker.

## REAL-WORLD APPLICATIONS

✔ You want to create a complicated image comprised of parts of many files. You use the Clipboard and cut and paste to bring these images together into one document.

✔ Create a logo that has a strong photographic image flowing through type. You use the Paste In command to paste the image into a Type Mask for an eye-catching Advertisement.

✔ You have to piece together multiple photos into one document. Rather than copying and pasting over and over, you drag and drop and save tons of time.

## Visual Quiz

The image here shows a cool cityscape stuffed inside of text. How was it done? What other options can you apply to the text? Can you do this on your own?

_____

_____

_____

_____

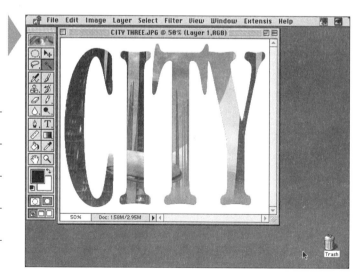

CHAPTER **6**

MASTER
THESE
SKILLS

▶ Using the Smudge, Blur, and Sharpen tools

▶ Softening with the Blur Filter

▶ Clarifying with the Sharpen Filter

▶ Touching Up Using the Toning Tools

▶ Cloning with the Rubber Stamp Tool

▶ Cloning between Documents

▶ Erasing to History Images

▶ Using the History Brush

# Editing in Photoshop

All of the editing tools provide you with the opportunity to fine-tune your creations, and to hone and smooth and otherwise give finish to your Photoshop art. All of these tools have counterparts in the nondigital world, which traditional photographers and illustrators use to tightly manipulate their work to gain the desired finish. The Photoshop editing tools should be viewed in that light. The really spectacular results you might have seen in Photoshop were most likely honed with one or more of these tools. Gaining proficiency with them will help you polish your Photoshop work.

The editing tools use the Brushes palette to determine the shape of their affected area. All the brush shapes are available, including those in the supplementary brushes folder provided by Adobe and any custom brushes you might have created. The Mode pop-up menu on the Brushes palette also offers a choice of editing modes. There are no opacity choices, but rather, variations of exposure and pressure.

Editing tools manipulate only the image that exists already. They do not apply any additional paint to the screen (with the exception of the Smudge tool Fingerpaint option). Editing tools, however, can blur, sharpen, lighten, and darken the pixels they interact with, thereby creating the effect of painting.

In order to gain proficiency, spend some time working with the editing tools in various ways. Put aside some time when you're not on deadline to play with each tool. That is, go through the exercises, push and prod each tool, and gain a thorough understanding of its capabilities. Think about what it might do in different circumstances and how you might use it. That way, when the time comes, you'll know to reach for the Dodge tool instead of the Sponge tool when you're working on a special project that requires just that touch.

Remember that you can also use the editing tools in a very localized way by selecting a specific area of your image with a Marquee, Lasso, or Magic Wand and working only in the selected area. This can give you control of a very tight portion of your image and — when working on a zoomed image — permits you to edit a few pixels at a time. Combining the editing tools with text can open even more Photoshop possibilities.

# Using the Smudge, Blur, and Sharpen Tools

In Photoshop 5, the Smudge, Blur, and Sharpen tools are accessed from the same location on the toolbar. This seems to be a bit of programming convenience on Adobe's part, since the Sharpen and Blur tools are quite different from the Smudge tool, and they edit differently too.

If you were to drag a finger through wet paint, you'd be duplicating the action of the Smudge tool. It grabs the color at the beginning of your stroke and pushes it toward the place where you're stroking. The Smudge tool is good for creating soft, feathery effects, such as adding wisps of hair to a portrait, creating cloud effects, soft textures, or fabric folds, blending colors together, or applying a special drawing technique for fine arts projects.

The Smudge tool is not good for retouching sizable parts of a photograph because it can create an unnatural effect when used in large areas. For example, to fix a blemish on a portrait, it's better to use the Rubber Stamp tool to clone a nearby sample of good skin over the imperfection. You'll learn more about the clone tool in Task 5 of this chapter. If the Fingerpainting mode is clicked in the Smudge tool's Options palette, the foreground color is smudged at the beginning of each stroke.

The Blur tool takes the hard edges off things; it reduces detail. You might use the Blur tool to soften areas of high contrast in a photograph or painting that might attract undesired attention, or subdue selected areas of a background. An alternate method would be to apply the Blur filter, which you will learn about in the next task.

Use the Sharpen tool to focus details. The Sharpen tool is essentially the antithesis of the Blur tool. Use it in spots where you want to bring out the detail in a small area. The Sharpen tool increases the contrast of the pixels you brush over to 'crisp-up' an image. The Sharpen tool must be handled carefully. Too much sharpening can create a pixellated look.

If you are wondering why there are blur and sharpen tools as well as filters, each has its own particular use. The tools enable you to apply the effect with a brush while the filter applies the effect to the whole or the selected part of the image.

The Smudge, Focus, and Sharpen tools won't work with indexed color or bitmap files. To use one of these tools on a file of that type, first change to a different mode by selecting Image ⇨ Mode ⇨ RGB or whatever other file type you think is appropriate.

## TAKE NOTE

### RETOUCHING BY LAYER

When using any of the editing tools — Blur, Smudge, or Sharpen — you can work on either all of the layers in the open document or only one at a time. To work on all layers at once, make sure the Use All Layers box is clicked in the tool's Options palette. To work on only one, deselect the Use All Layers box and highlight the layer you want to work on in the Layers palette.

## CROSS-REFERENCE

For more on image adjusting, see Chapter 8.

## FIND IT ONLINE

For information on Photoshop for PCs, check out http://www.netins.net/showcase/wolf359/adobepc.htm.

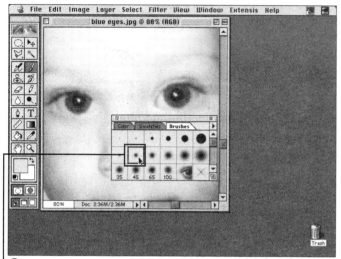

**1** *Click and hold on the Blur tool in the toolbox. Drag over to the Smudge tool to make that tool active. Choose a Brush that is small and has a soft edge.*

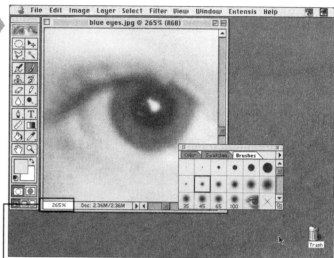

**2** *Zoom in by typing in a number in the Zoom window; for instance 265.*

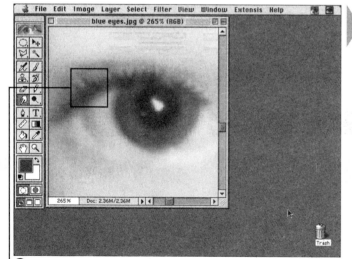

**3** *Starting at the base of the eyelashes, stroke outwards to fill in more eyelashes.*

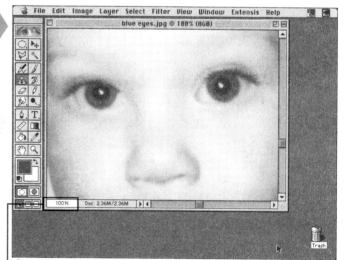

**4** *Zoom back out to 100% so you can see how the eyes look with fuller lashes.*

# Softening with the Blur Filter

The other way to use a Blur with an image is to use the Blur filter found in the Filter menu. Using filters is a great way to affect a large area surrounded by a selection. Your Blur choices are Blur, Blur More, Gaussian Blur, Motion Blur, Radial Blur, and Smart Blur.

The Blur filters will soften the edges of the pixels to create a fuzzy effect. Blur and Blur More are two blurs that don't bring up a dialog box. A predetermined or default blur amount is applied to your selection, which cannot be adjusted. Blur More just applies a larger blur amount to your selection or whole image.

If you want to see the blur and adjust it to your will, then choose Gaussian Blur. The Gaussian Blur dialog box lets you choose the Radius in pixels of the blur and you can check the Preview box to see how your image is being affected. There is a plus (+) and minus (–) that lets you zoom in and out to see the whole image. If you place your cursor over the thumbnail image, the cursor turns into a hand so you can move the image (if you are not zoomed out all the way).

Motion Blur does what it sounds like. It applies a blur in a direction simulating motion in your selection or whole image. The Motion Blur dialog box has an Angle that you can enter numerically, or you can drag the line in the circle to the angle you want. When you choose an angle the pixels will be dragged out a particular distance along the line of that angle. For instance

if you chose 45 degrees as your angle and 10 pixels as your distance, your Motion Blur would show dragged pixels for 10 pixels along a 45-degree angle. You also choose the Distance in pixels. The distance refers to how far the pixels will be dragged in a direction from the original position. If you set the distance really low, you may not see much of a moving blur. If you set the distance too high, you'll lose definition of your image. This filter is pretty cool to use to apply a motion to a selected object or to a background.

The last of the Blur filters is the Smart Blur. The Smart Blur filter will apply an exact blur based on your input. Your Options are Radius, Threshold, Quality, and Mode. You can alter the Radius and Threshold or keep the defaults. The Quality choices are Low, Medium, and High. Your Mode choices are Normal, Edge Only, and Overlay. The Edge Only is great to use when you have pasted an image and the edges are harsh. The Edge Only will slightly blur the edge so it blends better to the background image.

## TAKE NOTE

### BLURRING MORE NATURALLY

To apply a more natural blur, use Gaussian Blur set at a small amount and repeat by pressing Command [Ctrl]+F.

**CROSS-REFERENCE**

For more on copying and pasting see Chapter 5.

**FIND IT ONLINE**

This Web site at **http://pw1.netcom.com/ ~relan/index.html** shows you a wide array of artwork.

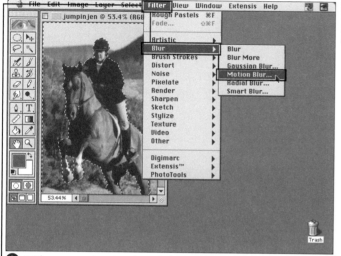

**1** With an area already selected, choose Filter ⇨ Blur ⇨ Motion Blur.

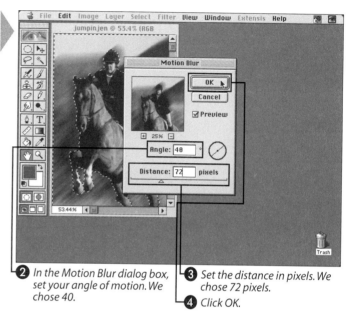

**2** In the Motion Blur dialog box, set your angle of motion. We chose 40.

**3** Set the distance in pixels. We chose 72 pixels.

**4** Click OK.

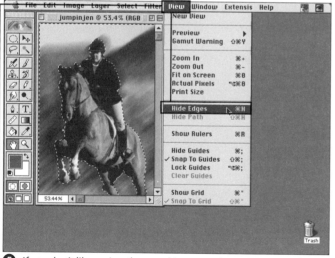

**5** If you don't like seeing the marching ants, choose View ⇨ Hide Edges. We like to choose this option so you can see without the distraction of your selection.

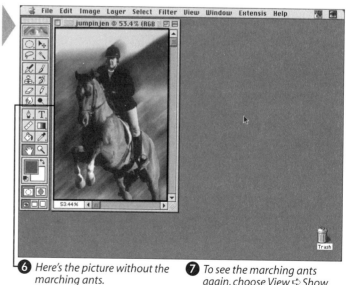

**6** Here's the picture without the marching ants.

**7** To see the marching ants again, choose View ⇨ Show Edges.

131

# Clarifying with the Sharpen Filter

The Sharpen filter lets you crisp-up your selection or the whole image. You can use the Sharpen tool, but it will only let you apply the effect in a brushing manner. The Sharpen filters are Sharpen, Sharpen Edges, Sharpen More, and Unsharp Mask.

Sharpen and Sharpen More filters are set up the same way as Blur and Blur More filters: they sharpen your image or selection by a predetermined amount. Sharpen More will apply the filter at a higher amount than Sharpen.

The Sharpen Edges filter will boost the contrast between the pixels in the selection border and the adjacent background pixels. The pixels side-by-side are more contrasty around the edges of your objects. Photoshop determines where the edges are by reading the areas of different colored pixels.

The most common and best way to sharpen an image is to use the Unsharp Mask filter. The phrase "unsharp mask" refers to how a photographer would fix a blurry image the old-fashioned way. An image tends to blur if there is movement when taking the picture, a bad scan from your scanner, resampling of the image size, or a bad print. The Unsharp Mask filter reads the pixels that are different from the pixels in the area and adds contrast according to your input. Your choices in the Unsharp Mask filter are Amount, Radius, and Threshold. Amount is how much you want the pixels to contrast. Radius is the size of the area affected. A low radius mostly affects the edges of the pixels, while a high radius affects more pixels. Threshold determines how much of a difference there is between the surrounding pixels. The Threshold range is between 0 and 255. A low Threshold means that most, if not all, of the pixels will be affected.

## TAKE NOTE

### THE BEST WAY TO SHARPEN

Unsharp Mask is the best filter to choose when you want to fix a blurry image. Set the Amount to a low value and repeat the filter until you get the desired effect. If you try to get the focus fixed in one shot, you'll tend to get pixelized, harsh edges.

### SHARPENING AND BLURRING MORE NATURALLY

It may sound strange but if you want to get a good sharpen or blur, don't use the Blur or Sharpen tools. Instead, use the Unsharp Mask filter and Gaussian Blur tool to get a more natural effect. Unsharp Mask enables you to specify the amount of sharpening that will be applied to your image or selection, and you can see a preview of it before you click OK. Gaussian blur on the other hand will enable you to apply a specified blur to your image or selection and show you a preview before you choose OK.

## CROSS-REFERENCE

For more on filters, see Chapter 14.

## FIND IT ONLINE

The Web site http://www.geocities.com/MadisonAvenue/9546/ shows you Outland Graphic Design Services' portfolio.

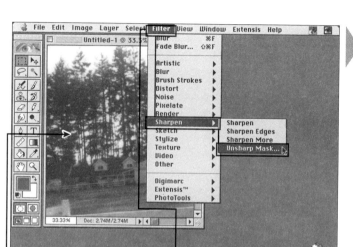

❶ Choose an image that is blurred.

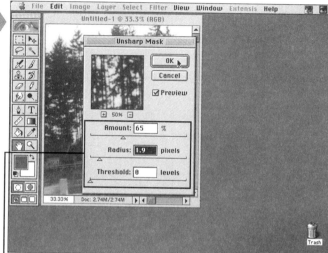

❷ Choose Filter ⇨ Sharpen ⇨ Unsharp Mask.

❸ We entered a value of 65% for amount. That let us see some sharpening amount without making harsh edges. You adjust the values by entering a number or dragging the slider. Don't try to do it all in one shot by entering high numbers in the settings, it will only make the image harsh and over-contrasted.

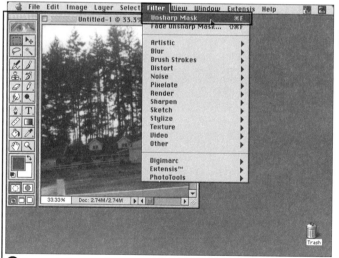

❹ Instead, choose a low setting and keep applying it until you get the results you want.

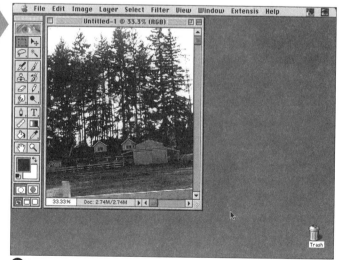

❺ You can choose the last filter from the Filter menu or press Command (Ctrl)+F.

# Touching Up Using the Toning Tools

The phrase "dodge and burn" refers to the way a photographer makes a portion of a print lighter or darker during the enlarging and printing processes. *Dodging* means preventing light from reaching the photosensitive paper, thereby keeping it lighter. Dodging is often done in shadow areas, so that they don't block up and lose detail. *Burning* is just the opposite of dodging. If a highlighted area is overexposed in the negative, the photographer will give extra exposure to that area so that details are brought out on the print. That is because the print is the opposite of the negative. The photographer may use his hands or a piece of cardboard to hold back light from the rest of the print so that only a selected area is burned or darkened.

When you use the Photoshop Dodge and Burn tools, you can lighten or darken an image without affecting the hue. These effects are applied with a brush for a more natural feeling. These two tools are grouped together in the Toning Tools palette, along with a third tool, the Sponge, which can be used to 'soak up' a particular color.

The Sponge can be used to selectively increase the saturation of a particular area of your image, thus brightening it up, or to reduce the amount of saturation, thereby bringing an area into the CMYK gamut. Because of the limitations of the printing press, CMYK colors are generally less bright and vivid than colors produced with the RGB model. Because it works only with color saturation, the Sponge cannot be used with indexed color (256-color) images or one-color (bitmapped, black-and-white) images. Likewise, you can't use the Smudge, Blur/Sharpen, or Dodge/Burn/Sponge Editing tools on the bitmapped image.

Like the other editing and painting tools you've explored, if you have a digitizing tablet with a pressure-sensitive stylus, you can set it to vary the size of the brushstroke or the exposure as you vary the pressure. You'll find these settings in the Dodge/Burn Options palette. To access the palette, simply double-click with your mouse on the Dodge or Burn tool in the toolbox.

The Exposure option in the Dodge or Burn Options palette enables you to control the amount of lightening or darkening with the Dodge or Burn tool. When you click and hold on the arrow in the Exposure option a slider appears, which you can drag to increase or decrease the amount of exposure.

When the Dodge/Burn tools are active, the Toning Tool Options palette shows a different pop-up menu that enables you to control where the lightening or darkening effect occurs—in the Shadows, Midtones, or Highlights of an image.

## TAKE NOTE

### ► TOGGLING BETWEEN DODGE AND BURN
Release the mouse button and press the Option (Alt) key while you're using the Dodge tool to change immediately, or *toggle*, to the Burn tool and back.

**CROSS-REFERENCE**
For more on adjustments, see Chapter 11.

**FIND IT ONLINE**
Check out Andy's Web at **http://www.andyart. com/index2.html** site for a plethora of Photoshop tips, Web stuff, and a cool portfolio.

**1** With an image already open, choose a large, soft-edged brush. We chose the 65-point brush.

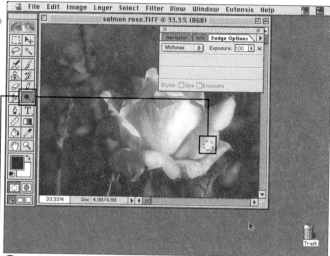

**2** Select the Dodge tool and brush on the areas that you want to lighten.

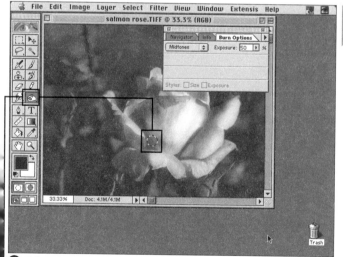

**3** Select the Burn tool and brush on the areas that you want to darken.

**4** With the Sponge tool set for Desaturate, paint around the edge of your object so the background becomes grayscale and your object remains in full color.

# Cloning with the Rubber Stamp Tool

The Rubber Stamp tool provides much of the magic associated with Photoshop. With the humble Rubber Stamp, you can sample one part of an image and paint what you've sampled on another part of the screen. This is also called *cloning*. You can even clone an image from one window into another.

All the painting modes apply (Lighten, Darken), and you can control opacity just as you do with other painting tools. For more on the Painting modes and painting in Photoshop see Chapter 9.

The Rubber Stamp tool can be used in a wide variety of Photoshop functions. For example, you can use the Rubber Stamp to add a tree where there wasn't one before or to move people closer together. You can also use it to edit in tight areas. I've found it useful to reproduce hair and skin textures in photo composites or where time has eroded image quality, such as in scratched old photographs that you'd like to repair.

If you double-click the Rubber Stamp tool, this brings to the front the Rubber Stamp Options palette. In the Options palette there is an Aligned check box. If you have this option checked then when you are rubber stamping the image constantly resamples your image and paints the resampled pixels wherever your brush is. In other words, the plus sign that you see stays aligned to the Rubber Stamp tool. When you take a sample (by holding down the Option [Alt] key), then start to rubber stamp, the position between the sample and where you are rubber stamping stays the same.

If the Aligned box is unchecked, then your sampled image stays put and keeps repeating from the original sampling. If you click a person's eye and want to repeat the eye over and over, then make your initial sampling of the eye, then click and drag and let up with your mouse repeatedly. The key is to click and drag and let up with your mouse, then click and drag and let up.

You can also set the opacity of the Rubber Stamp. At 100% you'll get the initial sample at full opacity. To soften the image or to show transparency, set the Opacity to 50% or less. There are many great uses for this tool such as adding more trees to a landscape, removing any unsightly blemishes (perhaps a person who walks into your picture), filling in between the border where you reflected a copied image, and more.

## TAKE NOTE

### CHEATING WITH THE RUBBER STAMP TOOL

If you uncheck the Align box and use the Rubber Stamp tool without letting up on the mouse button, you can get the same effect as having the Aligned box checked.

## CROSS-REFERENCE

For more on layers, see Chapter 11.

## FIND IT ONLINE

The Web site at **http://members.aol.com/sourcetile/** has a bunch of cool backgrounds.

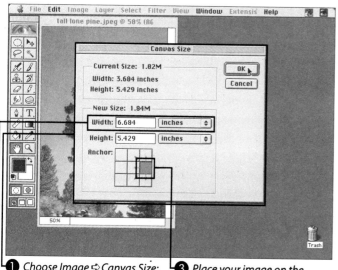

**1** *Choose Image ⇨ Canvas Size; the Canvas Size dialog box displays.*

**2** *Double the width.*

**3** *Place your image on the "canvas" by clicking one of the Anchor squares. Leave enough blank canvas on which to clone the image.*

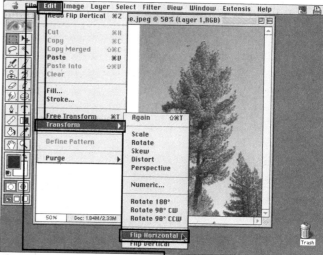

**4** *After selecting the right half of your image, press Command (Ctrl)+C to copy, then Command (Ctrl)+V to paste your copy.*

**5** *Choose Edit ⇨ Transform ⇨ Flip Horizontal.*

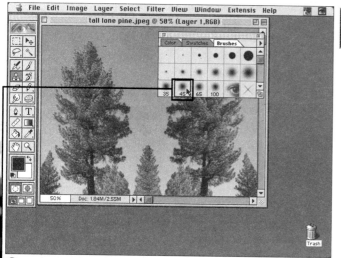

**6** *After moving the flipped image to the left side of the canvas, choose a large, soft-edged brush.*

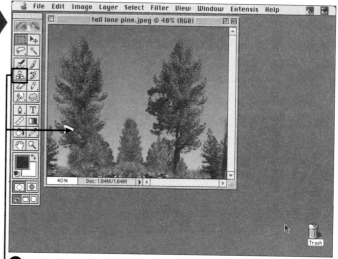

**7** *Use the Rubber Stamp tool to fill in more trees and rocks to make the image look less symmetrical.*

# Cloning between Documents

The Rubber Stamp tool lets you create amazing effects. You can use it to fix up an existing image, add to an image, fill out an image, and more. One of the really amazing things you may not realize is that you can use the Rubber Stamp tool between documents. Let's say that you really like part of an image, and you want to combine it with another image. You can use the Rubber Stamp tool to bring the images together.

If you are looking to repeat a section of an image, deselect the Align box in the Rubber Stamp Options palette. The key to successfully using the Rubber Stamp tool is to keep your eye on the crosshairs. The crosshairs tell you where the sampling is coming from. If you get close to the edge of your image, then watch out. If you hit an edge with the crosshairs and you are rubberstamping in the middle, then the part you are painting will get a sharp edge to it.

The Rubber Stamp tool has many different possibilities. We have used it to take the age off a model's photograph, blend away blemishes, and add parts to an image without using Copy and Paste. Using the Rubber Stamp tool can give a soft edge which

blends better than a pasted image. We have also found this tool particularly useful when removing objects or scratches in a photograph. If you are working with a landscape and accidentally mar the sky, fear not. If you select the sky using the Color Range command found under the Select menu, you can select the whole sky and blend two colors of blue to fix it. This trick has been used many times to fix a sky or make a prettier one.

## TAKE NOTE

### RUBBER STAMPING ON A LAYER

If you are like many artists and don't want to alter your original, you can work your Rubber Stamp magic on a layer that you can remove or to which you can apply other effects. The key to doing this is that you have to click the layer that you want to Rubber Stamp from first to make your sampling, then click the new layer to Rubber Stamp.

## CROSS-REFERENCE

For more on selection options, see Chapter 4.

## FIND IT ONLINE

For more on the Rubber Stamp tool, check out :http://www.treeo.com/PhotoDigiWorkshop/photoediting.html.

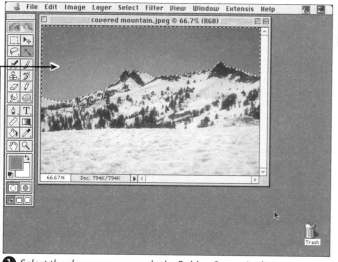

**1** Select the sky so we can apply the Rubber Stamp in that area without spilling over into the foreground.

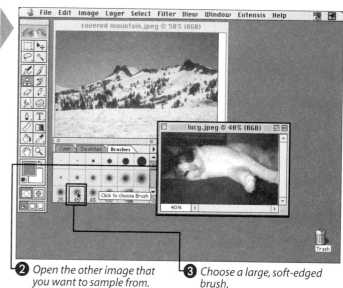

**2** Open the other image that you want to sample from.

**3** Choose a large, soft-edged brush.

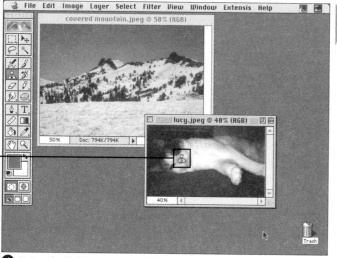

**4** Using the Rubber Stamp tool, make your sampling on the second image by pressing the Option (Alt) key to "suck up" a sample.

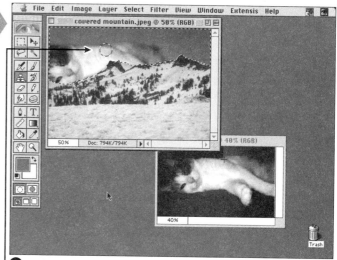

**5** With the Rubber Stamp tool, apply the sampled section to the first image in the selected area. Click and drag the image over the sky.

# Erasing to History Images

You can use the Eraser tool to erase part of an image. When you erase, you will always reveal the background color underneath. The background color is chosen from the background swatch in the Toolbox. What you're actually doing is changing the image's pixels as you drag past them.

The Eraser tool will only work on the active layer in the document. So remember, if you're working in a document with more than one layer, you need to go to the Layer Palette and highlight the layer you wish to erase from.

Let's say that you've saved an image that you've been working on. Then you make some changes to it, but you need to undo some of those changes. You can restore portions of the saved image with the Magic Eraser. Select the Eraser tool from the toolbox. Position the eraser over the area you want to restore to the saved image. Press the Option [Alt] key before pressing the mouse button and drag the eraser over the part of the image you want to restore. The eraser turns into the Magic Eraser, a square with an arrow going up and around the square. The original saved image will reappear in place of the changes you made. If holding the Option (Alt) key is a hassle, simply check the Erase to History box found in the Eraser Options palette. You can access the Eraser Options palette by double-clicking the Eraser tool in the toolbox.

The key to doing anything in Photoshop is to save often. This especially comes into play when using the Magic Eraser. Photoshop will look for the last saved version of the file you are working on and pull from that to replace the pixels you are erasing. This feature is pretty cool to use when you want to restore a section, but not the whole image. With the Magic Eraser, you can control with your brush what parts of the image come back. Rather than using the standard Magic Eraser (the square with the arrow), you can set your Preferences for Display and Cursors to show your Painting Cursors by Brush size rather than Standard. This will show you the exact brush size you are working with rather than the tool's icon.

If you want to erase something very small, it might make more sense to use a small brush or pencil (1 pixel in diameter) and to use it with the foreground color set to the color of the screen. The eraser can be used to erase one pixel at a time, but only if you are zoomed in to a 16:1 enlargement of a file. To restore the entire image from the last saved version on your hard disk, select Revert from the File menu.

---

**TAKE NOTE**

### ERASE TO HISTORY OPTIONS

The Erase to History check box in the Eraser Options palette lets you erase to your last saved version of your image. You can also use the History palette to erase or remove unwanted effects to your image. In the History palette you can pick and choose the effects you want and don't want to see.

---

**CROSS-REFERENCE**
For more on the History palette, see Chapter 12.

**FIND IT ONLINE**
For more information on the Eraser tool, see
http://www.extropia.com/tutorials/photoshop/
eraser_tool.html.

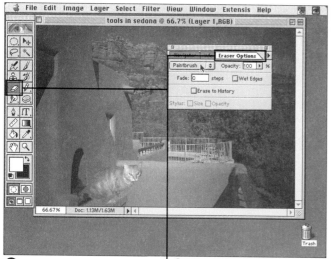

**1** You realize the fire you added to your image just isn't cutting it, so you want to remove just that area.

**2** Choose the Eraser tool, and double-click it to get the Eraser Options palette.

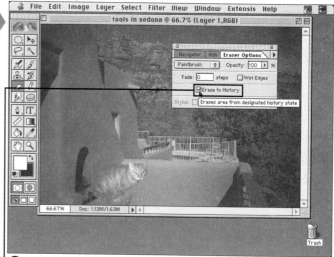

**3** Click the Erase to History box.

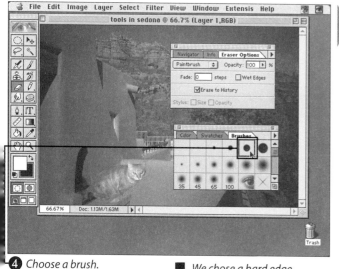

**4** Choose a brush.

■ We chose a hard edge because we wanted to completely remove the fire.

**5** Start erasing the image (the Eraser tool is set to display a brush in this figure).

# Using the History Brush

The History brush is a new tool to Photoshop 5. This amazing brush lets you paint back parts of an image from a previous snapshot. A snapshot is what you create in the History palette to remember how your image looked at that moment. To access the History palette, choose Window ⇨ Show History. To create a snapshot, you'll need to click and hold the arrow in the upper right of the History palette to access the pop-up menu. In this pop-up menu you can make a new snapshot. You can create many different snapshots of your image as you are working on it. This is the alternative to saving and it takes a lot less time, and you have multiple images to work with rather than just one.

The History brush takes the Erase to saved option even further. You can utilize many more 'saved' versions and be very picky on what parts you want back and what parts you don't. It seems in this new version of Photoshop, Adobe has paid attention to the user's complaints of only having one undo option. Adobe has given you many different options to restore parts of your image or the whole image.

You know how we have been saying to work on a layer so you don't affect the original? Well, if you use the History brush and update your snapshots, you can work right on the original without any fear of destroying it. Updating your snapshots is like saving often. If you update the snapshot frequently, then you are accepting the work you have done so far on your image. You need to update as often as you feel comfortable. If you don't update and try to use the History Brush, then you'll end up reverting your image back further than you may have wanted.

The options in the History Brush Options palette include Painting Modes, Opacity, Impressionist, and Stylus. The Painting Modes for the History brush are the same as all of the Painting tools (such as Normal and Difference). For instance, you can set the opacity so you brush back a transparent effect. The one that intrigues us the most is the Impressionist option. The Impressionist option will paint back, but also drag the pixels around, simulating an Impressionist painting. This can make for a cool artistic effect to the whole image or just a central object of your image.

The History brush can be used with a stylus, so a pressure-sensitive tablet is a must. If you don't have one, you should seriously consider purchasing one. Having a tablet will enable you to apply varying pressures to control how much of the image comes back.

## TAKE NOTE

### ► CLICKING THE SNAPSHOT FIRST

Be sure to select the snapshot (found in the History palette) before using the History brush. If you want to change the snapshot you can do so each time you brush if you like.

## CROSS-REFERENCE

For more on the History palette, see Chapter 12.

## FIND IT ONLINE

For more Photoshop tips, go to **http://www.algonet. se/~dip/photoshop/tips/tips_00.html**.

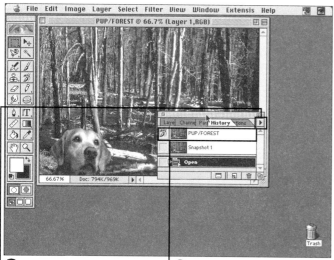

**①** *Open the History palette. Click the arrow in the upper-right corner of the History palette and hold. Drag down to New Snapshot to make a snapshot.*

**②** *Click the snapshot you want to use the History brush with to activate that snapshot.*

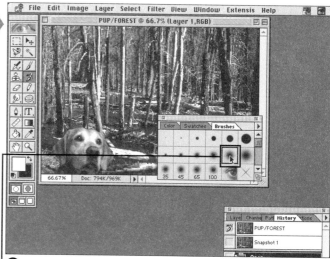

**③** *Choose a brush from the Brushes palette.*

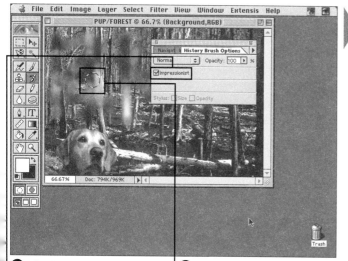

**④** *Check the Impressionist box in the History Brush Options palette.*

**⑤** *Start brushing to create the Impressionist effect. We chose to apply this effect to the trees by painting up the tree length.*

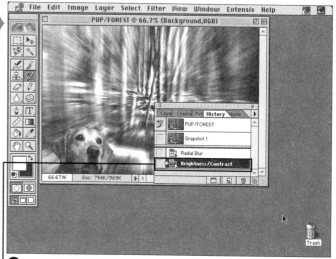

**⑥** *To see the effect and turn off the effect you can click off or on the name of the effect in the History palette.*

# Personal Workbook

## Q&A

**1** What is the purpose of the editing tools?

_____

_____

_____

**2** Where does the phrase "dodge and burn" come from?

_____

_____

_____

**3** Why would you use the Smudge tool?

_____

_____

_____

**4** Name the retouching tools.

_____

_____

_____

**5** Name the toning tools.

_____

_____

_____

**6** When should you use the Sponge tool?

_____

_____

_____

**7** How can you apply cool filter effects to text?

_____

_____

_____

**8** How does the History Brush compare to the Magic Eraser?

_____

_____

_____

ANSWERS: PAGE 336

## EXTRA PRACTICE

1. Open a practice file and use all of the Retouching tools. Check what each one does in each of its settings.

2. Use each of the Toning tools in a practice file. Use each one in each of the available settings.

3. Use the Navigator to get in very close. Then use it again to stand back and look at your work.

4. Find a photograph that is too light or too dark in some places. Use the Toning tools to make it more visually acceptable.

5. Use the Erase to History option to bring back parts of your image for which you didn't like the editing.

## REAL-WORLD APPLICATIONS

✔ Someone comes to you with a photo they'd like retouched to make them look ten years younger. You could put on your surgeon's cap and use the Toning and Retouching tools to smooth wrinkles and remove sags.

✔ Someone else appears with a photo of their Uncle Joe that they really like, but it's been sitting in a drawer for 40 years getting pushed to the back by socks and handkerchiefs. It's worn and torn looking. You could scan the photo and use the Retouching tools to bring Uncle Joe back to youthful health.

✔ You want to create a really distinctive border around a photograph. You could use the Smudge tool to create something entirely original.

## Visual Quiz

Can you tell if this "before and after" image was an actual doctor's photograph for plastic surgery or a Photoshop creation?

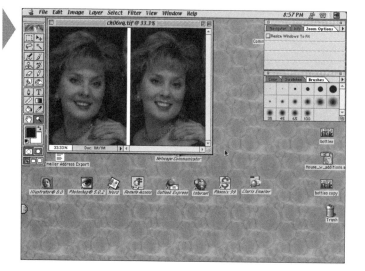

_____

_____

_____

_____

_____

# PART

## III

Contents of 'Desktop'

Name

My Computer

Network Neigh

Internet Explor

Microsoft Outloo

Recycle Bin

My Briefcase

3252-9

3259-6

3261-8

3262-6

3281-2

3296-3

DE Phone List

Device Manager

In

Iomega Tools

# Color, Painting, and Image Adjusting

# CHAPTER 7

# Creating with Color and Gradients

Now that you are really getting into Photoshop, you probably want to create your own colors, fills, and patterns for your images. Before delving into color you first must determine what color mode you'll be working in. The color modes are important for your output purposes. Working with a color mode is different from choosing a color to work with in Photoshop, but they do go hand in hand. Color modes affect what colors are available in the Color Picker. You'll use Color Picker to make your own colors to use in Photoshop. Color Picker lets you create any color you'd like in a variety of ways. After creating an amazing color, you can save the color for future use in your Swatches palette.

Like many other aspects of Photoshop, fills and gradients are easy to use once you get the hang of it and spend a bit of time experimenting with possibilities. They can add finish and polish to your work as well as structure to your basic designs. The Fill command enables you to lay flat color into selections and type very easily, but you can also fill in areas with gradients or patterns. The Gradient tool extends this filling capability by providing you with the ability to create effects that appear three-dimensional, as well as enabling you to apply special effects to type to give depth and richness to flat color.

You have several ways to create fills in Photoshop:

▶ Use keyboard shortcuts to fill an area with either the foreground or background color.
▶ Use the Fill command found under the Edit menu to fill a selection with a solid color or pattern.
▶ Use the Paint Bucket tool to create anti-aliased or aliased solid or patterned fills.
▶ Use the Gradient tool to create a variety of gradations of tone and/or color.

# Changing Color Modes

Photoshop's color modes are essential when it comes to outputting your images. When you have determined how your image is going to be viewed, imported, or printed, then you should choose the appropriate color mode in which to work and save the file. There are eight modes from which you can choose. You'll find the mode choices under the Image ⇨ Mode menu. You also can choose between 8 Bits/Channel and 16 Bits/Channel for each mode. The more bits per channel, the larger the file, and the more colors there are with which to work.

**Bitmap.** Displays only two values: black and white.

**Grayscale.** Displays up to 256 tones of gray.

**Duotone.** Displays up to 256 tones of gray and 256 tones of another color. For a third (Tritone) and fourth (Quad) color, you get 256 more tones per color.

**Indexed Color.** Displays up to 256 colors but reads the file and displays only the number of colors necessary.

**RGB Color.** Displays 255 tones of black and white for each color, resulting in 255 reds, 255 greens, and 255 blues.

**CMYK Color.** Displays 255 tones of black and white for each color, resulting in 255 cyans, 255 magentas, 255 yellows, and 255 blacks.

**Lab Color.** Creates consistent color that is not dependent on output.

**Multichannel.** Creates 256 tones of gray for each channel (you can have up to 24 channels).

If you convert your image to Indexed Color, you can access the Color Table from the Image ⇨ Mode submenu. The Color Table lets you change or edit the colors of an indexed mode file. This option is a quick and cool way to change the color in your image without the hassle of selecting. If you want to convert your image to RGB, CMYK, or Grayscale, then choose the Profile to Profile option.

A note of caution: Changing an image's mode multiple times will result in the original pixel information being lost and a compromise in the resolution. One change is fine, but the more you do, the more you lose.

## TAKE NOTE

### ▶ KNOCKING OUT WITH SPOT COLOR

Sometimes, you want your color on top to be a clear color and not blended with the color below. To create this, you'll need to have the color on top knock out the color below where they cross. If you are looking to use a Spot color for knocking out parts underneath your image, then you'll want to look at using another program like Adobe Illustrator. Illustrator allows you to use Spot colors and assign colors to knockout or overprint much easier than Photoshop.

## CROSS-REFERENCE

For more information on Modes, see Chapter 2.

## FIND IT ONLINE

This website shows you some real cool images that were created using Illustrator first, then Photoshop to finish: http://www.artworksstudio.com/awsprint.htm.

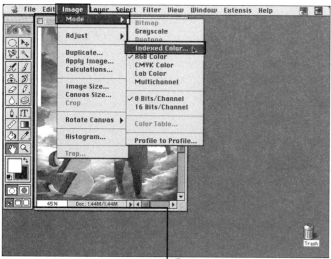

■ *This task prepares your image for the Web in Indexed mode. To change to another mode, simply choose Image ➪ Mode ➪ RGB or whatever mode you wish.*

❶ *Choose Image ➪ Mode ➪ Indexed Color.*

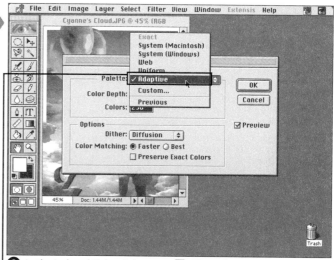

❷ *In the Indexed Color dialog box, choose Adaptive for Palette so the image will adapt to whatever system is being used to view it.*

■ *The Color Depth and Colors will default to the best choice, but you can change them if you'd like.*

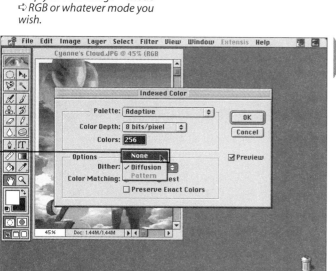

❸ *In the Options area, choose None for Dither to display the colors as they appear in the original.*

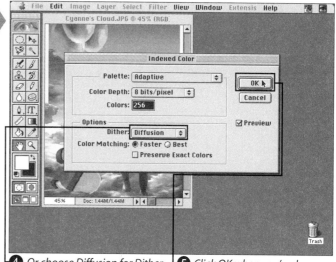

❹ *Or choose Diffusion for Dither to even out the flat colors by adding pixels of different shades in the flat area.*

❺ *Click OK when you're done.*

# Understanding the Color Picker

Photoshop's Color Picker can be accessed by clicking the foreground or background color swatch in the Toolbar or from the Color palette. There are eight different options in the Color Picker dialog box. The four numerical entries are

- ▶ **HSB.** Also known as hue, saturation, and brightness. The *hue* is the main chosen reflected color. *Saturation* is the intensity of the color specified in the hue box. *Brightness* represents the lightness or darkness of color.
- ▶ **RGB.** Also known as red, green, and blue. This color mode represents red, green, and blue in values from 0 to 255. The lower the value, the more black will show in that color. The higher the value, the more white. Your monitor displays in RGB so your color will look like what you choose on screen.
- ▶ **Lab.** Consists of lightness and two chromatic properties. The *a* stands for the green to red properties, while *b* stands for the blue to yellow properties. This color model was created to display consistent color regardless of the device you are creating on or printing to.
- ▶ **CMYK.** Also known as cyan, magenta, yellow, and black. This color mode is the best choice for printed images. With CMYK, the value you

enter creates a color. CMYK is the total of all four colors. The higher the value in one color field, the more of that color you'll see in the final result. You can work a file in RGB to see how it is on screen then change to CMYK for printing purposes.

You can also choose a color from the Color Field, which displays in the left area of the dialog box, and change the Color Field base color using the Color Slider to its right. The boxes to the right of the Color Slider show you the original color on the bottom and the new color on top.

You can use Custom Colors by clicking the Custom button and choosing from various options in the pop-up menu. Photoshop defaults to Pantone Coated because these are the most frequently used custom colors. If you know what color you want, simply enter the number and your color will be selected.

---

**TAKE NOTE**

▶ **RETURNING TO DEFAULT**

If you have totally mangled the foreground and background colors and want a quick way to get back to the default black and white, press the D key for default.

---

**CROSS-REFERENCE**

For more on color basics, see Chapter 1.

**FIND IT ONLINE**

http://www.artdude.com/portfolio/area1/videodata .html shows the power of using Photoshop to blend photos and illustrations.

① Select the white background of your image using the Magic Wand tool.

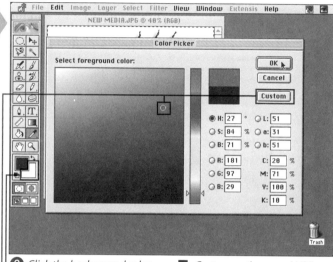

② Click the background color swatch to display Photoshop's Color Picker.

③ Enter a color numerically, with the color circle, or by clicking the Custom button.

■ Custom options are ANPA color, DIC Color Guide, FOCOLTONE, PANTONE Coated, Process, ProSim, and Uncoated, TOYO Color Finder or TRUMATCH.

④ Click the foreground color swatch to display the Color Picker again.

⑤ Click the Custom button to display the Custom Colors. Pick a color and click OK.

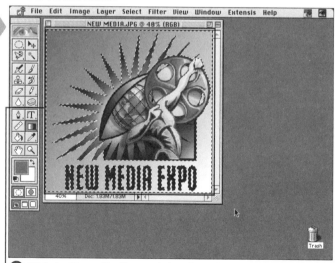

⑥ With the Linear Gradient tool, drag from the top of your image to the bottom to create a nice gradient from your foreground and background swatch colors.

# Using Swatches

Swatches are a great handy item to use when choosing color for your image in Photoshop. The Swatches palette gives you some default swatches to choose from and room to add your own colors.

The options found in the pop-up menu are Reset Swatches, Load Swatches, Replace Swatches, or Save Swatches. You access the pop-up menu in the Swatches palette's upper-right corner arrow.

**Reset Swatches.** You can reset the Swatch palette back to the original default colors. When you choose this option, you get a dialog box asking you if you want to Replace current swatch colors with the default colors. You can click Append, Cancel, or OK.

**Load Swatches.** Any saved Swatch palettes can be loaded by using Load Swatches. The Load Swatches will add the selected saved Swatch file to the end of the existing Swatches in the Swatches palette.

**Replace Swatches.** The Replace Swatches option will replace the existing Swatches in your document with the saved Swatch file you choose.

**Save Swatches.** The Save Swatches option lets you save the existing Swatches in your document. You can use the Save Swatches to keep a library of your client's specified palettes. When I save a Swatch file, I usually create a folder in Photoshop's application program that is called Swatches, so I can find the saved Swatch palettes easily.

With the Swatches palette you can change the foreground or background colors in a snap. To replace the foreground color, just click the swatch that you want. To replace the background color, hold down the Option (Alt) key and then click the swatch that you want.

I love using the Save Swatches option to create custom palettes for each of my clients. That way I can easily load the Swatch palette I need for whichever client's job I am working on for that day. Also because we know all clients change their mind at some point, you can update the Swatches palette easily.

Think of the Swatches palette as a painter's palette. You can keep colors that you access on a regular basis there and not have to re-create the color each time you want to use it. Keep reading to see how to add and remove Swatches.

## TAKE NOTE

### FIXING DEFAULT SWATCHES

A great way to fix any strange Photoshop happenings is to throw out the Photoshop Preferences file. The Photoshop Preferences file is found in the Photoshop application folder, inside the Adobe Photoshop Settings folder. Don't worry about throwing out what may seem like an important file, Photoshop will automatically regenerate a new preferences file with the standard defaults. You can only do this when Photoshop isn't running.

## CROSS-REFERENCE
For more on changing color in Photoshop, see Chapter 1.

## FIND IT ONLINE
This Web site at **http://www.dreamlight.com/gallery/ paint/index.htm** shows you many great images that were created using only Photoshop.

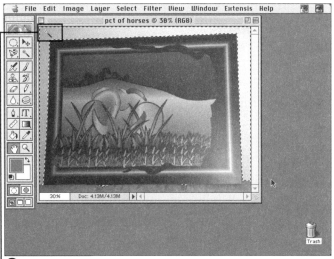

**1** *Using the Magic Wand tool, select the background of an image.*

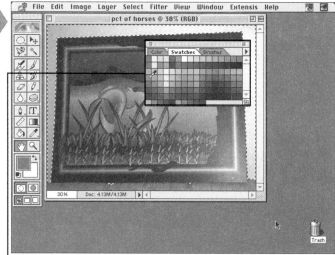

**2** *If the Swatches palette isn't open, choose Window ➪ Show Swatches. Click a Swatch in the Swatches palette that you want to use to replace your background color.*

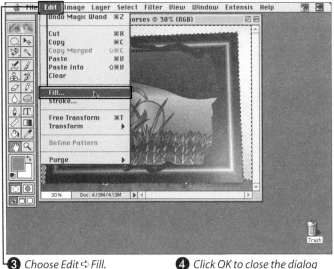

**3** *Choose Edit ➪ Fill.*

■ *Choose background Color, 100% opacity, and Normal mode.*

**4** *Click OK to close the dialog box.*

**5** *Your new Swatch color fills in the selected area. You could also press Option+Delete (Alt+Delete) to fill the area.*

# Adding and Removing Swatches

Now that you get the gist of the Swatches palette, I am sure you want to customize it. In the Swatches palette you can add and remove swatches with the click of your mouse.

Before you can add a swatch, you need to define a color. You can define a color by using the Color Picker and entering values. You can enter HSB, RGB, Lab, or CMYK values. Or you can choose a new color in the Color Field area and use the Color Slider to adjust to the range of colors you want. By clicking the Custom button, you can pick from many different types of custom colors.

If you are creating a totally new custom palette, I suggest that you remove all of the swatches first, then add your new colors one at a time. This task may seem tedious and it may take a while, but it will pay off in the long run if you have repeat business from a big client that uses a certain color palette. After creating a new Swatch palette, be sure to save it in your Photoshop folder for easy retrieval later. You can save as many Swatch palettes as you'd like, provided you have the disk space.

Your limit on the number of Swatches depends on the size of your monitor. On my 15-inch monitor I can drag the Swatches palette as large as it goes and can make a whopping total of 736 Swatches. A quick way to remove Swatches is to hold the Command (Ctrl) key down and click the first swatch repeatedly until all of the swatches are gone. That way you can start with a fresh empty palette.

Duplicating a Swatch is easy to do. You have to select the Swatch you want to duplicate and then click in an open area of the Swatches palette to have that duplicate color show up there. You may want to do this because you like the color tone, but maybe want it a bit lighter or darker. You can change it by entering a smaller number to make it lighter, or adding black to darken.

If you want to replace a Swatch with another color, create the color first, then press Shift and click the existing color you want to replace.

One great use of creating your own swatch palettes is that you can save palettes per customer. When you need to access that particular customer's palette for any revisions, it is a breeze to load the palette. We recommend that you save the swatches either with the client's job, or if you name the swatches after the client (i.e. Adobe9901 for the first job for Adobe in 1999) and save all of the swatches in a swatches folder right inside the Photoshop folder.

## TAKE NOTE

### NAMING YOUR SAVED SWATCH PALETTES

You should save your new Swatch palettes with a name you can relate to the job, such as Bezier logo palette, instead of 1, 2, or 3. You'll never remember which client belongs to which number.

## CROSS-REFERENCE
For more on the Photoshop window, see Chapter 1.

## FIND IT ONLINE
This Web site at **http://www.ebergman.com/postcards.html** shows you an interesting way to promote and sell your work.

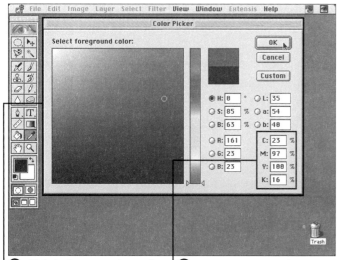

1. Click the foreground swatch in the Color palette to launch the Color Picker dialog box.

2. Enter your CMYK values.

3. With the new color in the foreground color swatch, put your cursor over a blank part of the Swatches palette.

4. The cursor changes into a Paint Bucket tool.

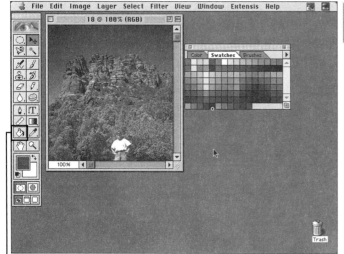

5. Click with your Paint Bucket in the blank area and your new color swatch appears in the palette.

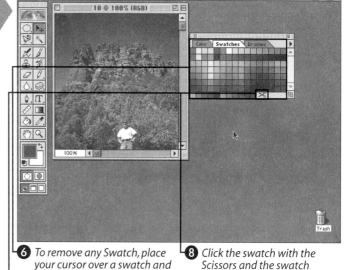

6. To remove any Swatch, place your cursor over a swatch and hold the Command [Control] key.

7. You'll notice your cursor changes to a pair of Scissors.

8. Click the swatch with the Scissors and the swatch disappears.

157

# Adding Fills to Your Image

When we talk about Fills in Photoshop, we're really talking about one of four things: filling an area with the foreground or background color, filling a selection with a color or pattern, using the Paint Bucket tool, or using the Gradient tool. While these methods produce strikingly dissimilar results, they all push some type of color into a previously specified area.

When you choose Edit ⇨ Fill, the Fill dialog box appears. In the Contents area, use the pop-up menu to choose your fill color. You have seven choices: Foreground Color, Background Color, Pattern, History, Black, 50% Gray, and White.

You can also choose to blend your fill. In the Blending area of the Fill dialog box, enter a percentage from 1% to 100% in the Opacity box to specify how much of the color you want to fill with. The higher the percentage, the more opaque the fill.

The Blending Mode option is much more complex. You have a whopping 19 options to choose from. Popular modes include

- **Normal.** Replaces the entire selected area with the color.
- **Dissolve.** Creates a speckled or rough airbrush look to your selection.
- **Overlay.** Overlays the selected color and lets the color and texture underneath show through.
- **Soft and Hard Light.** Apply either a diffused light or spotlight effect to the selection.

- **Difference.** Removes the selected color from the original color.

The Paint Bucket tool can be very helpful in certain situations. If you have a bunch of selections and only want to fill certain ones, the Paint Bucket is perfect. In some ways it is very much like the Magic Wand tool, except that it fills adjacent pixels that are similar in color with a new color of your choosing, rather than creating a selection. You select the pixels to be affected by determining the pixel Tolerance, just as you do with the Magic Wand tool. Use the Paint Bucket tool to fill either a selection or a solid-colored area with no pixels selected.

The Paint Bucket is a little tricky to use as an entirely precise tool. When you click the point of the Paint Bucket's drip on an area you sometimes get an entirely different reading with areas quite close together. You can adjust the Tolerance to get the Paint Bucket to fill as you'd like.

The Paint Bucket tool will fill areas with solid color. If you want to fill an area with a blend or a gradation of colors, then the Gradient tool would be the one to use. For more on the Gradient tool see the next task.

## TAKE NOTE

### ACCESSING THE FILL DIALOG BOX

To access the Fill dialog box quickly, press Shift+Delete (Shift+Backspace).

### CROSS-REFERENCE

For more on filling with the Paint Bucket tool, see Chapter 6.

### FIND IT ONLINE

Artist Randy Livingston has quite a cool slide show that you can view by visiting **http://zoom.bradley.edu/webwork/bfw3/fatboy.htm**.

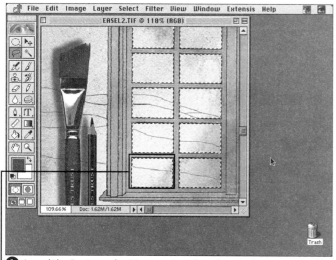

**1** *I used the Rectangular Marquee to select the window panes in this image. By holding the Shift key, you can continue to add to the original selection.*

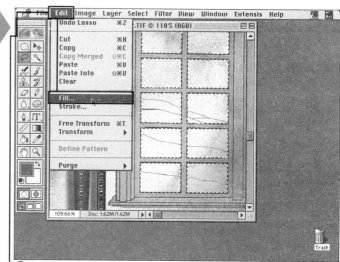

**2** *After choosing a color from the Swatches palette (I chose a pale yellow), choose Edit ⇨ Fill. The Fill dialog box opens.*

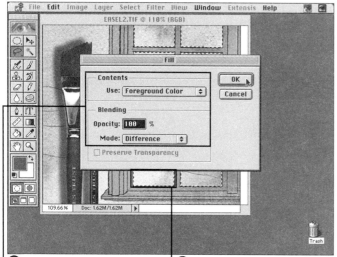

**3** *Set the Use pop-up menu to Foreground Color, the Opacity to 100%, and the Mode to Difference.*

**4** *The Difference mode will fill with the opposite of your chosen color in an overlay fashion. Since I chose a pale yellow, my fill will end up being a dark blue.*

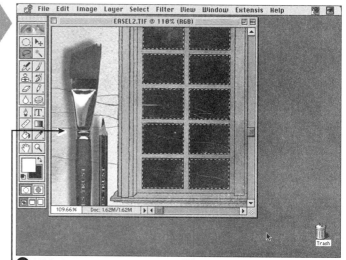

**5** *With the Marquee tool, click in another area of your image to deselect the selection (marching ants).*

■ *Or, you can also use View ⇨ Hide Edges to remove the ants.*

# Using the Gradient Tool

The Gradient tool is wonderful for creating a fill that is a smooth blend of multiple colors. You can use it to create special effects like chrome that would be difficult to produce otherwise. The gradient is applied only within a selected area or to the whole document if nothing is selected.

The many fills that Photoshop provides and the immeasurable combinations of color and fill type are what make the Gradient tool really fun and versatile. You can choose a default Gradient Fill in the Tool Options Palette or you can create your own. The default Gradient fills include Foreground to Background, Foreground to Transparent, Black/White, Red/Green, Violet/Orange, Blue/Red/Yellow, Blue/Yellow/Blue, Orange/Yellow/Orange, Violet/Green/Orange, Yellow/Violet/Orange/Blue, Copper, Chrome, Spectrum, Transparent Rainbow, and Transparent Stripes.

Five Gradient types are found in the Gradient tool's pop-up tools.

- ▶ Linear fills are applied in a straight line from the beginning point to ending point, no matter what the shape of the selection may be.
- ▶ Radial fills radiate out from a center point, like the glow radiating from the sun.
- ▶ Angular fills shade a counter-clockwise motion around the indicated starting point.
- ▶ Reflected fills use symmetric linear gradients on both sides of the indicated starting point.

▶ Diamond fills shade out from your starting point in a diamond shape. The defined ending place resembles a corner of the diamond.

Sometimes the effect you're looking for can't be found with the existing gradient fills. Photoshop lets you easily create and edit your own fills by clicking the Edit button in the Gradient Options palette. In this dialog box you can make a new gradient, rename, remove, duplicate, load, or save gradients (more on this in the next Task).

The opacity of the fill at different locations on the gradient is controlled by the Transparency Mask. The Transparency Mask is set to 100% by default but you can manipulate the transparency to have it fill gradually, blending into a color with less opacity.

You can save grayscale gradients as selections. When the selections are loaded, they can be used to apply effects, color corrections, and filters in a selective and graduated way.

## CROSS-REFERENCE

For more on selections, see Chapter 3.

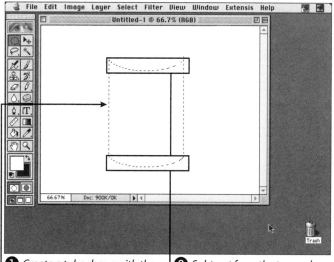

**❶** Create a tube shape with the Rectangular marquee tool.

**❷** Subtract from the top and add to the bottom with the Elliptical marquee tool.

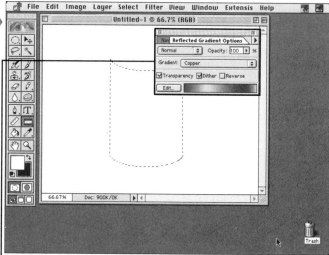

**❸** First, you'll have to choose the Reflected Gradient from the Gradient tool's pop-up tools. In the toolbar choose Copper from the Gradient pop-up menu.

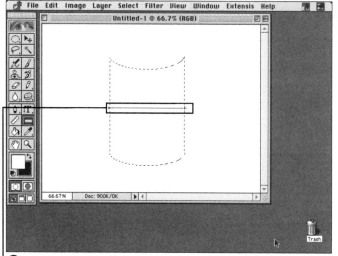

**❹** Drag the Reflected Gradient's cursor from the left to the right side of the tube.

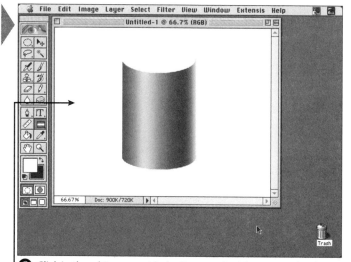

**❺** Click in the white area with the Rectangular Marquee to deselect the selected area.

161

# Creating a Custom Gradient

Now that you have worked with the default gradients that Photoshop has to offer, it is time to create your own. There are two ways to go about this. The first way is to jump in head first and start with a new gradient. The second way is to duplicate an existing gradient to see how it was constructed.

Following are the areas that you need to know about when creating a gradient:

**Name.** Displays the list of current gradients.

**Adjust.** Controls the gradient color and transparency. The Color option is selected, but you can select the Transparency option and you'll go to its dialog box.

**Gradient bar.** Add, duplicate, or move the color stops to create the gradient you want on this bar.

**Color stops.** Click a Color stop to make it active so you can move, duplicate, delete, or change its color. To remove a Color stop drag the stop down away from the Gradient bar. You can add up to 32 Color stops in a gradient.

▶ **Color selection box.** Displays the active Color stop.

▶ **Foreground and Background.** The Foreground (F) and Background (B) areas let you automatically put the Foreground or Background color into the active Color stop.

▶ **Color Swatch.** The Color Swatch is where you activate the Color Picker. Here you can use any color you create in your gradient.

▶ **Midpoint.** The little diamonds above the Gradient bar show you the exact midpoint between two colors. You can adjust this midpoint.

The Buttons on the right side of the Gradient Editor dialog box are New, Rename, Remove, Duplicate, Load, and Save. The buttons are generally self-explanatory. You click the New button to create a new gradient. If you want to delete a gradient, click the Remove button. I like the Duplicate button. That way I can take apart and edit an existing gradient without changing the original

The Transparency dialog box opens another door in creating a gradient. You choose the opacity of each Color stop. When you access the Transparency options, you start with a beginning and an ending Transparency stop. You click the stop to change the transparency in percentage. You'll see a preview in the Gradient bar below. Just like the Color stops, you can have up to 32 Transparency stops in a gradient.

You can create many amazing effects using the Gradient options. You can create cool metallic effects, a curtain-like effect, three-dimensional shading, and more.

### TAKE NOTE

▶ **USING PANTONE COLORS IN GRADIENTS**

One note to keep in mind, if you decide to use custom colors or Pantone colors in your gradient, Photoshop will convert those colors to CMYK.

### CROSS-REFERENCE

For more on importing an Illustrator file, see Chapter 2.

### FIND IT ONLINE

Glenn Riegel's website at **http://users.nbn.net/glimage/ gallery.html** shows you art done with Illustrator and Photoshop. His images are astounding.

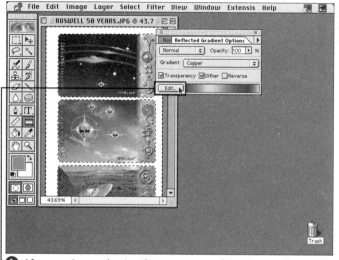

**1** After creating a selection that you want to fill with a gradient, click the Edit button in the Reflected Gradient Options palette.

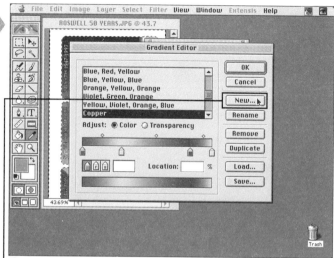

**2** In the Gradient Editor dialog box, click the New button.

■ Enter a name for your new gradient.

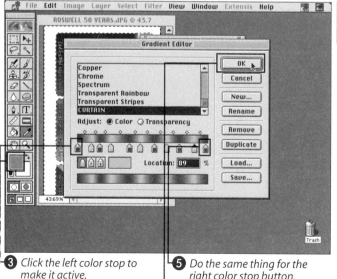

**3** Click the left color stop to make it active.

**4** Click the color swatch to activate the Color Picker, then give that swatch a color.

**5** Do the same thing for the right color stop button. Repeat the two colors. Place them close to each other.

**6** To copy a button, click it, then click the Gradient bar to place it. Click OK when you're done.

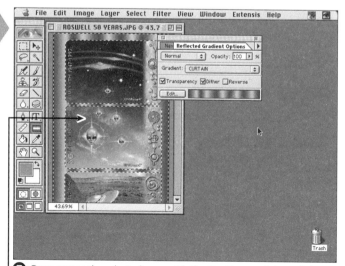

**7** Drag across the selected area with the Gradient tool, then click with the Marquee to deselect the selection.

# Personal Workbook

## Q&A

**1** What is a *fill?*

_____

_____

**2** What is a *gradient?*

_____

_____

**3** What can be filled?

_____

_____

**4** How do you access the Custom colors?

_____

_____

_____

**5** How can you save a custom Swatches palette?

_____

_____

_____

**6** When would you use a gradient?

_____

_____

**7** What is the key command to fill with the foreground color?

_____

_____

**8** How you change the default gradients?

_____

_____

_____

**ANSWERS: PAGE 337**

## EXTRA PRACTICE

1 Select an eye in a portrait and change its color using the different fill modes.

2 Create a block of type with the Type tool and use the Fill command to change the color of the type.

3 Practice changing the color of your selections and type with the keyboard shortcuts.

4 Use the Paint Bucket tool to fill areas of a color photograph with flat color.

5 Edit a gradient using the Gradient Editor button from the Gradient Options palette.

6 Make your own custom curtain gradient.

## REAL-WORLD APPLICATIONS

✔ The image you are creating is fading away into a white background. You want to sharpen it up (do something that will visually lift your new graphic from the page). You could highlight the file's background layer and fill it with a soft, contrasting color.

✔ The photo you're enhancing has gone through a funny color shift. You *know* the subject's hair is not as red as it appears, and you want to just select the hair so you can adjust the color. You use the Paint Bucket tool to select the necessary pixels and then colorize away.

✔ You have to create a logo that looks like chrome. You set the type, then use the Chrome settings of the Linear Gradient tool to finish the look.

## Visual Quiz

This portrait image has bars made with the Gradient Editor that fade to the underneath image. How was it created?

_____

_____

_____

_____

_____

_____

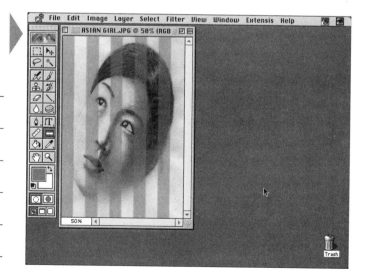

# CHAPTER 8

# Image Adjusting

Ultimately in Photoshop you'll come across an image that isn't quite up to par. Photoshop offers a variety of means to fixing any bad photograph. For the beginner, Auto Levels (found under the Image menu) works just fine without having to know anything about Photoshop. The next step into image adjusting would be using the Levels command. This feature takes a bit more knowledge and understanding on what is happening to the photograph. Curves is probably the most difficult of all of the image adjusting commands to use. With a little understanding and practice, you'll get the hang of it. Brighten and Contrast round out the basic of image adjusting to clean up your image.

Next in our image adjusting is adjusting color in an image. Curves can also be used to adjust colors. Color Balance is another way to adjust an image that has too much of one or more colors overpowering an image. The Hue and Saturation command lets you control the color, lightness, and intensity of a single color. You can also adjust all of the colors at once in terms of saturation and lightness. Variations lets you adjust multiple color facets in one dialog box. In Variations you can manipulate midtones, shadows, highlights, saturation, lightness, and darkness.

Not only are these adjustments helpful, but you can combine effect on top of effect. Using the Adjustment Layer option you can apply an adjusted effect to one or more layers and remove them easily. If you opt not to use the Adjustment layer option, then you can still remove effects via the History palette. Many images look pretty good at first glance, but working with these various image adjustments will really make your photographs stand out. If you are tracing images in another program like Adobe Illustrator, you can clean up the image in Photoshop using Image Adjusting so your tracing will be a breeze.

Extensis Corporation has a wonderful plug-in product for Photoshop that makes adjusting your image easy. Intellihance Pro 4.0 combines all of Photoshop's adjusting effects into one dialog box. You have choices to apply a preset from the pop-up menu, Fine Tune, or Power Variations (all found under the Mode menu of Intellihance Pro 4.0). You can find Intellihance Pro 4.0 and other Extensis products by checking out their Web site at **http://www.extensis.com**.

# Using Levels and Auto Levels

Auto Levels and Levels are a great way to fix the shadow and highlights of your image. Auto Levels is found under the Image menu under the Adjust submenu. When you choose Auto Levels, Photoshop automatically adjusts the shadow and highlights. With Auto Levels, Photoshop brings in the white (highlight) and the dark (shadow) increments by .05%. While this may seem to work well, it mainly works with images that need only minimal tweaking.

The Levels command is a tad more complex. When you open the Levels dialog box, you'll find a variety of sliders and eyedroppers to manipulate. At the top of the Levels dialog box is the Channel pop-up menu. You can choose to adjust the individual channels, or all channels at the same time. For basic and overall use we recommend that you adjust all of the channels at the same time by choosing RGB, or CMYK from the pop-up menu.

The Input Levels command is below the Channels pop-up menu. You can enter the values numerically, or with the sliders in the window showing the Histogram. The numerical boxes are in conjunction with the sliders. By that we mean the far left box/slider is for the darkest (shadow) value. The middle box/slider is for the midtone value. The far right box/slider is for the lightest (highlight) value. When you drag the sliders, the numerical field will enter the number you have dragged to.

The eyedroppers you see on the right side of the dialog box let you do the same thing as the sliders, but with a bit more ease. Of course you have to have an eye for your shadow, midtone, and highlight in your image. With the black eyedropper you'll click the darkest part of your image (to do this, you'll need to drag the dialog box so you can view your image). Next, we like to use the white eyedropper to click the lightest part of your image. Many times the black/white adjustment is all your image will need. Be sure to have the Preview box checked so you can see exactly what is happening to your image. The gray eyedropper is the tricky one. If you miscalculate the actual midtone range, you're likely to make your whole image look out of whack.

The Output Levels slider found at the bottom lets you change the overall dark and light tone. We like to use it for dimming images, or sections of an image. You can save and load settings with the Save and Load buttons. If you have totally mangled up the levels and want to start over, simply hold the Option (Alt) key down and press the reset button found under the OK button.

## TAKE NOTE

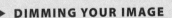

### DIMMING YOUR IMAGE

You may want to dim an image because you are putting it in a page layout program and want to see the type over the image. Using the Output levels slider, drag the black (left) slider towards the right until it is dimmed to your satisfaction.

## CROSS-REFERENCE

For more on images, see Chapter 2.

## FIND IT ONLINE

To make good clean scans for the web, see **http://photo.net/wtr/thebook/images.html** for great tips.

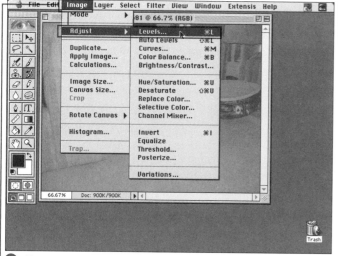

① *Choose Image ➪ Adjust ➪ Levels or press Command (Ctrl)+L.*

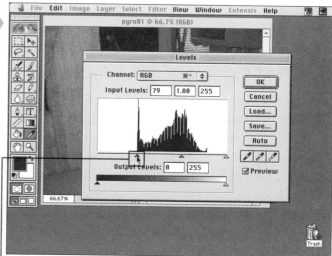

② *Drag the black slider to the beginning of the histogram curve on the left.*

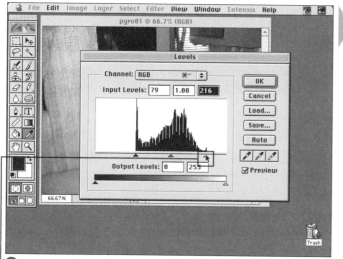

③ *Drag the white slider to the beginning of the histogram curve on the right.*

④ *Click OK to see the results.*

# Using Curves to Adjust Your Image

The Curve command found under the Adjust submenu of the Image menu is a bit more daunting to work with. We are going to make using curves easy with two main ways to use Curves. First let's discuss the Curves dialog box. Just like the Levels dialog box you first choose whether you want to adjust all color channels or each color channel individually. The difference between Levels and Curves is that Curves lets you adjust more than just three tones.

The next area that you'll see is a grid with a straight line that goes from the bottom left to the top right. You can move the endpoints of the line up, down, left, or right. By moving the points to the left or right, you get a straight-lined S shape. When you click the line you can create a new endpoint that can be moved. The endpoints that you make in the middle of the line create a curve on the line. You can play with the curves that you create to see some spectacular results. You'll only see the results if you have the Preview box checked, and your Curves dialog box is moved to the side so you can see your image as you adjust the curve.

Another way to adjust the curve is to use the Pencil option. With the Pencil option you can drag out your own curve and it will appear and adjust your image. After drawing out a curve, you can switch back to the curve editing option. When you use the Pencil option, you have the option to Smooth the curve found under the Save button. If you click the Smooth button the line will smooth out from the original. If you continue to click the Smooth button, the line will slowly go back to straight.

The Auto button will automatically adjust (similar to Auto Levels) the curve. The eyedroppers under the Auto button work the same as in Levels. You click with the black eyedropper on the darkest part of the image, the gray eyedropper on the midtone range, and the white eyedropper on the lightest part of the image.

The easiest way to use Curves is to think of the S curve. You can adjust your image by creating a slight S-shaped curve with two interior points, and just work with those two points, slowly adjusting until your image looks just right. The other way is to drag the lower left point to the right and the upper right point to the left. Slowly adjust by dragging to the right or left until the image looks just right.

## TAKE NOTE

### ▶ ADJUSTMENT LAYERS

If you want to experiment with using Curves, but don't want to totally trash your image, use an Adjustment layer first. Choose Adjustment Layer from the Layers menu (New submenu), and choose Curves from the pop-up choices.

## CROSS-REFERENCE

For more on layers, see Chapter 11.

## FIND IT ONLINE

Check out **http://www.photo-art.com/howto.htm** to see how an image was adjusted using Curves.

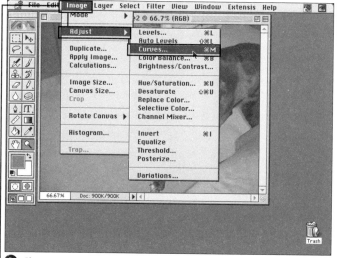

**1** *Choose Image ⇨ Adjust ⇨ Curves or press Command (Ctrl)+M.*

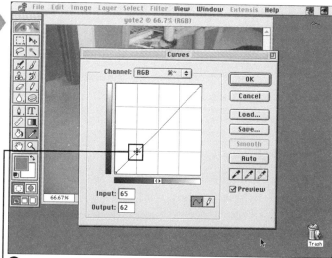

**2** *Click about 3/4 inch up from the lower left to create the first point of the S curve.*

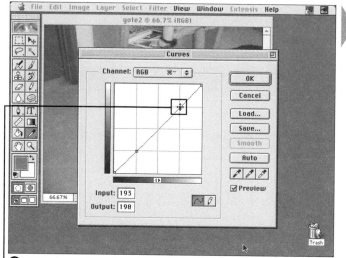

**3** *Click about 3/4 inch down from the upper right to create the other part of the S curve.*

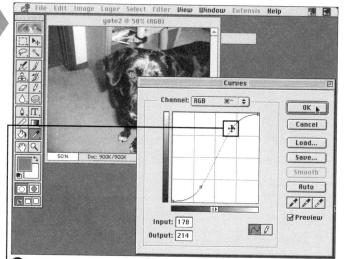

**4** *Drag the points in an S shape until you get the adjustment you'd like, then press OK.*

# Fixing Color with Color Balance

Color adjusting can be done using Color Balance found under the Adjust submenu of the Image menu. Color Balance affects color cast or colors with too much or not enough saturation. The Color Balance dialog box has the colors Cyan, Magenta, Yellow, Red, Green, and Blue. What you are adjusting is the tonal balance in the shadows, midtones, or highlights.

As with most dialog boxes, you can either check or uncheck the Preview box. Yeah, you are probably wondering why you would ever want to uncheck the Preview box. Well, if you are working on an extremely large file that takes a while to redraw, then unchecking the Preview box will speed things up. Of course, you can't see what is happening to your image until after you click OK, but you can always Undo.

The other check box in the Color Balance dialog box is to Preserve Luminosity. By checking this option, your RGB images will retain their tonal balance even while you change colors. Many images tend to get a cast to them. By that we mean that the image may have an overall greenish tone to it. To remove this green cast, you'll use Color Balance. To use Color Balance you'll drag the Green Slider towards the Magenta direction (to the left) until the cast is gone. Of course the catch is that you need to have the Preview option checked so you can see what is happening to your image. To apply a more subtle effect

try checking the Shadow or Highlights button to apply or remove a cast in the shadow or highlights of your image.

The other thing Color Balance can do is to apply a cool color effect to the whole or just parts of your image. One thing we like to do is to copy an image and repeat it on a whole page. Then select each image one at a time and apply a different color balance to each image. That creates quite an interesting poster-like image.

Now that you are seeing many ways to adjust an image, keep in mind that you can combine an effect on top of another effect endlessly until you get the results that you want. Another option to keep in mind is that you can make a selection and apply a Color Balance to that particular selection rather than the whole image. This opens the door to a whole new arena. You can emphasize a certain object by selecting just that object and adjusting the Color Balance.

## TAKE NOTE

### ▶ RED EYE

One way to fix an image with red eye is to use Color Balance. Using the Elliptical Marquee, select the red eyes, then use Color Balance to decrease the Red and Magenta (increase the Cyan and Green) and add a touch of Blue.

## CROSS-REFERENCE

For more on using Selection tools, see Chapter 3.

## FIND IT ONLINE

To read an article on using Color Balance check out **http://uk.macworld.com/dec96/media/expertgraphics.html**.

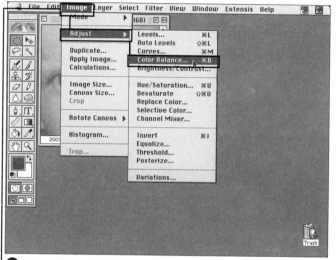

❶ Choose Image ➪ Adjust ➪ Color Balance or press Command (Ctrl)+B.

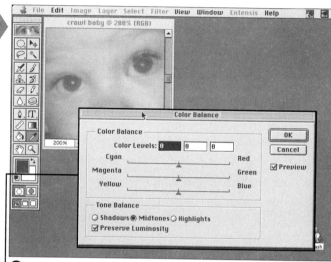

❷ Move the Color Balance dialog box alongside your image so you can see your adjustments as you work.

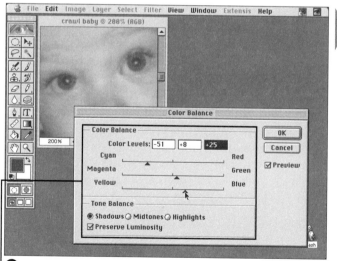

❸ Click the Shadow button first. Drag the top slider towards Cyan, drag the middle slider towards Green, and drag the bottom slider towards Blue.

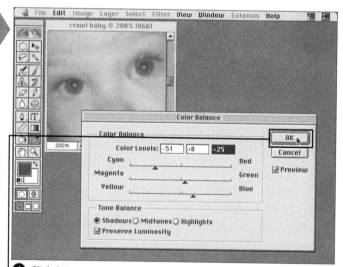

❹ Click OK.

173

# Dramatizing Your Image with Brighten/Contrast

A great way to jazz up your image is to use the Brighten/Contrast command. The Brighten/Contrast really cleans up those blasé images by adding contrast and light. The gist of the Brighten Contrast dialog box is pretty straightforward. If you drag the Brightness slider towards the right (positive numbers) the image or selection will brighten. By dragging the slider towards the left (negative numbers) the image or selection will darken. If you drag the Contrast slider towards the right, the image's darks and lights will be more pronounced. By dragging the Contrast slider towards the left, the image or selection will become more muddled and graytoned.

Beyond adjusting, you need to have some sort of understanding of your monitor and adjusting your Gamma. Gamma is the way your monitor gauges brightness and then translates it. Adobe Photoshop ships with a Gamma utility that you can drag from your Photoshop folder into your Control Panel. By adjusting your monitor with the Gamma utility you are much closer to actually getting what you see on your screen as a printout.

The correct gamma setting for a Macintosh monitor is strikingly different than that for a Windows system. What looks like a perfectly color-corrected image on a Web browser on your Mac will look quite dark and hideous on your Windows's browser. Fortunately for Windows users, the reverse is not true. That's because, due to their monitor's gamma settings, they have already made the image lighter than the Mac user would have done.

The easiest way to deal with gamma is to ignore the whole issue if you're a Windows user because the largest percentage of Web surfers use Windows, so images corrected to your gamma will look good to most people. Also, an image that is slightly lighter than perfect can be viewed acceptably. An image that is too dark looks bad from any angle. Images corrected for Windows gamma will look too light on the Mac. Images corrected on Windows will look too dark on the Windows system.

If you take this road, your Mac images must be made slightly lighter than they would normally appear so that Windows monitors won't render the image too darkly.

---

## TAKE NOTE

### SHOOTING THE GAMMA GAP

The most common gamma setting on Windows is 2.5, whereas it's 1.8 on the Macintosh. With this in mind, the easiest way to compensate for the way other people will see your images is to "shoot the gamma gap," which is, essentially, to compromise. If you split the difference at home, where you create images, you'll set your own gamma at around 2.2. This is a solution that's easy to do, but isn't perfect.

---

## CROSS-REFERENCE

For more on channels, see Chapter 12.

## FIND IT ONLINE

Macintosh users can find a useful gamma correction tool on the Internet at **http://www.flash.net/~rolandg/thanks/**. GammaToggleFKEY is freeware created and distributed by Roland Gustafsson.

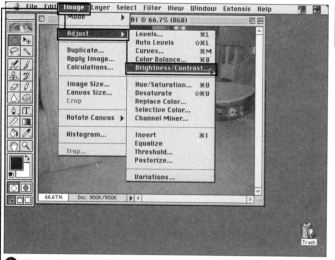

**1** *Choose Image ⇨ Adjust ⇨ Brightness/Contrast.*

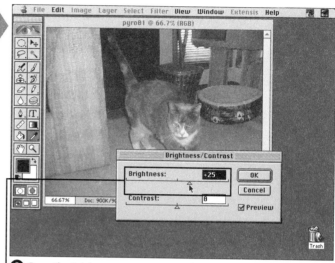

**2** *Drag the Brightness contrast towards the right.*

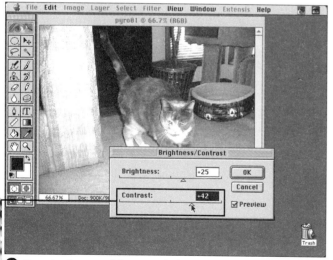

**3** *Drag the Contrast slider towards the right.*

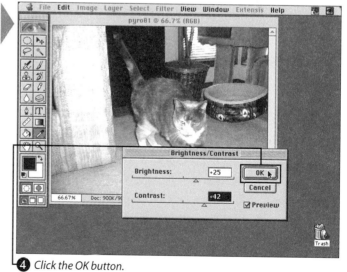

**4** *Click the OK button.*

# Altering Colors with Hue/Saturation

Another way to alter the colors in your image is with the Hue/Saturation command. The Hue/Saturation command lets you adjust the hue, saturation, and lightness of an image or selection. Within the Hue/Saturation dialog box you have many variables to work with. You can adjust what is called the Master (all colors) or individual colors. You can also choose to check the Colorize box which lets you add overall color to a grayscale image that has been converted to a color mode.

The colors you can choose other than Master from the pop-up menu are Reds, Yellows, Greens, Cyans, Blues, and Magentas. You'll notice the eyedroppers are only available when you choose a color. They are grayed out when you choose Master.

The Hue slider (with the Master chosen) will rotate the hue when dragged to the left or right. This can give a totally new perspective to your image or selection. If you watch the color bars at the bottom of the dialog box, you'll see just where the hue is rotating to. If you have an image that has a big red section and you rotate the hue to +60, the red area will take on a yellow color with a tinge of green. The more you apply a rotation, you can follow what the colors will change to.

The Saturation slider (with the Master chosen) will flood more color in when you drag the slider to the right. If you drag the slider to the left, the color will be drained from your image or selection. To really make an object pop out, select everything but that object and totally desaturate everything to grayscale. The Lightness slider (with the Master chosen) will lighten or darken the tones of the whole image or a selection. Under the Cancel button is the option to Load (an already saved settings of the Hue/Saturation dialog box) and the option to Save your settings. As with the other adjustment dialog boxes, if you press the Option (Alt) key, the Cancel button changes to a Reset button that will reset the numbers back to default.

By checking the Colorize box, you can change your image to look like a Duotone image. We like to create our own textures by using a new document, filling with 999% Noise, then using Hue/Saturation to Colorize the texture into one basic tone. This method offers you some texture with a basic color.

## TAKE NOTE

### RESET

As we have been mentioning throughout, you can reset all of the settings back to default by pressing the Option (Alt) key. That changes the Cancel button to a Reset button.

**CROSS-REFERENCE**

For more on Photoshop basics, see Chapter 1.

**FIND IT ONLINE**

The Web site at **http://macworld.zdnet.com/pages/ january.96/Column.1652.html** shows you some effective uses of Hue/Saturation.

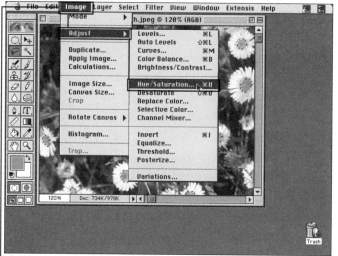

**①** Choose Image ➪ Adjust ➪ Hue/Saturation or press Command (Ctrl)+U.

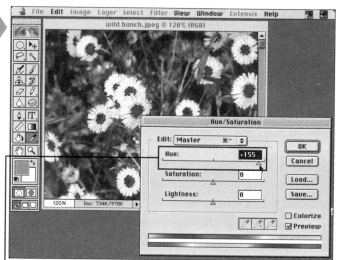

**②** Since we have just the daisy centers selected that is what will be affected. Drag the Hue slider until you see a color you like for the daisy center.

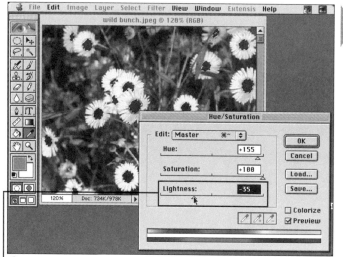

**③** Drag the Saturation slider to the fullest at 100%. Drag the Lightness slider to the left to darken the daisy centers.

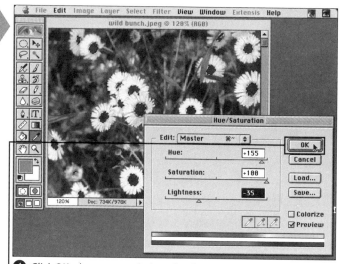

**④** Click OK when you reach the color that you want.

# Applying Variations

Variations are found under the Adjust submenu of the Image menu. Variations combines color adjusting with a lighten/darken option. What makes Variations unique is that you have a giant dialog box that shows you the original and the image after you apply some effects. You can work within this dialog box until you get the results that you want.

The top part of the dialog box shows you the Original and the Current Pick. The Original never changes so you can always see what your image looks like before applying anything. Underneath the Original and Current Pick is the Color application area. You can apply more Yellow, Red, Magenta, Blue, Cyan, and Green. Notice how the colors are set in a circular way. Each color has an opposite color across from it. If you add More Red, then add More Cyan, nothing will change. Cyan is the opposite of Red and will void the application of Red. The same concept goes for each color around the circle. The boxes on the right side of the screen are the Lighter and Darker options. The Current Pick will be displayed in the middle. You click the Lighter box to lighten your image. By clicking the Darker box, you darken the image.

How much is applied depends on the Fine/Coarse slider. The closer you drag to the Fine area, the less effect will be applied. A good way to use this feature is to set the slider all the way to Coarse (far right) to see how the colors and lightness/darkness affect your image. Then set the slider close to the Fine side so a small amount is applied at a time.

The areas you can affect are the Shadows, Midtones, Highlights, and Saturation. You'll notice that many of the adjustments affect these areas but the default is always set to Midtones. That is because most images can be corrected and adjusted using only the Midtone setting.

The Show Clipping checkbox will display when a particular area is at its highest setting. When you choose the Saturation button, your center color choices switch to Less Saturated, Current Pick, and More Saturated. If you notice the colors in the More Saturated box are strange and flat looking, then those particular areas are already fully saturated with color.

As with most dialog boxes with settings, you have the option to Save or Load existing settings. This can be particularly helpful if you have a batch of photographs that have the same error. No matter the error, an existing setting will make the changes much quicker.

> ## TAKE NOTE
>
> ### RESET YOUR IMAGE
> You can reset the settings by holding the Option (Alt) key and clicking Reset. Another quick way to reset is to click the Original image at the top of the dialog box.

## CROSS-REFERENCE
For more on applying multiple effects, see the next task in this chapter.

## FIND IT ONLINE
This Web site at **http://www.it.rit.edu/~icsa320/ 320-03a/** offers insights on image adjusting.

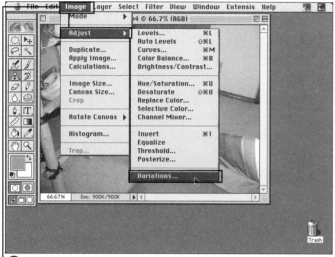

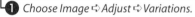

**①** *Choose Image ⇨ Adjust ⇨ Variations.*

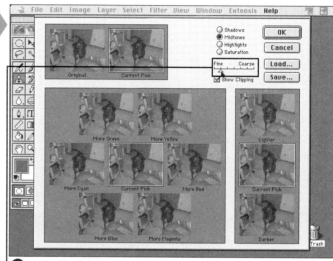

**②** *Move the slider towards the Fine setting.*

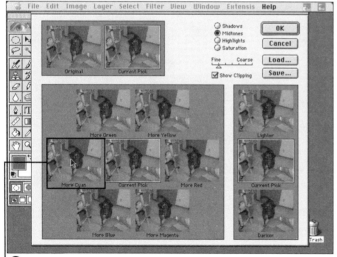

**③** *Click the Cyan box until the color looks just right.*

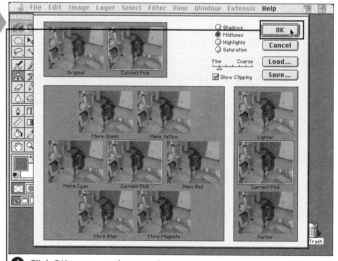

**④** *Click OK to accept these settings.*

# Using Extensis' Intellihance Pro to Fix Your Image

Intellihance Pro provides a full arsenal of tools for enhancing images, located conveniently in one location, allowing you to see how multiple changes affect your image all at the same time. In addition, you can compare up to 25 different versions of enhancements at once.

Possibly the easiest way to use Intellihance Pro to make your images look better is by simply selecting a preset from the Extensis ⇨ Intellihance Pro menu. Intellihance Pro ships with 25 different presets, each of them customized for a variety of different image types. Once you select one of the presets, your image is enhanced (or the selection is enhanced, if you had one). It's pretty painless.

But the real fun comes from going into Intellihance Pro and making adjustments to the presets — or creating brand new settings. The Intellihance Pro interface allows you to modify several versions of your image at once. To view multiple presets, choose one of the options from the layout menu (like, for instance, 1 × 5, which will display 5 horizontal strips of the image). By default, the image will be split into five sections. You can opt to show the same portion (or all) of the image by choosing Repeating Image from the View menu. Click the pane you wish to modify (a red border will appear around it, indicating that it's active). Then adjust the settings to the right of the image.

An even more interactive way to change the settings of each preset is to use Intellihance Pro's Power Variations, which go way beyond the Variations that Photoshop has to offer. With Power Variations, you can view up to 24 "stepped" changes on your image of any type. For instance, you can view changes to your image in terms of brightness, with each pane representing a slight change from the currently active pane. The amount of change can be adjusted by moving the Visual Adjustment slider. Click the modified image that you wish to use, and that becomes your active image. Power Variations has several different settings that aren't available in Photoshop's Variations, such as sharpen, cast, and contrast. Plus, you can zoom, pan, and split the image to your heart's content while in Intellihance Pro's Power Variations.

You can use Intellihance Pro to fix images with multiple problems without having to go back and forth in Photoshop's adjustment menu. This great program takes the best of Photoshop and puts it in one area. To make Intellihance Pro even more appealing, it is easy to use and lets you save adjustments. This comes in handy if you have a pile of photographs that have all been underexposed or overexposed. You can simply fix one, then save the settings, then apply the same adjustment to the rest of the photographs.

## TAKE NOTE

### QUICK ENHANCE

To let Intellihance Pro 4.0 do the work for you, choose the Quick Enhance option.

## CROSS-REFERENCE

For more on filters and plug-ins, see Chapter 14.

## FIND IT ONLINE

Visit the Extensis Web site at **http://www.extensis.com** for more information on Intellihance Pro 4.0 and other products.

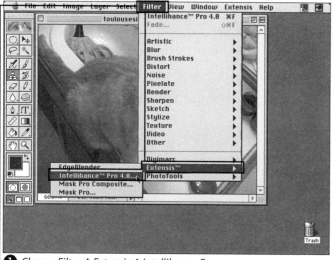

**①** Choose Filter ➪ Extensis ➪ Intellihance Pro.

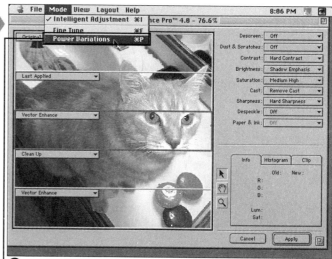

**②** Change the Mode (pull-down menu) to Power Variations.

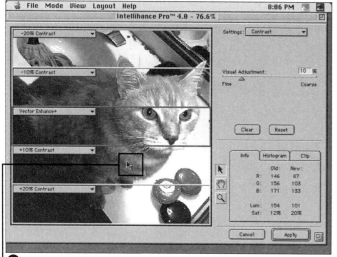

**③** Here we worked with the Brightness pop-up menu, and added −10% to darken the image. Then we chose Contrast from the pop-up menu and increased the contrast in increments of 10%.

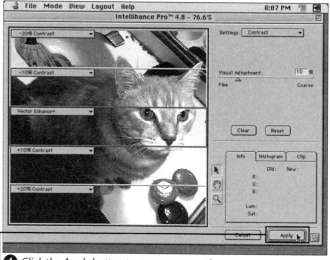

**④** Click the Apply button to accept your settings.

**181**

# Personal Workbook

## Q&A

**1** What are the eyedroppers used for in the Levels dialog box?

_____

_____

_____

**2** How do you dim an image using Levels?

_____

_____

_____

**3** What is the easiest way to use Curves?

_____

_____

_____

**4** How can you fix redeye in a photo?

_____

_____

_____

**5** What adjust feature do you use to increase the darks and whites in your image?

_____

_____

_____

**6** How can you change the color of a section of your image without filling in with color?

_____

_____

_____

**7** How can you adjust color, saturation, and lighten your image all at the same time?

_____

_____

_____

**8** How can you view many variations of the image that you are adjusting using Intellihance Pro 4.0?

_____

_____

_____

ANSWER: PAGE 338

## EXTRA PRACTICE

**1** Open an image that needs some clarification and use the eyedroppers in the Levels dialog box to pick the darkest and the lightest colors.

**2** Fix an image more accurately by using the S curve in the Curve command.

**3** Correct the yellow cast in your image using Color Balance.

**4** Bring out some snap in your image using Brighten/Contrast.

**5** Change the color of a bunch of flowers (not the stems or background, just the flowers) by using Hue/Saturation.

**6** Totally fix an image using Levels, Color Balance, and Brighten/Contrast.

## REAL-WORLD APPLICATIONS

✔ You have a pile of photos that have been overexposed and need to be corrected. You use the Levels command and save your settings so you can use them for the whole batch of photos.

✔ Your client has given you an old photo with a red cast to it. You use Color Balance to bring the luster back to the image and have it reprinted in time for his parent's anniversary.

✔ You need to fix an image, but don't know what color cast it has. You use Variations to get an idea of what colors you need to add to fix the cast.

✔ You are tired of using multiple adjustment features to fix an image, so you buy Extensis' Intellihance Pro 4.0 to make your life much easier.

## Visual Quiz

What adjustment option was used to give this photo a poster effect?

_____

_____

_____

_____

_____

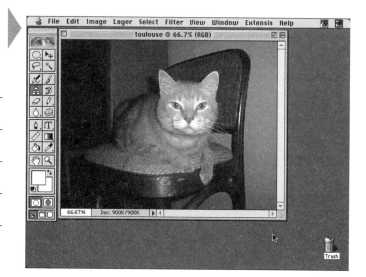

**CHAPTER 9**

# Painting with Photoshop

The images you work on in Photoshop will either be scanned or given to you on some form of transfer like diskette, CD, Zip, or Jaz cartridges, or created in an illustration program like Illustrator or FreeHand. You probably won't use Photoshop to create images from scratch; instead you'll use the painting and drawing tools Paintbrush, Pencil, Airbrush, and Eraser to manipulate existing images.

When you look closely at any image, you see that the pixels surrounding object edges gradually transition in color until they match the background. In the normal view, however, all you see is a smooth edge. The smoothing of a line, shape, selection, or a piece of type with respect to its background is called *anti-aliasing*. Many of Photoshop's tools feature anti-aliasing, either as an option or as a built-in feature.

Before painting in Photoshop, you need to understand the Foreground and Background swatches. When you paint, you are accessing the foreground color with which to paint. Foreground and background in Photoshop refer to two different concepts. The foreground and background colors are those defined on the Color palette and also in the Color Control box as the current color you paint with *(foreground)* and the color that would remain if you used the Eraser tool to erase part of the present image *(background)*. The foreground and background colors are used as the beginning and ending points of a gradient blend. The other foreground/background concept relates to the image you are looking at. If you have a photograph of a person standing in front of the Eiffel tower, then the Person is the foreground, and the Eiffel tower is the background.

If you want to change the foreground color, you can click the upper left of the color swatch, either on the Color palette or in the toolbox. This activates the Color Picker. A double border then highlights the active color swatch. Move your mouse pointer over to the small color swatches (it turns into an eyedropper). Click to make your choice. You can also use the Color Picker to choose your color. Change the background color by clicking the lower-right large color swatch. Select your background color as you did the foreground color.

# Using the Paintbrush

Photoshop brushes are very adaptable tools: they're like millions of brushes in one! You can use them to paint freeform or straight, smooth, fuzzy, or rough-edged lines. Their shapes can be round, oval, calligraphic, or a shape that you create. The paint can be applied continuously, intermittently, or as a dotted line, and the paint can range from opaque to completely transparent. You can even paint in different brush modes that allow you to lighten or darken only selected pixels in an image.

To start working with brushes, open the Brushes palette by choosing Window ➪ Show Brushes and then choose a brush size and style and you can paint to your heart's content. Play with it a bit. Experiment with different brush diameters and degrees of hardness. Pressing the Shift key enables you to paint in 45-degree straight increments. The Shift key constrains your brush movements to 45-degree angles. That way if you want to paint in a straight line up, down, or at 45 degrees, you can do it by pressing the Shift key. If you are looking to create a harsh aliased edge, you'll use the hard-edged brush. If you want a smoother transition between your painting and the background, then choose a soft-edged brush.

A powerful and easy-to-use editing option is the Paint Opacity control. The Paint Opacity controls how see-through the paint will be. You can have the color painted with total opacity (not see-through at all), or adjust it so you can see underneath to the background. You control Paint Opacity from the Options Palette, which you open by double-clicking the painting tool you're using with your mouse You can double-click any tool with your mouse to access that particular tool's options. Alternately, select Windows ➪ Options and then select the tool you'll be working with. The appropriate Options Palette will appear.

The opacity of any Painting tool can be varied from 1 to 100%. Press the number keys to enter the opacity in multiples of 10 (1 = 10%, 2 = 20%, and so on). One hundred percent opacity (complete coverage) is 0. You can also change the foreground color while using a painting tool. While using the Paintbrush, release the mouse button and press the Option (Alt) key and your Paintbrush will turn into an eyedropper.

If you click and hold the mouse button as you drag the eyedropper over the image, you are sampling the color, and the foreground swatch color box will change accordingly. When you let go of the Option key and click the mouse button again, you will be painting once more and not sampling color, so be careful. You can set the eyedropper to sample individual pixels or a color that is the average of a 3 × 3 or 5 × 5 pixel area around the pixels the eyedropper passes over. Use the Eyedropper Options palette to set this by double-clicking the Eyedropper tool with your mouse in the toolbar.

**CROSS-REFERENCE**

For more information about tools, see Chapter 1.

**FIND IT ONLINE**

Ron Chan's Web site, **http://www.ronchan.com**, is a fantastic portfolio of abstract images done in Illustrator and Photoshop.

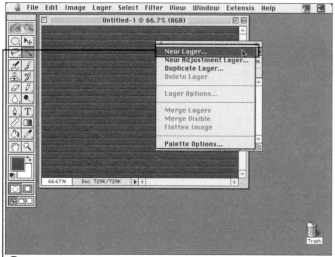

**1** Create a new layer first by clicking Layer ➪ New ➪ Layer and (you can easily delete the layer later if you don't like it).

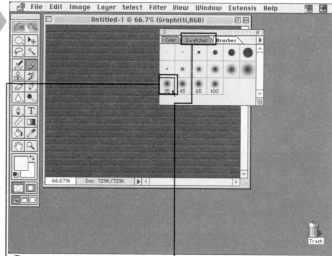

**2** If the Brushes palette isn't visible then choose Window ➪ Show Brushes. Choose a brush with a soft edge; for instance, the 35-pixel brush.

**3** If you don't want to use the default color, click the Swatches tab and choose a color.

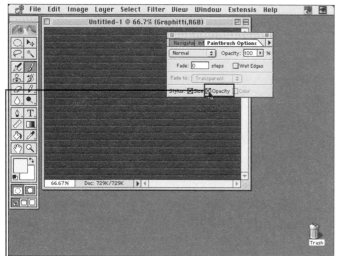

**4** To access the Paintbrush Options, double-click the Paintbrush tool. If you are using a pressure-sensitive tablet, click the Stylus Opacity option.

**5** The harder you press, the more opaque the color is applied, and vice versa.

**6** Try your paintbrush.

■ For instance, add graffiti to a brick wall

**7** Switch brush sizes and colors by repeating steps 2 and 3. We don't recommend doing this in real life, because in real life, you can't throw out the layer or choose Undo!

# Picking the Right Brush

Now that you've seen the number of brushes Photoshop has to offer, the next step is to choose the right brush for your task. If you are looking to add a soft touch to your image, then you'll want to choose a soft-edged brush in the size that you feel comfortable with. If you are covering large areas with paint, then choose a large brush. If you are doing some fine intricate painting, then choose a smaller brush. Keep in mind that you can always zoom in or out for more accuracy. Maybe you are looking to create a cool repeating pattern, well then check out some of Photoshop's brush libraries for some default shapes like an eye, bird, star, deer, and many more.

You can also change the settings of any custom or default brush, at any time. Simply select the brush and then select Brush Options from the pop-up menu on the Brushes Palette or double-click the brush you'd like to change. In both instances, the Brush Options Dialog Box will appear.

When you use the Paintbrush tool, there are several options available on the Paintbrush Options Palette. You can change the Mode, Opacity, Fade steps, Wet Edges, Fade to, and Stylus options. Each produces a different effect while painting.

Mode is the style of blending that you choose for your Paintbrush. Fade steps refers to the distance in pixels over which the brush stroke will last before it fades out. Use Fade steps to create the effect of a real paintbrush running out of paint at the end of its stroke. If you choose to Fade the effects of the

Paintbrush, two more Paintbrush options become active. Select Transparent if you want the brush stroke to become transparent and disappear at its end. Select Background if you want the brush stroke to start with the foreground color and finish with the background color.

Wet Edges gives your brushstroke the illusion of a watercolor effect. The closer to the edge of the brush stroke, the more intense the color. In the center of the brush stroke, it is more transparent and watery.

The Stylus options are used only if you are using a pressure-sensitive digitizing tablet. You have three stylus options that you can set according to your creative objective. *Size* enables the brush stroke to be thicker or thinner, depending upon how much pressure you use. *Opacity* changes the brush stroke to become more opaque with more pressure. *Color* changes the color of the brush stroke. Light pressure gives you the background color, medium pressure gives you a color between background and foreground, and the heaviest pressure gives you the foreground color.

## TAKE NOTE

### ▶ BRUSH COLOR

If you create a custom brush stroke while using a color brush, it will seem semi-transparent when you paint with it, even when you paint with solid black paint. If you want a custom brush to be totally opaque when used, create the brush in black.

## CROSS-REFERENCE

For more on picking colors, see Chapter 7.

## FIND IT ONLINE

For some cool custom brushes, check out **http://www.geocities. com/SiliconValley/Lakes/7447/brushes.html**.

❶ First create a new layer by choosing Layer ⇨ New ⇨ Layer so you don't alter the original image.

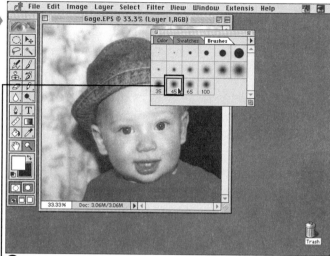

❷ We selected a large ( 45-pixel), soft-edged brush. That way we can create the moustache with a soft edge in one stroke

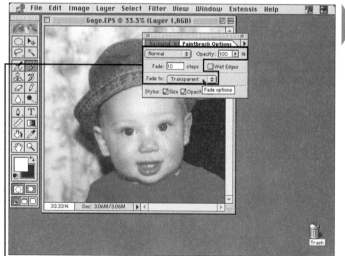

❸ Double-click the Paintbrush tool in the toolbox with your mouse to access the Paintbrush Options palette. Set the Paintbrush Options to Normal mode, Opacity of 75%, Fade 10 steps, and Fade to Transparent. These settings enable you to paint so the color isn't totally opaque and fades out to the background slowly.

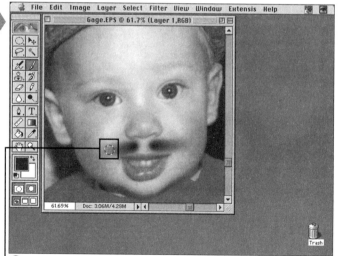

❹ A subtle mustache was added to this otherwise cute baby using the Paintbrush.

189

# Creating and Saving Brushes

Photoshop's Default Brushes palette contains 16 brushes. You can load several other types by choosing Load Brushes from the pop-up menu on the Brushes Palette. Brushes are automatically installed in the Photoshop 5.0 ⇨ Goodies ⇨ Brushes folder on your hard drive These extra brushes are sorted by type so you can load the ones you need. *Assorted* brushes are brushes of odd or varied types and textures. For example, one interesting brush is shaped like a goose in flight. Another is like an elk. *Shadows* brushes are brushes with a built-in shadow. These can be useful for creating special effects and textures. *Square* brushes are all square in shape. You might use these to fit into tight corners when a round brush just won't cut it.

While you'll likely find the included brushes adequate for most purposes, Photoshop enables you to create custom brushes of different sizes, shapes, angles, and degrees of hardness. This can be great for really specific jobs where existing tools just don't work. To create a custom brush, open the Brushes Palette, click the right arrow at the top of the scroll bar, and select New Brush from the pop-up menu. The New Brush dialog box appears. You can generate a new brush by entering different numbers. Watch your new brush take shape in the box in the lower-right corner as you adjust these settings:

▶ **Diameter.** The larger the number, the larger the diameter of the brush (measured in pixels).

▶ **Hardness.** This sets the softness or hardness of the brush, as measured by the percentage of the brush that is hard.

▶ **Spacing.** Use this to determine the amount of space between brush-tip impressions in a full stroke.

▶ **Angle.** You can rotate the brush tip in any direction to simulate the angle at which you might hold a brush.

▶ **Roundness.** You can also change the shape of a brush. For a stylized look, you may prefer to have a chiseled brush tip, like the nib of a calligraphy pen.

If you've created a brush you like or you've made changes to a particular brush that you'd like to keep around, select Save Brushes from the pop-up menu on the Brushes Palette and enter a name for your new brush. This will save any changes you've made to your default brushes.

---

**TAKE NOTE**

**ACCESSING THE BRUSH TOOL**

To quickly access the Brush tool from the toolbox, press B.

---

**CROSS-REFERENCE**

For more on editing in Photoshop, see Chapter 6.

**FIND IT ONLINE**

Check out **http://www.ultimate-photoshop.com/filters/brushes/** for more brushes and customized brushes.

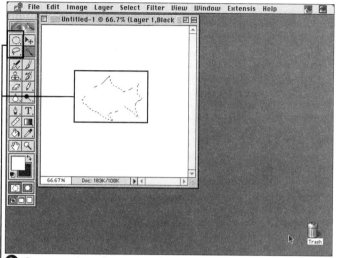

**1** Create a unique shape using the Selection tools. Here we used the Ellipse and Lasso tools to create this fish shape.

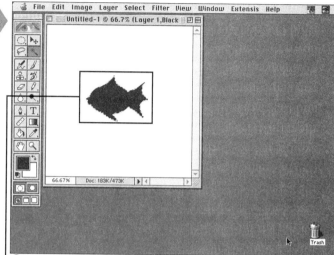

**2** Press the D key on your keyboard to make sure your Foreground and Background colors are the default black and white. Choose Edit ➪ Fill. Fill the Selection with 100% black by pressing OK in the Fill dialog box.

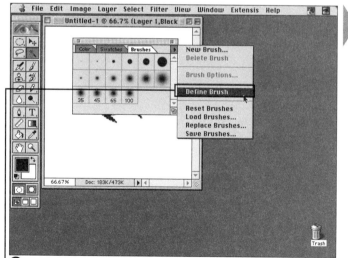

**3** To access the Brushes palette choose Window ➪ Show Brushes. To access the pop-up menu click the arrow in the upper-right corner of the Brushes palette. Choose Define Brush from the Brushes palette pop-up menu. In the Brush options dialog box, you can set the size, shape and softness of the brush

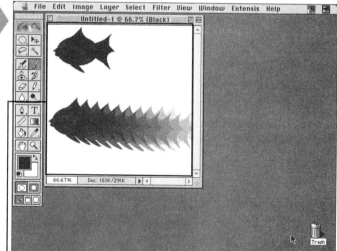

**4** Start Brushing. The top row of this image shows what happens if you click one time, you get just the shape. The next row has the brush set to fade to transparent.

# Understanding the Painting Modes

Photoshop offers several different painting modes: Normal, Dissolve, Behind, Multiply, Screen, Overlay, Soft Light, Hard Light, Color Dodge, Color Burn, Darken, Lighten, Difference, Exclusion, Hue, Saturation, Color, and Luminosity. You'll find these modes on the pop-up menu at the top left of the Paintbrush Options palette. All painting modes are available with the Paintbrush, History Paintbrush, Pencil, Airbrush, and Rubber Stamp tools. The best way to understand the function of each mode is to try them yourself.

*Painting modes* are created by the effect of the overlying brush stroke on the underlying pixels. Each mode affects pixels in a unique way. Keep in mind that each color is the numerical representation of its RGB values. To understand how these modes work, you need to think of three different colors involved in the process: blend, base, and result.

Mode explanations follow, but try them on your own to see the effect for yourself:

▶ **Normal mode.** The blend color covers underlying base pixels completely when in the 100% opacity mode.
▶ **Dissolve mode.** The blend color replaces the underlying base pixel color at random, based on the density of the applied paint at any specific pixel location.

▶ **Behind mode.** The behind mode is used when you are working with layers.
▶ **Multiply mode.** This mode darkens the image by multiplying color values according to a mathematical formula.
▶ **Screen mode.** Lightens the pixels you're painting over while giving them a tint of the blend color.
▶ **Overlay mode.** The base color is mixed with the blend color, preserving the highlights and shadows of the original image while overlaying the new color on top.
▶ **Soft light mode.** Provides the effect of shining a diffused spotlight on the image.
▶ **Hard Light mode.** Provides the effect of shining a harsh spotlight on the image.
▶ **Color Dodge.** Examines each channel's color information and then brightens the base color.
▶ **Color Burn.** Examines each channel's color information and then darkens the base color.

## TAKE NOTE

### VIEWING YOUR BRUSH

One of our favorite Preference settings is to set the Painting cursors (under Display and Cursors) to Brush Size, that way you see exactly where the brush is covering.

## CROSS-REFERENCE

For more on RGB color mode, see Chapter 2.

## FIND IT ONLINE

For more tips on Photoshop see **http://www. mccannas.com/pshop/photosh0.htm.**

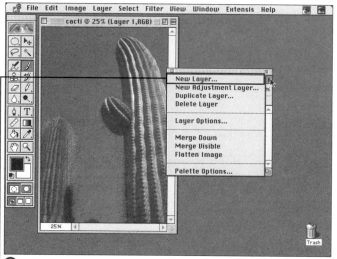

**1** To experiment with the different painting modes, first create a new layer so you don't alter the original image. To create a new layer choose Layer ⇨ New ⇨ Layer.

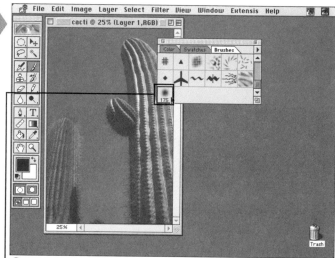

**2** Choose any large brush with a soft edge from the Brushes palette. If the Brushes palette isn't visible, choose Window ⇨ Show Brushes.

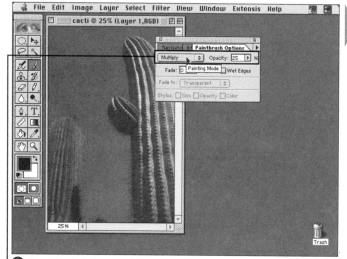

**3** Double-click the Paintbrush tool with your mouse to access the Paintbrush Options dialog box. Choose Multiply in the mode pop-up menu and set the Opacity to 25%.

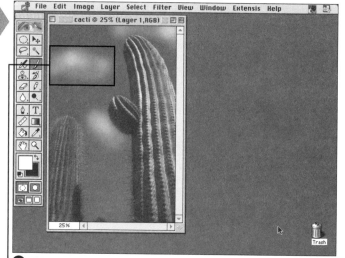

**4** This example shows a brush using Multiply mode and an Opacity set to 25%. Slowly paint in clouds in this blue sky. The soft edge makes nice wispy clouds and the more you go over a spot the more color of the clouds appear to add depth.

# Understanding the Painting Modes *Continued*

The blend color is the one you're using to paint with. The blend color can be applied with complete opacity (100%) or some degree of transparency, selected from the Options palette's slider. The base color is the underlying color of the image or background you're painting over. The result color is the color that you get after applying the blend color on top of the base color.

The painting modes are as follows:

▶ **Darken mode.** Only base pixels lighter than the blend color are changed

▶ **Lighten mode.** Only pixels darker than the blend color that you are painting with are changed. So here's a brain twister. How can you paint gold over blue in lighten mode and get pink? The answer is simple — the higher number (lighter value) dominates.

▶ **Difference mode.** Calculates the difference between the blend and base color. The result color is the value that is determined.

▶ **Exclusion.** The effect is the same as Difference, but less pronounced.

▶ **Hue mode.** Changes hue to that of the blend color, but pixels maintain their saturation (intensity) and luminosity (a measure of brightness).

▶ **Saturation mode.** Changes the saturation of the underlying base pixels but leaves their hue and luminosity alone.

▶ **Color mode.** Changes underlying base pixels to the blend color. The hue and saturation of the pixels are changed, but not the luminosity. This mode is good for colorizing grayscale artwork (like photographs) without changing the gray levels.

▶ **Luminosity mode.** Only the lightness of the pixels are affected, not the color values. The luminosity mode is the exact opposite (inverse) of the color mode. Use this mode when you want to change pixel lightness while leaving the hue alone.

## TAKE NOTE

### CHANGING OPACITY

One of the greatest things you can do in the Paintbrush options palette is to change the opacity of the paint application. This way you can add subtle effects that overlay the original image.

## CROSS-REFERENCE

For information on using the History Brush, see Chapter 6.

## FIND IT ONLINE

For some great tips on using the Brush tool, customizing brushes, and modes, visit **http://www.stars.com/Authoring/Graphics/Tools/Photoshop/customizing_brushes.html**.

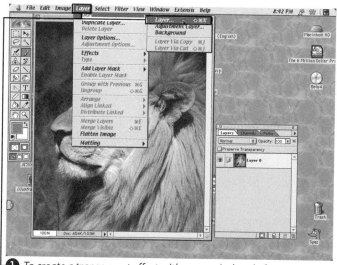

**1** To create a transparent effect with your paintbrush, first create a new layer by choosing Layer ⇨ New ⇨ Layer. This makes it easy to remove if you don't like the effect.

**2** Choose any large brush with a soft edge (so the edges won't be harsh) from the Brushes palette (Window ⇨ Show Brushes).

**3** Double–click the Paintbrush tool with your mouse to access the Paintbrush Options dialog box. Choose Overlay from the mode options in the pop-up menu and set the Opacity to 50%.

**4** This image shows the foreground enhanced by using the Overlay option to soften the background colors.

# Using the Pencil Tool and Other Options

The pencil is considered to be a painting tool even though it paints a hard-edged line that is visibly aliased. Use the pencil whenever you want a coarser look. All the brush sizes, painting modes, and opacity options apply, just as they do with the Paintbrush and Airbrush. Set the Fade and Stylus Pressure options for the pencil by double-clicking the pencil icon, just as you did for the Paintbrush and Airbrush.

We like to use the Pencil tool in Quick Mask mode to really tighten up selections. To switch to Quick Mask mode, click the icon, or press the letter Q. Zoom in on your selection. You can tighten up a selection border by using the Pencil tool to paint in pixels. If you make a mistake and go outside of your border simply press the X key (which toggles between foreground and background colors) and paint out that spot. Many times we use the Quick Mask mode to make the whole selection. You can change the Brush size to get the rough outline, then use a smaller brush to paint in the edge in Quick Mask mode. If you create a soft-edged brush you can get the feathered soft-edge mask. If you forget, you can always choose Feather from the Select menu.

Some of the other painting options we haven't mentioned yet are Airbrush and Eyedropper. Use the Airbrush for soft retouching effects, especially when colorizing grayscale drawings and photographs. The Airbrush paints a soft spray of color that is unequaled for hazy glows and sheer overlays of hue. For some realism, use a pressure sensitive digitizing tablet.

The Eyedropper tool is fabulously helpful when working on any number of projects in Photoshop. It makes it easy to "grab" hard-to-mix colors from an existing document and very simple to match a specific color in a logo or other corporate identification. As well, the Eyedropper can be useful in straight-up manipulations. When you're smoothing a cheek, say. Or unruffling feathers.

Unlike the Paintbrush, with the Airbrush, paint builds up when you continue to hold it in one place and press the mouse button. It "puddles" just as a real airbrush does. You set Brush Options for the Airbrush as you do for the Paintbrush in the Brush palette. The Airbrush Options (Fade, Stylus Pressure: Color and Pressure) are the same as the Paintbrush. What is called opacity (on the Brushes palette) is called pressure when the Airbrush tool is active. Increasing pressure increases the darkness of the stroke.

## TAKE NOTE

### MAKING STRAIGHT LINES WITH THE PENCIL

You can make a straight line using the Pencil tool by pressing the Shift key as you drag out a line. The Shift key constrains the line to 0 or 90 degrees.

## CROSS-REFERENCE

For more on Quick Mask, see Chapter 3.

## FIND IT ONLINE

Take a look here for some great Photoshop techniques: http://www.pixelfoundry.com//techniques.

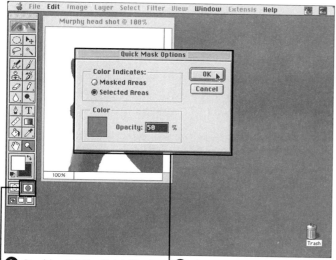

❶ Double-click the Quick Mask mode to set the options.

❷ If you want the masked image to show through, click the Selected Areas option and set the Opacity to 50% or less.

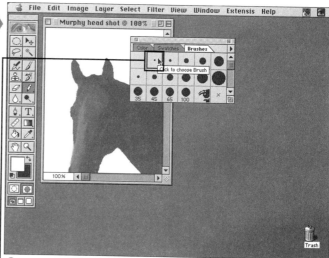

❸ Choose the Pencil tool from the Toolbox. If the Brushes palette isn't visible, choose Window ➪ Show Brushes. Choose any large brush to do the large areas, and any small brush to do the edges.

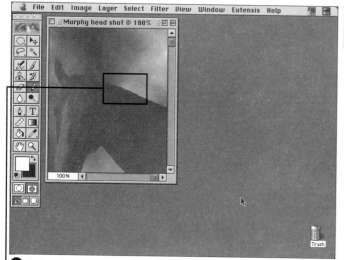

❹ Using the Pencil tool, adjust the edge of your object by painting the edge.

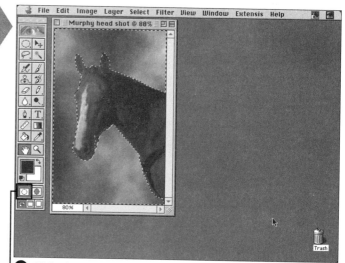

❺ Click Edit in Standard Mode, which is to the left of the Quick mask button in the toolbox, to see the selection (marching ants).

# Adding Lines with the Line Tool

You can use the Line tool to draw straight lines of any length and width. The Line tool is located on the main Toolbar. Find it by clicking the Pencil tool and keeping the mouse button depressed. The Line tool appears in the pop-up tools.

As you use the Line tool, you will notice that the boxes that usually give you RGB and CMYK information in the Info Palette are instead filled with useful information about the line you are drawing. The box on the left measures the movement of the end of the Line tool with relationship to the starting point on the screen's X, Y grid.

The triangle to the left of the X and Y is the Greek symbol delta, which represents change. As you drag the mouse, what you are measuring is the change in X and the change in Y. If you hold down the Shift key, you can constrain the line to the X axis so that there is no change in Y. The same would happen if you held down the Shift key and drew a line straight up (there would be no change in X, only a change in Y).

In the second new box that appears, the A represents the angle from the horizontal, and D represents distance, or the length of the line you have drawn.

The Line tool can be useful for drawing a straight line with an arrowhead. This can be helpful when rendering maps or other documents where precision and a sense of direction are important.

If you are looking to put a line with an arrow on your image, you'll need to access the Line Tool Options palette. The arrowhead selections are found by choosing the Shape button in the Line Tool Options palette. In this palette you can enter a percentage for the line width, and check the Arrowheads at the Start or End box. You can select a pixel width for the arrowhead width as well as a numeric value for its length. You can adjust the concavity of the arrow by entering a number. (Concavity is the amount of curvature of the sides of the arrowhead.) When you click and drag with your mouse and release the mouse button, the arrowheads appear. Make your arrowhead wide enough for the pixel width of the line so it looks proportional.

Straight lines are also useful for delineating a Heading or for creating borders. Another great use for the Line tool is to create callouts leaders for your type. Because of Photoshop's increasing type ability, you may be able to create a whole image with text and leader lines all with one program.

---

**TAKE NOTE**

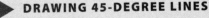

**DRAWING 45-DEGREE LINES**

To draw a line at a perfect 45-degree angle, press Command (Ctrl)+Shift and drag the mouse in the desired angular direction.

---

**CROSS-REFERENCE**

For more on text, see Chapter 4.

**FIND IT ONLINE**

The Web site at **http://www.DiPweb.com** shows you Photoshop in depth.

**1** To create a line with arrowheads first double-click the Line tool with your mouse to access the Line Tool options palette. Set your line options for a 3-pixel-weight line and arrowheads at start. Once you enter your pixel weight, the palette will remain on your screen. You may have to drag it out of your way so you can work

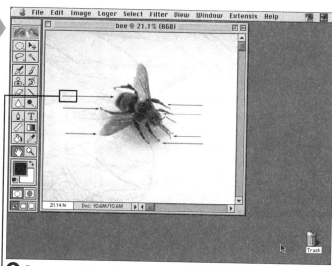

**2** Drag towards the object to create a leader line that points to it.

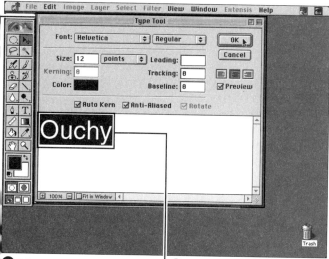

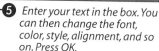

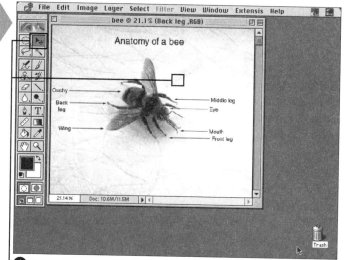

**3** After creating all of your leader lines, click the Type tool at the end of a leader line.

**4** The Type tool dialog box is where you can enter your text, style, color, and so on.

**5** Enter your text in the box. You can then change the font, color, style, alignment, and so on. Press OK.

**6** Repeat steps 3 to 5 for all of the text that you want to enter. Click the Move tool to make final adjustments.

# Personal Workbook

## Q&A

**1** What is *anti-aliasing?*

_____

_____

_____

**2** How do you create your own special *Paintbrush* in Photoshop?

_____

_____

_____

**3** How do you control paint opacity?

_____

_____

_____

**4** How do you draw an arrowhead with Photoshop?

_____

_____

_____

**5** Where can you find extra brushes in Photoshop?

_____

_____

_____

_____

**6** When should you use the Eyedropper tool?

_____

_____

_____

_____

**7** How do you add just one arrowhead to point to an object in Photoshop?

_____

_____

_____

_____

ANSWERS: PAGE 338

## EXTRA PRACTICE

① Use all of the brushes, even if you just make one stroke with each in a single file. Get to know the exact differences between a hard-edged brush and a soft one.

② Alter the properties of an existing brush. Make it bigger or harder or angle it differently.

③ Make your very own brush in the form of a design that you need to repeat, such as a logo.

④ Experiment with paint opacity. See how changing the opacity alters the way paint is laid down.

⑤ Use every single painting mode found in the Paintbrush Options palette. Use them against each other and on existing images. See what each mode does and think about how you might use it.

## REAL-WORLD APPLICATIONS

✔ You want to create a logo that includes a series of evenly spaced ellipses. You could customize a brush so that it creates these ellipses when you use it.

✔ You want to create a distinct halo around a photograph. You could choose the Dissolve painting mode and paint around the edge of the image.

✔ You have added arrowheads to all of your leader lines in your medical image to point out different areas. The client wants just plain lines. Fortunately for you, the arrows and lines were on their own layer, so you can re-do easily.

✔ You need to make an exact selection, so you could use the Pencil tool with Quick Mask mode. Then you could apply a small feather to blend the edges.

## Visual Quiz

How was this gunshot-through-burlap-bag effect created?

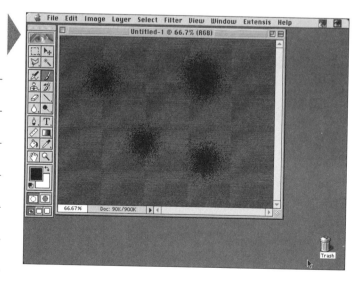

# Advanced Concepts

# CHAPTER 10

**MASTER**
**THESE**
**SKILLS**

- ▶ Using the Pen Tool
- ▶ Making a Path with the Magnetic Pen Tool
- ▶ Saving a Path
- ▶ Making Selections with the Paths Palette
- ▶ Creating a Clipping Path

# Creating Paths and Clipping Paths

Creating paths is essential to good Photoshop use. A path is a line created using the Pen tool. The actual path is like a guide, meaning that it isn't going to print out on your image. You can also make a path from an existing selection as well. You will love using the Pen tool and other tools to create paths. Paths created in Photoshop can be used to make selections, saved as channel masks, or copied and pasted into other programs such as Adobe Illustrator.

You can use the Selection tools, the Pen tool, or any means of making a selection to create a path. You can use a saved path to make a selection at any time. One great thing about saving paths, rather then saving selections as channels, is that you have more options when it comes to saving. For example, you can save as a TIFF, EPS, JPEG, and more by saving paths rather than selections. To activate the path into a selection, you need to select the path name, then choose Make Selection from the Paths palette pop-up menu.

The Pen tool has added a new partner in its pop-up menu in the toolbox. The Magnetic Pen is new to Photoshop 5, and like the Magnetic Lasso, it reads the edges of the pixels and creates a path based on that.

Saving a path rather than a selection is not only smart for saving purposes (you only have to save one file this way), but it also is handy if you want to export the path into other programs such as Illustrator.

Another great feature of paths is the Clipping Path. The Clipping Path lets you define a border for your image; when brought into another program, only the pixels within that border will be visible. Clipping Paths create a mask effect to your image. When you bring that image into a program like PageMaker, then only content that was inside the path's edges is displayed and saved. You can clip a large image in PageMaker using basic shapes, but the Clipping Path allows you to use irregular shaped paths for masking.

You'll find this chapter pretty essential if you work with other programs along with Photoshop. Once you learn the Pen tool logistics, you'll find you can use the Pen tool in any program. The Clipping Path option will seem like a miracle when you are working with large, complex files and only want a section used in your page layout program.

# Using the Pen Tool

There are three distinct Pen tools available to you from the Pen icon on the Main Toolbar. Of the three, the Pen tool allows the greatest precision when drawing. It's also the hardest of three Pens to learn and use effectively. The Magnetic Pen tool acts like a tracing tool. The lines you draw snap to the strongest edges in the image you're tracing. The Freeform Pen tool allows you to draw a loose irregular path. The anchor points are set down automatically as you draw.

There are some basic rules when using the Pen tool. If you click one time, you create a corner anchor point; click again in a different spot to create a straight line. Remember that a line is made up with at least two points. If you click and drag as you click, you create a smooth point; click and drag again and you'll create a flowing line.

The Smooth lines are made up of a smooth anchor point, direction handles, and a direction line. The direction line should remain tangent to the shape you are following. There is a 1/3 rule. Only drag out 1/3 of the total length of the line. Also, don't let the dragged handle cross the next handle or you'll get loops. If you are following a shape, then look at the image in terms of hills and valleys. Place a smooth anchor point on the hills and valleys. When you drag, the path creates an anchor point and direction handles. The direction handles are where you

can alter the shape of the line later. Always go in the same direction until you get around your object. Don't try to make up for an incorrect line by changing the next one. If you see the line is going awry, keep going; then you can go back later and fix it with your editing tools, found in the Pen tools pop-up tools in the toolbox.

To connect the path back to the original point, you'll see a small circle displayed beside the Pen cursor that indicates the Pen is over the original connection point. You can combine Smooth and Corner points at will. Remember to click and let up to make a corner point and click and drag to make a smooth point. To use the Pen tool successfully, you'll use a combination of both points. The editing tools will also let you fix any line by adding points, deleting points, and converting points. The Freeform Pen tool will follow the nuances of your hand to create your path. This may sound like the answer to your dreams, but have that second cup of coffee, and you'll see this may not work for everything.

## TAKE NOTE

### SAVING A PATH
You must save the new path by name before viewing the old path again, or your new work will be lost.

**CROSS-REFERENCE**
For more on making selections, see Chapter 4.

**FIND IT ONLINE**
Check this Web site for a tick on Photoshop (yes, ticks, you'll see): **http://www.iserv.net/~rtideas/.**

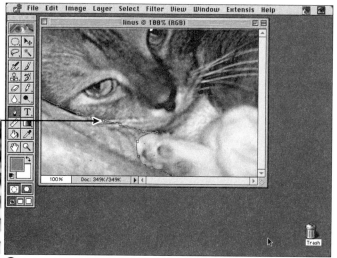

**1** Using the Pen tool, draw around the edge that you want to make into a path. Click and drag to create a smooth curve and click one time to make a square point.

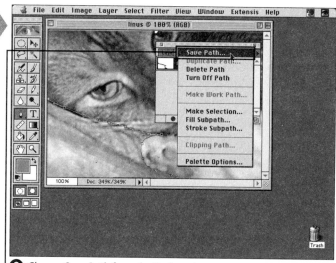

**2** Choose Save Path from the Paths palette pop-up menu. Enter a name for your path.

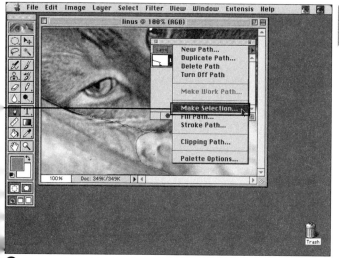

**3** Choose Make Selection from the Paths palette pop-up menu to make the path into a selection.

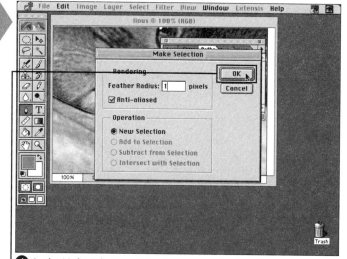

**4** In the Make Selection dialog box, enter a feather if you wish; if not, click OK.

# Making a Path with the Magnetic Pen Tool

The Magnetic Pen tool is new to Photoshop 5. The Magnetic Pen is similar to the Magnetic Lasso in that it reads the difference between pixel colors. To change the direction of the path, you can interrupt by clicking to place your own anchor point. When you get back to the original point, the Magnetic Pen cursor will display a circle letting you know that you are overtop a point that will connect the path.

It takes some work to get proficient enough with the Pen tool to do really outstanding work. But persevere, because once you get it, you'll wonder why you thought it was so difficult! Also, it's important to remember that every Anchor you put down isn't set in stone. There are tools and shortcut commands to help you fine-tune your creation.

From the Pen icon on the Main Toolbar, you can access a few tools to help you tune your drawing:

- ▶ The Add Anchor Point tool lets you place an anchor where there wasn't one before.
- ▶ The Delete Anchor Point tool lets you remove an anchor that's messing up your results.
- ▶ The Direct Selection Tool lets you select an anchor to move or reshape one or more segments of a path.
- ▶ The Convert Point Tool lets you alter the type of anchor from corner to smooth, or vice-versa.

If you create more shapes and lines while a path is selected, they will automatically be saved with that path. You do not have to save the path again. To create a new path, you must first deactivate the active path. Do this by clicking the arrow on any area outside of your saved path, but still within the Paths palette. The saved path's box becomes inactive and the path is hidden, although it's still saved. You can then begin drawing a new path on the blank screen. You'll note that as soon as you begin to draw, a new box labeled Work Path appears in the Path Palette, and you can see your new path begin to take shape there.

Fill Path and Stroke Path are powerful tools for creating precisely filled and outlined shapes. You can use them with all the painting and editing tools, in modes appropriate for those tools. Pen tool paths behave very much like selection borders. In fact, you can use a path to create a selection border. You will not be irreversibly converting the path into a selection; you will be using the path as a template from which to make a selection.

## TAKE NOTE

### ▶ COMBINING TOOLS

You can always combine the different Pen tools to create your path. To continue on an existing path, click and drag on one of the path's endpoints and you'll start drawing from that point.

## CROSS-REFERENCE
For more on making basic selections, see Chapter 3.

## FIND IT ONLINE
This Web site addresses the use of the Magnetic Pen tool. It is a great reference if you are having any trouble using it: http://www.escribe.com/software/photoshop/msg02448.html.

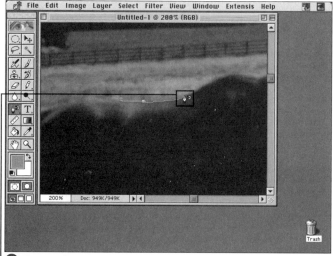

**1** To start the Magnetic Pen tool, click on the edge of the object you want to trace.

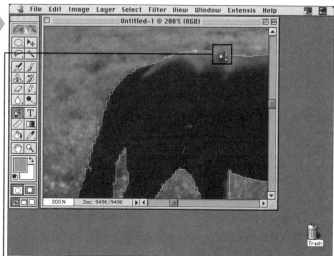

**2** Drag along the object you are selecting until you get back to the beginning point. When you are back at the beginning, the Magnetic Pen cursor will have a circle by it to indicate you are over the beginning point.

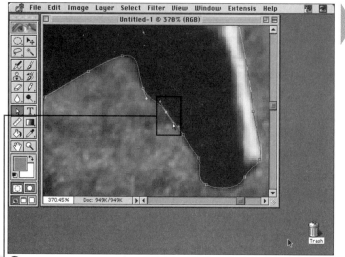

**3** Use the Arrow from the Pen tool's pop-up menu in the toolbox, to fix and adjust any lines. Add or delete anchor points by using the Add or Delete Anchor point tool found in the pop-up tools of the Pen tool.

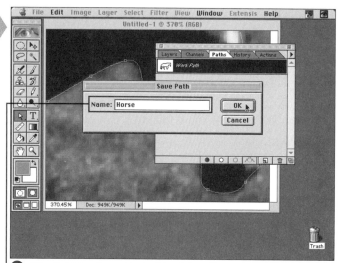

**4** After finishing the path, double click on the word "Work Path" in the Paths palette to give the path a name. We entered the name of the object.

# Saving a Path

The Paths palette is where you can activate, create, delete, and save paths. The Options found in the Paths palette pop-up menu are Save Path, Duplicate Path, Delete Path, Turn Off Path, Make Work Path, Make Selection, Fill Subpath, Stroke Subpath, Clipping Path, and Palette Options.

When you create a path, the Save Path option is activated. When you get the Save Path dialog box, you only get the choice to give it a name. If you don't choose a name, the default is to name it Path 1, Path 2, etc. You can Duplicate a path if you want to alter it, but not affect the original path. To Delete a path, you can choose Delete Path from the pop-up menu or just drag the path to the trashcan icon at the bottom of the Paths palette.

If you 've made a selection and you want that selection to be a path, then choose Make Work Path from the Paths palette pop-up menu. You'll have to give the path a name to save it in the palette. You can make any path you have created into a selection by choosing Make Selection from the pop-up menu. Fill Subpath will fill the path with the Foreground, Background, History, Pattern, Black, 50% Gray, or White. You can also choose Stroke Subpath with the Pencil, Paintbrush, Airbrush, Eraser, Clone Stamp, Pattern Stamp, History Brush, Smudge, Blur, Sharpen, Dodge, Burn, or Sponge. It will stroke the subpath with the Foreground color. Clipping a path will be discussed later in this chapter.

The Palette Options are the thumbnail size that you preview. You can choose none, small, medium, or large. The Paths Palette also has icons at the bottom of the palette that let you access a quick way to some of the options. The dark filled circle will fill your path with the foreground color, the white filled circle will stroke the path with the foreground color, and the dashed circle will make the path into a selection. The circle with the direction lines will make a path from a selection. The piece of paper will create a new path. Finally, when you drag the path to the trashcan icon, it deletes the path.

A document with saved paths can be saved in many different file formats, including Photoshop, Photoshop 2.0, Amiga IFF, BMP, Photoshop EPS, JPEG, PCX, Photoshop PDF, PICT File, PICT Resource, Pixar, PNG, Raw, Scitex CT, Targa, or TIFF.

## TAKE NOTE

### SAVING PATHS

You can save as many paths as you'd like. We recommend you name the path something that you can remember; that way. if you have a lot of paths you can find the one you want easily.

**CROSS-REFERENCE**

For more on saving files, see Chapter 1.

**FIND IT ONLINE**

For a great article on the Pen tool and paths, see: http://www.macworld.co.uk/sep98/media/ create_graphics.html.

**1** *Using the Pen tool, trace around your object. We chose this flower. When you get back to the beginning, the Pen cursor will display a circle letting you know that you are connecting the path.*

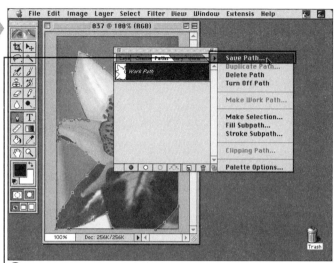

**2** *Choose Save Path from the Paths palette pop-up menu.*

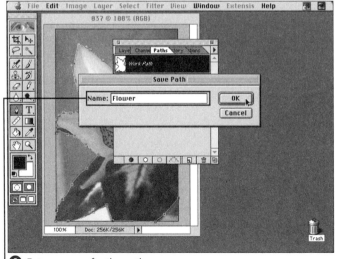

**3** *Enter a name for the path.*

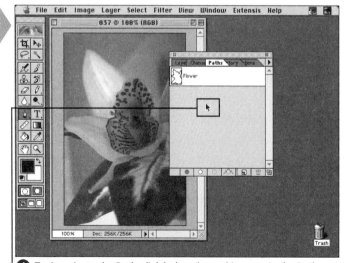

**4** *To deactivate the Path, click below the path's name in the Paths palette. To reactivate it, you simply click on the Path's name to see it displayed.*

# Making Selections with the Path Palette

If you have used a vector-oriented illustration program, or if you took serious drafting back in high school, you will recognize the Pen tool as a Bezier (Bez-ee-yay) curve drawing device. With the Pen tool, you can create lines and shapes that can be fine-tuned, saved as paths, filled with color or outlined (stroked), and used as the basis for selections. You can change selections into paths and edit them with the tools on the Paths palette. While you see paths on screen, they contain no pixels and don't print with the image.

The smallest part of a path is a segment: the line connecting two anchor points. Several segments, linked, make a subpath, and subpaths combine to form paths. A path can be either a line or a closed shape, a series of lines, a series of shapes, or a combination of lines and shapes. You can stroke and fill subpaths as well as paths.

It's very common to change the shape of a path after you create it. Working with paths is generally a practice of successive approximation until you create the shape or line just the way you want it.

While working with the Pen tool, notice that a new anchor point is darkened as it is created, indicating that it is selected. At the same time, the previous anchor point lightens, meaning that it is deselected. Release the mouse button.

Hold down the Shift key to constrain the placement of an anchor point to a 45° angle or a multiple of 45°, such as a 90° angle. This also works to con-strain the angle of a direction line to 45° or a multiple thereof. Both constraints are helpful for drawing some geometric shapes. The first time you click on a smooth point with the Convert Point tool, it converts it to a corner point. Clicking again and dragging converts it back to a smooth point. Press the Command or (Ctrl) key to display the arrow pointer whenever the Pen tool is in use.

Using fewer anchor points to define a curve usually gives better results. More is not necessarily better. However, there are times when you'll need to add points, especially when you're tracing around an irregularly shaped image.

Any path that you create can be made into a selection. Those selections in turn can be saved as an Alpha Channel. Any file saved with Alpha Channels is limited to Photoshop, Photoshop 2.0, PICT File, PICT Resource, Pixar, PNG, Raw, Targa, or TIFF. So if you are looking to save as EPS, then either save only the paths or save two versions of the file so you have the channels to go back into later. For more on channels and Alpha Channels, see Chapter 12.

---

**TAKE NOTE**

### USING PATH ICONS

The icons at the bottom of the paths palette are huge time savers. If you hold you mouse over an icon, the pop-up help will tell you what that icon does.

---

**CROSS-REFERENCE**
For more on printing files, see Chapter 15.

**FIND IT ONLINE**
For more information and step-by-step tips on using paths, see this Web site: **http://www.andyart.com/photoshop/ps_58.htm**

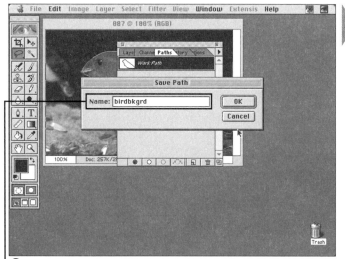

**1** After creating a path, save it by choosing Save Path from the Paths palette pop-up menu, then giving it a name.

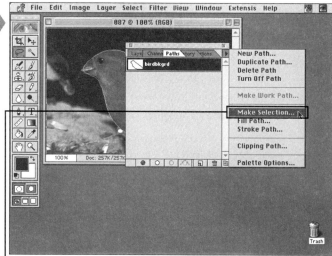

**2** Choose Make Selection from the Paths palette pop-up menu.

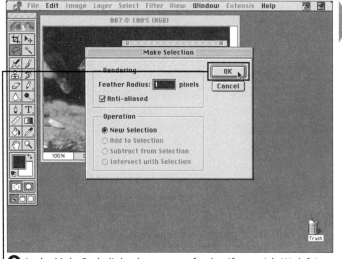

**3** In the Make Path dialog box, enter a feather if you wish. We left it at 0. Then click OK.

**4** Press Command (Ctrl) Shift I to select the Inverse, then press Command (Ctrl) I to create a cool inverse color effect.

# Creating a Clipping Path

Beyond the creating paths, a clipping path is useful in many other programs. A clipping path is a path created around the edge of an object because you only want that object to be displayed in another program. I know you're thinking—why not just put a white background and be done with it? Well, because if you save that file and take it into PageMaker, then the white background will come as well. Not only that, but even if you can hide the object's edges in PageMaker, you're still working with the full file size, including the white background.

A clipping path is a path that defines an edge; when you take that image into another program, then only what was within that edge will be displayed. If you have difficulty in printing your clipping path, you may be working with an older imagesetter, or a low-resolution printer. If you are still having problems printing, then you can delete the anchor points to make fewer segments. The fewer the segments, the smoother the path, but initially when you start working with paths you'll tend to use way too many points.

To create a clipping path you first must make a path either from a selection or from using one of the Pen tools. Then you need to give the path a name by choosing Save Path from the Paths palette pop-up menu. Then you need to choose Clipping Path from the Paths palette pop-up menu. In the Clipping Path dialog box, you'll need to find the name of your path in the Path pop-up menu. You can also set the flatness if you think the printer may have trouble with your path. We usually leave this blank. Finally when you save the file, you save it as a TIFF or EPS.

In conjunction with the clipping path is the *clipping group*. With a clipping group, you use the bottom layer as a mask for the above layers and groups. A grouped layer is made in the Layers palette. Before making a clipping group, first make sure the bottom layer is the mask that you want to use. To make a clipping group, you need to put the cursor on the line between the layers while pressing the Option (Alt) key. You'll see two circles appear, letting you know that it will make those layers a clipping group when you click. You'll notice the line between the layers is now dotted. The bottom layer (masked layer) will be underlined, and the clipping group layer names will all be indented to the right. To ungroup the layers, hold the Option (Alt) key down and place the cursor over the line between the layers and click.

## TAKE NOTE

### GROUPED LAYERS

Only layers in successive order can be used as a grouped layer.

**CROSS-REFERENCE**
For more on layers see Chapter 11.

**FIND IT ONLINE**
If you are having any trouble with Photoshop's clipping paths, see this note from Adobe at: **http://www. adobe.com/supportservice/custsupport/SOLUTIONS /fcbe.htm**

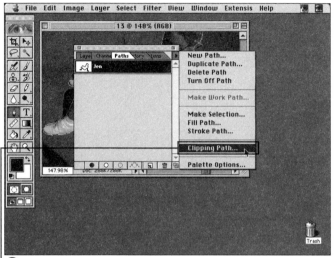

**①** *After saving your path, choose Clipping Path from the Paths palette pop-up menu.*

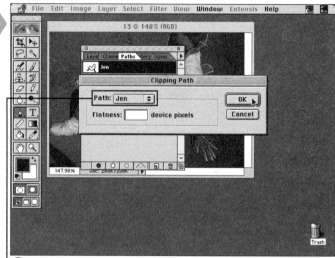

**②** *Choose the path's name from the pop-up menu.*

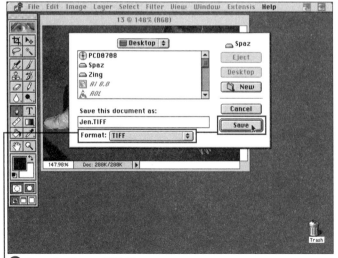

**③** *Save the file as a TIFF file.*

**④** *Place the image in a PageMaker file to see how the clipping path worked.*

# Personal Workbook

## Q&A

**1** Name the Pen tools.

_____

_____

_____

**2** How can you add an anchor point where there wasn't one before?

_____

_____

_____

**3** What does the Magnetic Pen do?

_____

_____

_____

**4** What is a *path*?

_____

_____

_____

**5** Which gives you more saving options, saving with Paths, or saving selections as Alpha channels?

_____

_____

_____

**6** What is a *clipping path*?

_____

_____

_____

**7** Why would you use a clipping path?

_____

_____

_____

**8** What is a *clipping group*?

_____

_____

_____

ANSWERS: PAGE 339

## EXTRA PRACTICE

1. Open an image with lots of curves. Use the Pen tool to create a path around an object.

2. Use the Magnetic Pen to select an object that is more complex and surrounded by different pixels.

3. After creating a complex path, save the path for later, then turn the path into a selection so you can apply effects to that area.

4. Create a clipping path and take that path into a page layout program to see the results.

5. Bring the same image as you did in number 4, but don't create a clipping path. Notice the difference.

6. Create a mask on the bottom layer and use the clipping group to affect all of the layers.

## REAL-WORLD APPLICATIONS

✔ You have created this stunning logo on a psychedelic background. Your client wants to see a variety of backgrounds, so you use the Pen tool to trace the logo out, and save the path so you can make selections easily.

✔ There is this great profile of an eagle that you'd love to illustrate. You use the Pen tools to create an accurate and smooth path, then you export the paths to Illustrator where you fill in the path with colors and blends.

✔ There is this great image that you composited from some old photos. You only want to use the picture of your cousin Filbert in your newsletter, so you use the Pen tools to make a path and then create a clipping path that you save. In PageMaker, the placed image looks great with only cousin Filbert showing.

## Visual Quiz

What did we use to make the person in this newsletter show without a background?

_____

_____

_____

_____

_____

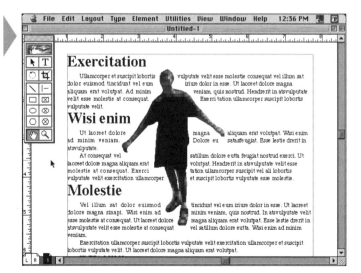

CHAPTER **11**

MASTER
THESE
SKILLS

▶ **Creating and Editing Layers**
▶ **Using Layer Masks**
▶ **Applying Adjustment Layers**
▶ **Adding Layer Effects**
▶ **Linking Layers**
▶ **Flattening Layers**
▶ **Managing Layers**

# Working with Layers and Adjustment Layers

Layers (and adjustment layers) offer some of the real basic power in Adobe Photoshop because they give you full control of all aspects of the images you create. Everything you know about channels and masks will help you understand layers. *Channels* relate to a single color aspect of the entire image, *layers* relate to each individual aspect of the image.

Layers are a kind of "super channel" with many capabilities and options. The chief limitation of a channel is that it is essentially a grayscale image. You can modify the brightness and contrast or other grayscale characteristics of a channel. Each of Photoshop's layers, in contrast, can be a complete full-color image of its own. You can paste a picture of a yellow taxi in one layer, a stout tree with lush green foliage in a second layer, and then combine them in flexible ways. Layers are transparent until you place something on them. Think of each layer as a separate document with color channels of its own. If you can think of layers as a kind of full-color "channel" with many of the properties

of the channels you've already used, you'll be halfway to understanding this feature.

As you work with layers, you may need to change the order in which layers are arranged so that some objects are in front of or behind others. As with channels, you can copy, move, or duplicate layers within a document or between documents by dragging and dropping from one window to another, or delete a layer by dragging it to the trashcan icon at the bottom of the Layers palette.

When you are done working with a document, you "flatten" the layers together, merging them into a final, background-only image that is your finished work. Of course, there is nothing to keep you from saving the "final" version under a new name, keeping the layered document for additional manipulations later on.

Adjustment Layers allow you to manipulate a layer or series of layers without actually affecting the image. An adjustment layer acts like a layer mask, but the changes you make are stored within the adjustment layer itself.

# Creating and Editing Layers

Like many things in Photoshop, the steps involved in working with layers are easy. But it's how you combine the steps in creative and ingenious ways that makes Photoshop such a powerful tool.

You create a new layer in two ways: either by using the New Layer command from the Layers Palette (choose New Layer from the pop-up menu or click the New Layer icon) or by pasting a new item into the document you're working on. When you create a new item with an editing tool, such as a filled marquee box or a swathe of color with the Paintbrush, some human intervention is required to add a new layer. It is quite easy to choose Layer ⇨ New ⇨ Layer from the Layer menu or to press Command+Shift+N (Ctrl+Shift+N). In any of these scenarios, the newly created layer will be instantly reflected in the Layers Palette.

Once created, layers can be manipulated quite endlessly from the Layers palette. You can change their order by dragging them to a new position. Make a Layer invisible by clicking the Eye icon that corresponds to that particular Layer (click again to make the Layer visible again).

To make a Layer active and ready to edit or work on, simply click the Layer icon in the Layers palette. A darkening of that Layer's representative indicates the active Layer. Also, a small square to the left of the active Layer's icon holds a paintbrush to let you know that it is active. It is a good habit to click the layer name rather than the icon, or you may change the visibility of that layer.

You can also link layers so they can be manipulated or moved together. When you click the square (where the paintbrush would be) in an inactive layer, it links it to the layer above it in the Layers Palette (more on this in "Linking Layers").

It's a good idea to practice working with individual layers. You'll quickly see how this capability gives you a great deal more flexibility in working with the components that make up a finished Photoshop document.

Being able to shift layers around fluently makes it possible to add real dynamics to an image. Working with type is a good example. Overlapping type can give you a really fresh look. If various lines of type are on different layers, experiment with the amount of overlap as well as which bit of type overlaps which. The results of this sort of experimentation can be startling in their differences.

## TAKE NOTE

### LAYERS IN PREVIOUS VERSIONS

Prior to Photoshop 3.0, all Photoshop documents had only a background layer and nothing more. If you are working with an image that was created in an earlier version, you will need to save it in a later format of Photoshop.

**CROSS-REFERENCE**
For more on type, see Chapter 4.

**FIND IT ONLINE**
Check this Web site out for frequently asked Photoshop questions: http://www.geocities.com/CollegePark/Quad/2237/ adobefaq.txt.

**1** *After making your selection, choose Edit ⇨ Copy.*

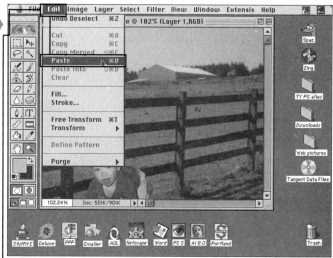

**2** *Paste your selection on another image by choosing Edit ⇨ Paste.*

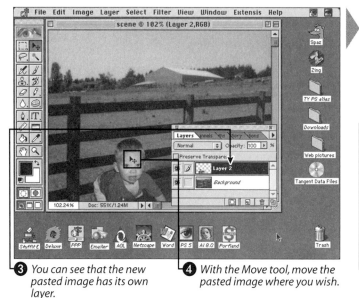

**3** *You can see that the new pasted image has its own layer.*

**4** *With the Move tool, move the pasted image where you wish.*

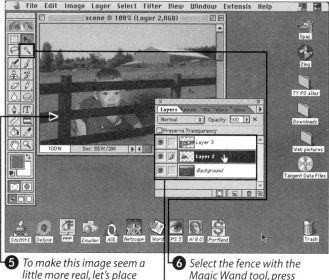

**5** *To make this image seem a little more real, let's place fence posts in front of the baby.*

**6** *Select the fence with the Magic Wand tool, press Command (Ctrl) C, then press Command (Ctrl) V.*

**7** *Rearrange the layers so the copied fence posts are on top.*

# Using Layer Masks

You can modify how a layer is combined with other layers by creating a separate Layer Mask. The Layer Mask lets you control how all of the elements on a specified Layer are hidden and how they are revealed. You can make changes to the layer mask and apply special effects to it without actually affecting the layer's pixels. If you don't like what you've done, you can remove the mask without applying it. Once you apply the Layer Mask to the layer, the changes become permanent. Using the Layer Mask allows you a bit of freedom and distance from your work—freedom, because it's easy to change and discard a Layer Mask without applying it, and distance, in that the changes you're making are a distinct and separate part of the image until applied. Layer Masks allow you the freedom to get into your Layer in a more intimate way than other methods. They're great for fine-tuning detail areas, when just a touch of lightness is required here or a blend of darkness over there.

Experiment with creating special effects with Layer Masks. Create effects not easily possible with other methods in Photoshop. Some of the special effects you can create using Layer masks are pasting an object into a specified shape, pasting a cool image into type, fading out a certain layer to transparent, and more.

Layer Masks can be seen onscreen in the Layers palette. They look just like an extra thumbnail to the right of the layer in the Layer's palette, and they are linked to the layer thumbnail to be affected. Black por-

tions indicate material that is hidden, while white indicates what will be revealed. Choose a medium gray to affect the Layer's opacity.

Adding a layer mask is easy. Simply click the Add Layer Mask icon from the tool bar at the bottom of the Layers palette. An additional thumbnail representing this layer will appear linked to the layer's thumbnail in the palette. The currently active portion of the layer (the mask or the layer itself) is surrounded by a black outline.

If you want, you can add a Layer Mask for each layer of a document. Remember, though: All of those layers within layers can add to your system's overhead and slow things down. Also, finished files will be more difficult to store and transport. Multi-layered documents with lots of extra selection channels can make for some really huge files. To keep file sizes manageable, it's important to remember to render your Layer Masks by applying them whenever possible.

*Continued*

*Continued*

## TAKE NOTE

### BREAKING THE MASK LINK

Though the Layer Mask is linked to its layer by default, you can break the link just as you would any Layers palette link by clicking the link icon that separates the Layer Mask from the Layer in the Layers palette. With the link broken, the layer and the Layer Mask can be moved around independently of each other, using the same methods you'd use to move anything in Photoshop—the pointing tool or the arrow keys.

## CROSS-REFERENCE

For more on moving pixels, see Chapter 3.

## FIND IT ONLINE

Check this out for great 3D type tutorials: **http://www.netins.net/showcase/wolf359/3dtext.htm**.

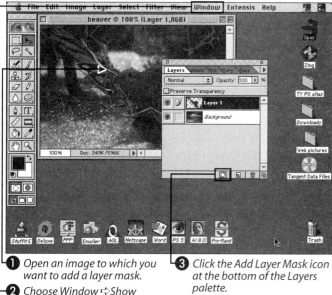

**1** Open an image to which you want to add a layer mask.

**2** Choose Window ➪ Show Layers to open the Layers Palette.

**3** Click the Add Layer Mask icon at the bottom of the Layers palette.

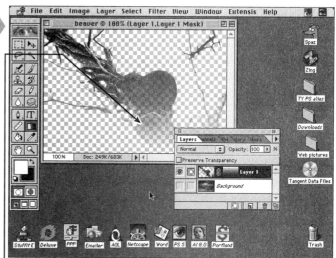

**4** Create your layer mask; for instance, drag the Blend tool from top to bottom to create a fade for your image.

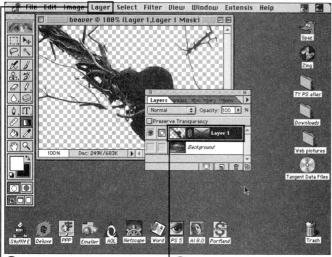

**5** To see your image without the Layer Mask (but without discarding it), choose Layer ➪ Disable Layer Mask.

**6** The Layer Mask disappears and displays on the Layers Palette with an X through it. If you want the effect to be a part of the layer, choose Layer ➪ Remove Layer Mask. At the prompt, click Apply.

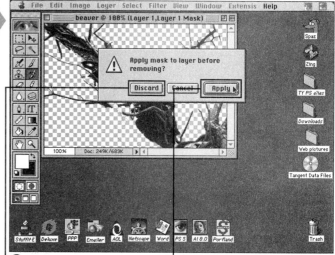

**7** To discard your mask, choose Layer ➪ Remove Layer Mask and click Discard.

**8** Or, choose Apply to render the mask to the layer before removing it or Cancel to continue. Saving a file with a layer mask is the same process as saving a file with any layer.

## Applying Partial Layer Masks

You don't have to apply a Layer Mask to an entire Layer. You can use one of the Selection tools to Select a portion of the Layer to work on. Before creating any type of layer masks—either partial or full layer masks—you need to be working on a layer other than the background layer. To create a new layer, you can click on the new layer icon (the middle one that looks like a piece of paper) at the bottom of the Layers palette. You can also create a new layer when you paste anything into your document or when you create type.

Next, you should decide whether you want to hide the unselected material of the Layer or show it. If you want to hide it, you need to choose Layer ⇨ Disable Layer Mask. That will put an X through the mask and display only the image on that layer. If you want to see it again, choose Layer ⇨ Enable Layer Mask. If you want to show it, click Option [Alt] and the Add Layer Mask button on the bottom of the Layers Palette. Creating and working with a selected portion of the Layer Mask is just the same as if you were working on the entire Layer.

## Summarizing Layer Masks

To review the gist of Layer Masks:

▶ The Layer Mask is actually an Alpha Channel within Photoshop.

▶ The Layer Mask controls how a layer's elements are hidden and revealed.
▶ Add a Layer Mask by clicking the Add Layer Mask icon in the Layers Palette or by selecting Layer ⇨ Add Layer Mask.
▶ Applying the Layer Mask makes it permanent to that layer.
▶ If not applied, no pixels in the document are altered.
▶ To hide desired portions of the Layer Mask, paint it with black.
▶ To subtract from the mask, paint with white.
▶ To alter the opacity of the mask, paint with varying shades of gray: light gray gives the least amount of coverage. Dark gray gives the most.
▶ To view the mask alone, click Option [Alt] and the Layer Mask icon. To return to the normal view, click any eye icon in the Layers Palette.
▶ To apply a Layer Mask to a portion of a Layer, select the desired area with any of the Selection tools.

**CROSS-REFERENCE**

For more on Quick Masks see Chapter 3.

**FIND IT ONLINE**

For great shadows on type, see **http://www.netins. net/showcase/wolf359/shadow.htm**.

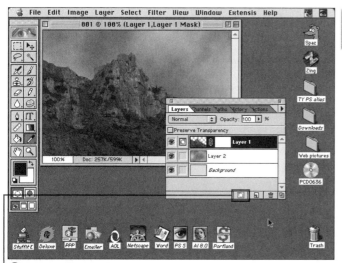

1 To create a partial layer mask, first create a Layer Mask on the top layer of your image by choosing the Layer Mask icon at the bottom of the Layers palette. The Layer Mask icon is the farthest left icon that looks like a rectangle with a circle inside of it.

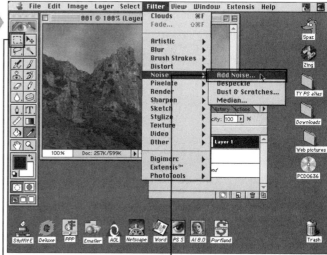

2 Use a Selection tool to select the portion of the image you want to work with.

3 For instance, you may choose to add a filter to create special effects on a portion of your image. This particular image used the Add Noise filter.

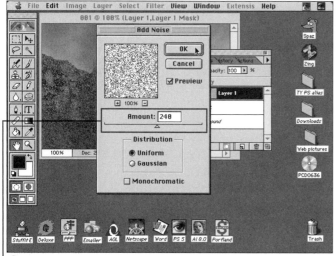

4 Add a high amount of Noise.

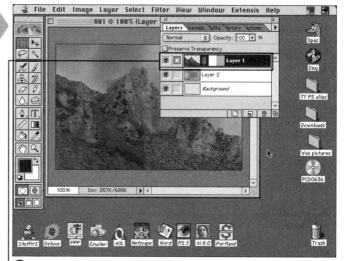

5 Check out the Layers palette and see that the effect was only applied to that selected half.

# Applying Adjustment Layers

Adjustment layers add an extra level of magic to Photoshop. The Adjustment Layer lets you make adjustments to a layer's color and tonality without actually affecting the image. Here again, think of playing with stacks of acetate, but this time, the changes you make are directly to a single piece of acetate. If you don't want the changes anymore, the acetate can be easily stripped out and thrown away or even just disabled for the future.

What this means in a practical sense is that you can actually see what a change might do without having to worry about causing difficult-to-get-out-of changes to your entire image. Also, you can play with radically different changes that will affect the look of your entire file with a couple of keystrokes.

The Adjustment Layer affects all the layers beneath it, and you can insert it between any layers you like. Adjustment layers have built-in Layer Masks. This means that you can easily mask out an area that you don't want affected by the Adjustment Layer.

Adjustment Layers are available to adjust an image's Levels, Curves, Brightness/Contrast, Color Balance, Hue /Saturation, Selective Color, Channel Mixer, Invert, Threshold, and Posterize. All of them work in the same manner as the one in the illustrated exercise, just as the same commands do in the Image ➪ Adjust menu. The difference, of course, is that in using Adjustment Layers, you aren't actually changing anything for the time being. No pixels are affected until the image is flattened or the layers are otherwise compressed.

Adjustment layers at a glance:

▶ Adjustment layers let you manipulate the image without actually changing the pixels.
▶ Adjustment layers affect all the layers beneath it, so you can move the adjustment layer to any location on the Layers palette.
▶ Adjustment layers have built-in layer masks, so you can choose to edit out areas you don't want affected by the adjustment layer.
▶ Create a new adjustment layer by selecting New Adjustment Layer from the pop-up menu on the Layers Palette or from the Layer ➪ New ➪ Adjustment Layer.

## TAKE NOTE

### USING ADJUSTMENT LAYERS AS LAYER MASKS

Adjustment Layers are really just a specialized flavor of Layer Mask. With that in mind, you can paint right on an Adjustment Layer in exactly the same way you do on the Layer Masks, using the same ratios of black to reveal the background, white to hide it, and gray to adjust opacity. To edit the Adjustment Layer Mask, use any of the editing tools to remove, add, or change the opacity of an effect. Painting in black removes the adjustment effect, painting in white displays the full effect, and painting in gray removes the adjustment effect only partially.

## CROSS-REFERENCE
For more on Layer Masks, see earlier in this chapter.

## FIND IT ONLINE
For basic tips on using Photoshop, see **http://www. netins.net/showcase/wolf359/tutorial.htm.**

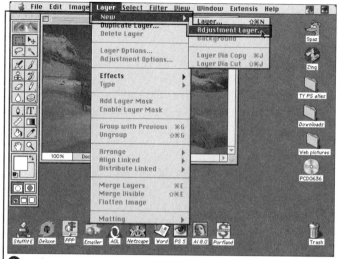

**1** *With your image open, choose Layer ➪ New ➪ Adjustment Layer.*

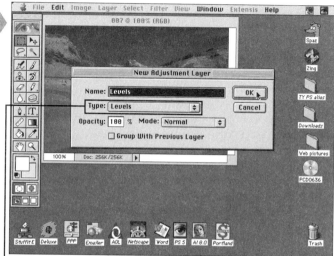

**2** *Choose the Levels under the Type pop-up menu. This option will let you adjust the tonality of the image.*

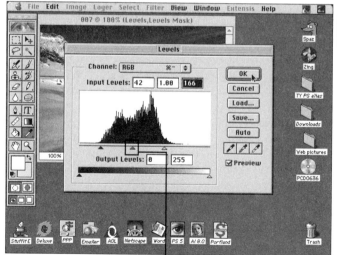

■ *Adjust the Levels. Here, the white slider was all of the way to the right, so we dragged it to the base of the curve starting on the right side to make the whites whiter.*

■ *Dragging the black slider to the base of the curve on the left makes the dark areas darker.*

**3** *Dragging the gray slider to the left lightens the gray tones.*

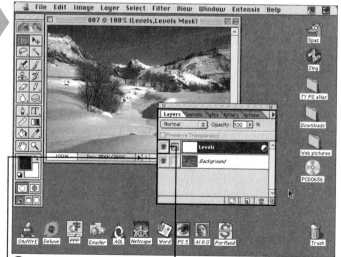

**4** *View the Layers palette to see the new layer that was created on top of the original layer. Your image will reflect the new changes to the tone.*

**5** *You can remove or turn off this layer. Click on the eye icon beside the layer in the Layers palette. Turn it back on by clicking the box where the eye icon was.*

# Adding Layer Effects

New Photoshop features often are the result of the designers at Adobe looking at what third-party filters are doing. One such feature is Layer Effects, which is new to Photoshop 5. Layer Effects make it possible to easily add sophisticated effects to layered files in Photoshop. Layer Effects, very challenging to achieve in earlier program versions, bring these great effects to the average and new user very easily.

Depending on the type of work you do, you might find many uses for Layer Effects. These effects can be especially useful if you do Web design. For instance, you can easily create type that appears to stand away from the page, boxes with bevels, and buttons with shadows. It is likely due to the Web's influence that we're seeing more and more of this three-dimensional look throughout various design mediums. Whatever the case, Layer Effects can add that extra punch to various types of graphics with very little effort on your part.

You use Layer Effects by highlighting the Layer you'd like to apply effects to, then selecting Layer ⇨ Effects. You can apply one or all of the five Layer effects to the same Layer. If you choose more than one, you can simply cycle through the Layers Effect's dialog box, applying the ones you wish and passing on the ones you don't want by selecting Next.

Each Layer Effect has its own controls, similar to those found in Photoshop's Filters. The default settings will produce an attractive effect. However, to truly make an Effect your own, experiment with each of the settings. Here's an overview, although results will vary depending on which Layer Effect is chosen.

*Angle* refers to the angle at which light is focused on the layer. When the Use Global Angle box is checked, the light appears to come from a uniform source throughout the various Effects.

*Mode* has the same meaning it has in all Photoshop functions. The result of a mode change will be seen in the same way it is with the painting tools.

*Opacity* affects how much light shines through the main part of the Effect. At 0%, the Effect will be invisible. At 100%, it will appear to be solid.

*Distance* refers to how much room will appear between the object and the Effect.

*Intensity* affects how strongly the Effect is seen.

---

### TAKE NOTE

#### ▶ CONVERTING LAYER EFFECTS TO LAYERS

Sometimes a Layer Effect Layer just isn't enough. An actual layer (rather than a Layer Effect Layer) has more options for you to work with. There'll be times when you want to work more closely with the effects after the Layer Effects have been rendered. You can convert a Layer Effect Layer to a regular layer accessible in the layers palette with an icon all its own. Do this by selecting Layer ⇨ Effects ⇨ Create Layer while the specified layer is highlighted.

---

### CROSS-REFERENCE

For more on third-party filters, see Chapter 14.

### FIND IT ONLINE

If you use Bryce, check out this Web site to see Photoshop and Bryce tips: **http://www.netins.net/showcase/wolf359/psbryce.htm**

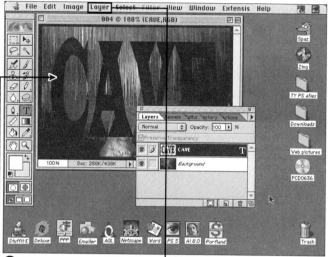

**1** This image shows the text already on its own layer. We're going to apply a cool effect to this text by using Layer Effects.

**2** Choose Layer ⇨ Effects ⇨ Bevel and Emboss.

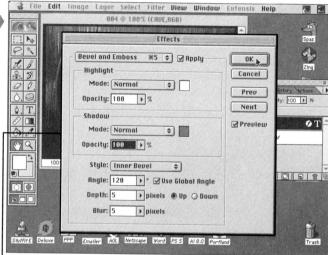

**3** The highlight and shadow areas are where you choose your mode, color and opacity. The third area is the style, angle, depth and blur. If you check the preview box, you can see how each of your settings affects the image.

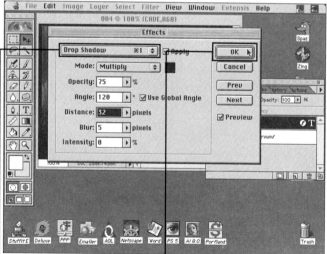

**4** To apply another effect at the same time, choose Drop Shadow from the pop-up menu in the Bevel and Emboss dialog box.

■ Adjust the settings and check the Apply and Preview boxes to see the results.

**5** Click OK when you're done.

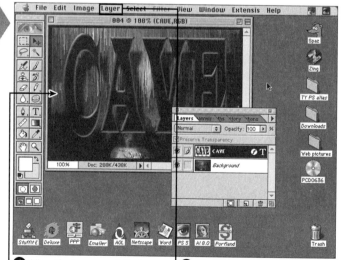

**6** View the Layers palette to see the changes you made to the palette. The image automatically shows you the changes once you click OK.

**7** You can remove the layer or turn off the effect(s) by choosing Layer ⇨ Effects ⇨ Hide All Effects.

**229**

# Linking Layers

To understand layers, it helps to think about how a basic document image is arranged. When you open a blank document using the File ⇨ New command, you might think of it as being empty: just a plain white canvas ready for your manipulations. In truth, the document is already filled with something: It has an opaque white background, as long as the default White button is checked in the Contents box of the New dialog box. New documents can also have a Background color or be Transparent. (It's hard to show transparency, or at least differentiate it from white, so Photoshop represents it with a translucent checkerboard pattern that can be modified in the Transparency and Gamut preferences.)

The other concept you need to understand is the idea of transparency. In that sense, layers are not like separate documents because they aren't automatically filled with opaque white. Layers are transparent until you place something on them. Think of a white art board as the base or background of your document. The order of individual layers is the third concept you need to understand. As you work with layers, you may need to change the order in which layers are arranged so that some objects are in front of or behind others. Fortunately, you can arrange layers in any order you like simply by dragging them in place in the Layers Palette.

Working with a multilayered image is almost as easy as working with a single layer image, because Photoshop allows you to link layers and work with more than one layer at a time. Linking layers is a breeze: You simply click the box of the inactive layer (the box that normally would show the paintbrush if that layer is active), and it links that layer to the layer above it. You may be wondering why you'd want to link layers. Well, if you have two objects on separate layers and want them to move together, then link them first and move. You can always unlink them by clicking the link icon (which looks like chains). You can also apply effects to multiple layers if they are linked. You can always re-arrange layers by dragging them above or below in the Layers palette.

## TAKE NOTE

### TURNING OFF LAYER THUMBNAILS

By default, the Layers palette thumbnails will be turned on. This is an element of Photoshop operations where there is room for both personal preference and operating system demands. It's nice to see large thumbnails of elements of your work in progress, but making thumbnails smaller or turning them off can save disk space and improve performance. Layer thumbnails can be turned on and off just like Channels icons, using the Palette Options choice from the fly-out menu.

## CROSS-REFERENCE
For more on Photoshop preferences, see Chapter 2.

## FIND IT ONLINE
Here is another gallery of art displaying Photoshop with other programs: **http://www.netins.net/showcase/wolf359/digimgal.htm**

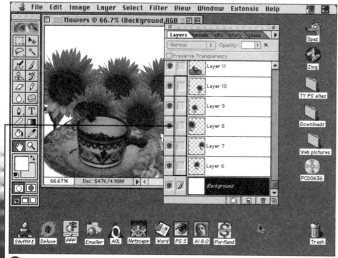

**1** To rearrange and resize the sunflowers in this image, open the Layers palette and click all the boxes where the paintbrush would be to link the five sunflower layers.

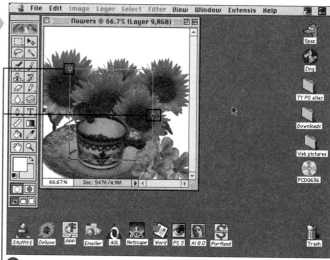

**2** Make your desired changes. Here, the flowers were resized pressing Command (Ctrl) T to activate the Transform bounding box and drag the handles.

■ Unlink layers as you wish to move the flowers around and to resize more if desired.

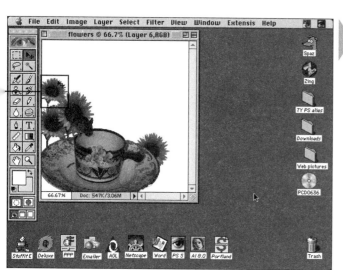

**3** Unlink one of the flowers, then use the Move tool to move the other two flowers.

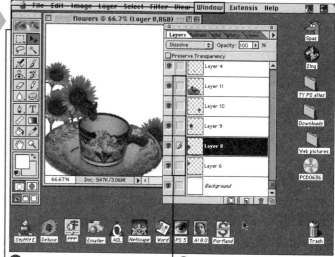

**4** Choose Window ➪ Show Layers to display the Layers palette again.

**5** Click all of the links to unlink the layers.

# Flattening Layers

**B**y now you are getting the hang of using layers. We are sure you have come across the Flatten Layers command by now and are wondering just what it means to you. Well, you can choose to *flatten* all of your layers to smush them all down to one layer. You would do this for a few reasons: One is to make the file smaller. Another reason is so you can save the file as something other than a Photoshop file.

When you flatten your layers, you essentially change all transparent areas to white and merge all layers, even the invisible ones. You will also get the message about flattening layers if you change modes. For example, if you are working in RGB and have layers and you change to Grayscale, a dialog box will come up asking if you want to Don't Flatten, Cancel, or Flatten. If you change to Indexed or Multichannel modes, you either have to flatten or you can't change to that mode.

You should take note that when flattening layers, what you see isn't always what you get. What we mean is that a file with layers is displayed a bit differently in Photoshop than the same file flattened. This is mostly noticeable with files to which you have done a lot of blending and added adjustments layers.

The best way to avoid losing your layers is to save your image both with layers and without. The quickest way to do this is to do a regular save (this will save the file as a Photoshop document) and then choose Save A Copy. When you choose Save A Copy, Photoshop automatically flattens the layers for you.

Layer Shortcuts:

▶ As with channels, you can copy, move, or duplicate layers within a document or between documents by dragging and dropping from one window to another.
▶ Delete a layer by dragging it to the Trashcan icon at the bottom of the Layers palette.
▶ Add a new layer by clicking the New icon at the bottom of the Layers palette.
▶ You can nudge the contents of a layer in one-pixel increments by pressing your keyboard's arrow keys in the direction you'd like the move. To nudge in 10-pixel increments, press Shift and an arrow key.

## TAKE NOTE

### DELETING CHANNELS ON A LAYERED FILE

When you have a layered file with channels on the layers, you must flatten the layers before you can remove a channel from that file.

## CROSS-REFERENCE

For more on Channels, see Chapter 12.

## FIND IT ONLINE

Here is a gallery of Digital Imaging: **http://www.west.net/~crash/gallery1.html**

❶ One way to flatten your layered image quickly is to choose File ➪ Save A Copy.

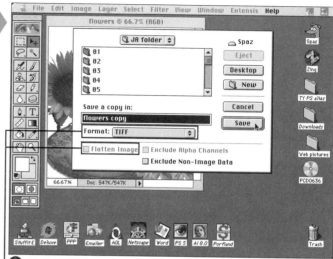

❷ Choose TIFF from the pop-up menu. You'll notice the Flatten Image box is checked and grayed out automatically because Photoshop has to flatten the layers to save as a TIFF.

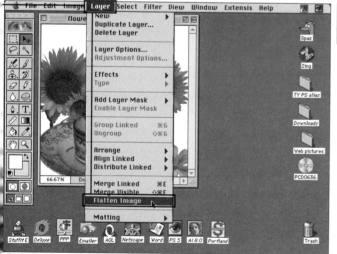

❸ Alternately, you can flatten layers by choosing Layer ➪ Flatten Image or by choosing Layer ➪ Flatten Image.

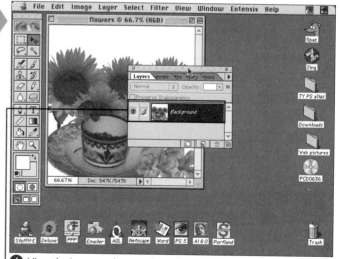

❹ View the Layers palette and you'll see that everything is now on one layer.

# Managing Layers

With all this layering going on, you'll find it's important to discover ways to keep track of your layers as well as to minimize the large files that can sometimes result from working in multilayered files.

In every file you work on, you'll see two file size numbers. In Windows, this number can be seen in the lower left corner of the screen. On the Mac, it's tucked in the lower left side of the image window. The higher number is the estimated size of the unflattened file. A flattened file is a file with one layer. It may have had many layers, but an option called Flatten Layers (found under the Layer menu) was applied to reduce the file size. An unflattened file will display all of the original layers. The lower number is the estimated size of the file if it were to be flattened. A file with many layers will be quite a bit physically larger than the equivalent file that is flattened.

Flattening a file's layers makes the file with layers physically smaller. This can be a good thing if storage size is an issue. It also means you can store the file in a different, more space-saving format. Saving the file as a GIF, for example, would mean a very small file size.

However, it should be noted that once a file's layers are flattened, there's no way back. If, at some future point, you want to go back and alter one of the layers, you won't be able to because they'll be gone.

If possible, save unflattened versions of files that might need touch-ups in the future. You can break the layers down and save each one as a separate file in any format you please. When you come back to work on the file, you can "reconstitute" your layers by copying and pasting each layer in a new Layered file, or you can just save the file in Photoshop format with all its layers.

Another space-saving idea is to use the Layers ⇨ Merge Visible command to blend specified layers into one. You do this by using the Eye icon to make the layers you *don't* want to merge invisible for the moment. After you've used the Merge Visible command, click the Eye icon to make the other layers visible again. Watch the file size in the lower left-hand corner drop as you do this. You can do this as many times as you like in the same file.

## TAKE NOTE

### STORING FILES

Not all Photoshop modes support layers. If you're going to change modes midstream, Photoshop will warn you before the layers are flattened. If you don't want to do it, you can Cancel from the prompt. Also, only the Photoshop format will preserve your layers intact for future use. Saving as a different file type will require you to flatten the layers before saving.

**CROSS-REFERENCE**

For more on saving formats, see Chapter 2.

**FIND IT ONLINE**

For some extremely cool fantasy art done with Photoshop, see **http://www.kansas.net/~duncan/portfolio.html**.

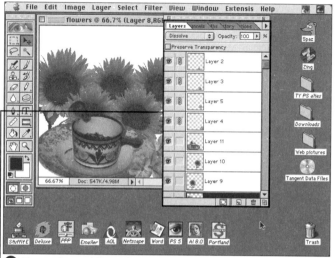

**①** Open a layered file and view the Layers palette (display it by choosing Window ⇨ Show Layers).

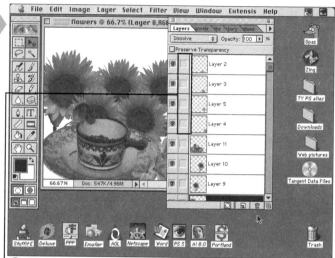

**②** Link layers with similar images by clicking the box beside the eye icon. When you click there, you activate the link icon, which means the layers are linked.

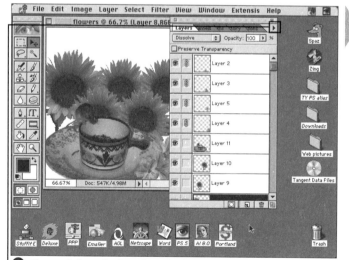

**③** Choose Palette Options from the Layers pop-up menu. You access the Palette Options by clicking on the arrow in the upper right corner of the Layers palette.

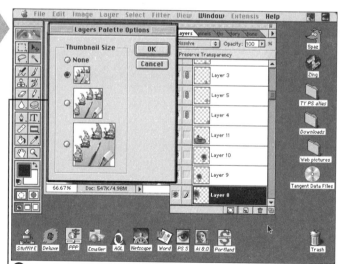

**④** Here is where you can turn off the thumbnails to speed up Photoshop.

# Personal Workbook

## Q&A

**1** How do you change the order of your layers in a Photoshop file?

_____

_____

_____

**2** How do you copy a layer?

_____

_____

_____

**3** How do you change the size of the thumbnail images that represent each layer?

_____

_____

_____

**4** How can you tell how large (or small) your file size will be once you flatten the document?

_____

_____

_____

**5** What is a *layer mask*?

_____

_____

_____

**6** Why is it good to apply layer masks before saving?

_____

_____

_____

**7** What does an adjustment layer affect?

_____

_____

_____

**8** When can you use Layer Effects?

_____

_____

_____

ANSWERS: PAGE 340

## EXTRA PRACTICE

**1** Open a file you've saved in PSD format with the layers intact to get a sense of the difference. You can even add a couple of layers just to see how file size is affected.

**2** Practice shuffling layers around the document you've created. Watch how the changes you make drastically alter the file. Think about the applications these changes could have in a file you care about.

**3** Add some new layers to the document. Open an image, copy and paste it into this document. Drop it in a couple of times and move them around independently of each other.

**4** Open a new file in Photoshop and paste in part of an image file so that the image is on a new layer by itself. Create a Layer mask and experiment with different ways of using this type of Mask.

## REAL-WORLD APPLICATIONS

✔ The very complicated file you've created is huge. It's as big as Toledo. You're done, yet you think you may have to make changes to it at some time in the future. You could save the file as a Photoshop document with all layers intact, and save a flattened TIFF version for your client so you can easily go back to the layered one to make any changes.

✔ An image you're manipulating seems almost perfectly exposed. You think, however, that if you could just lighten a certain part of the background it might be that much stronger. You could create a Layer Mask and apply a gray haze over the pesky background.

## Visual Quiz

Can we save this image just as it appears as an EPS file?

_____

_____

_____

_____

_____

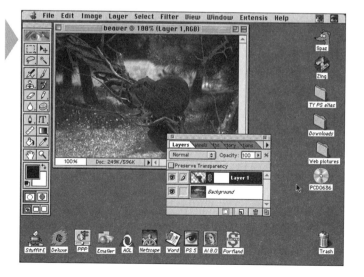

CHAPTER **12**

MASTER
THESE
SKILLS

▶ **Working with Channels**

▶ **Duplicating and Splitting Channels**

▶ **Fading with Channels**

▶ **Using Masks**

▶ **Using the History Palette**

▶ **Controlling the History Palette**

# Understanding Channels and History

The History function introduced in Photoshop 5.0 is totally amazing. Photoshop users have been screaming for multiple undo's since the program's earliest versions, but the History palette is more than multiple undo's. While we'll continue to wait for a keyboard-accessible, multileveled undo command, History gives us an easy way to access a Photoshop file's recent history. The last 20 changes to the image are reflected in a Palette as easy to use as the Layers Palette, and convey the same type of fluid feeling. History takes away a lot of the trepidation about trying a series of new things on a document in Photoshop.

Channels and Masks are two of the things that make the History palette such a joy. On first glance, Photoshop's Channels and Masks can look a little intimidating to the new user.

It might appear to bypass the whole issue of Channels and Masks and just go on with the Rubber Stamp and Smudge tools. If you're tempted to go this way, take a deep breath and jump in.

Channels on the other hand are the means by which you can save and load masks so that you can edit your images. Every document is composed of channels, with an RGB image composed of three color channels (one each for Red, Green, and Blue) and a composite channel. The CMYK channel is composed of four color channels. A document can have a total of 24 channels. Those extra channels, often called alpha or mask channels, are 8-bit grayscale images in which selections (masks) are stored. Each of these additional channels adds to the size of your overall file. Each channel is in perfect registration with every other channel, and all channels have the same size and resolution.

# Working with Channels

Channels and masks go together because Photoshop stores both things as Alpha Channels in the Channels palette. Each Photoshop document can have as many as 24 channels, including the necessary channels created automatically by Photoshop when you save a new document.

Each channel is an eight-bit grayscale image in which information is stored. Each one is stored in perfect register to the other channels in the palette. Here we find an analogy to things in the traditional printing world: Channels are the sheets of acetate the traditional graphic artist uses to create an image with color and depth. Like that traditional graphic arts acetate, each channel and mask is labeled with an appropriate name. The name is either a color, in the case of RBG and CMYK channels, or a name that you assign it in other cases.

In some ways, channels behave very like selections or layers. But they're different in some very key ways:

▶ A masked area is an area that you cannot paint on, edit, filter, or manipulate in any way. A masked area is protected by a mask, which, by default, is represented by the black area in the channel. Think about the way that a rubylith overlay is used in traditional graphic arts.

▶ A selected area is an area that you can paint on, edit, fill, filter, flip, or rotate or to which you can apply effects. A selection by default is represented by the white area in the channel.

▶ A visible channel is one whose eye icon is turned on.

▶ An editable channel is one whose Paintbrush icon is turned on.

▶ The Target channel is one you have selected for editing. You create a channel as a Target channel when you click on it and it becomes highlighted.

Sometimes it's a good idea to create a duplicate of a channel you will be changing as a backup, just in case your calculations slip. All won't be lost, as you can just delete the botched channel and continue working with the duplicate as though you'd never messed up at all.

It can also be a good idea to duplicate channels into a new file. This allows you to keep a database of channels in another file where their presence won't bog down your work file. These duplicated channels can be loaded into the desired document at your leisure.

## TAKE NOTE

### A SHORT CUT
Another way to create a duplicate channel within the same file is to simply drag the old channel into the Create New Channel icon at the bottom of the Channels palette.

## CROSS-REFERENCE
For more on printing, see Chapter 15.

## FIND IT ONLINE
To see channel offsetting, check out **http://axesgw. axes.co.jp/~hisashin/tips-tricks/mam03/mam0304. html**.

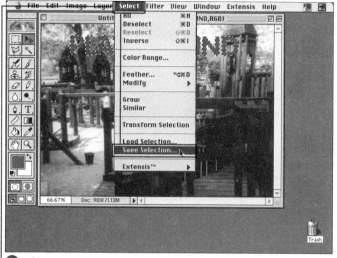

**①** After creating a selection, choose Selection ⇨ Save Selection. Deselect the selection by pressing Command (Ctrl)+D.

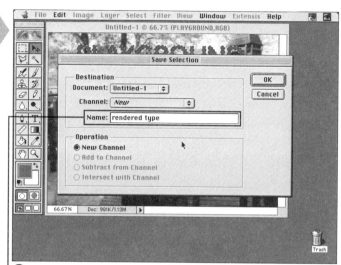

**②** Name your selection; we chose to name this Rendered Type.

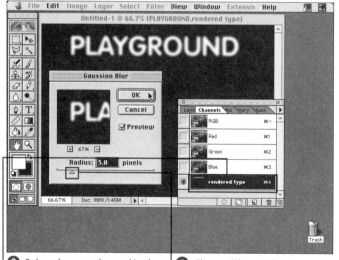

**③** Select the new channel in the Channels palette.

**④** Choose Filter ⇨ Blur ⇨ Gaussian Blur and apply a higher amount to the selection. Click on the RGB channel.

**⑤** Create a new layer in between the Background and text layer.

**⑥** Load the new selection by choosing Selection ⇨ Load Selection.

**⑦** With the Marquee tool, move the selection down and to the right.

**⑧** Fill the selection with Black (creating a soft shadow) by pressing Option (Alt)+Delete.

# Duplicating and Splitting Channels

Photoshop allows you to split channels into separate files simply by using the Split Channels command. Images that are composites of channels, such as RGB and CMYK, may be split into their components with this technique. You can do this if a file is too large to be manipulated as a whole. Split channels can be merged back into one document when you've finished processing each one.

Each channel will be placed into its own document and the original document will be closed, but not destroyed. The RGB documents produce three files, the CMYK documents produce four, and the multichannel documents produce as many files as there were channels in the original document.

If you delete a channel in the middle of the list, the higher-numbered channels will all move up while retaining the names you've given them. It is not necessary, by the way, to name a channel; it is only for your convenience when working with complex images with many masks.

When you have at least one mask channel, you can turn off all the Eye icons for the R,G, and B channels (or the C, M, Y, and K channels) by clicking the eye icon for the composite image.

You also may want to duplicate a channel to try various effects to it. To duplicate the channel, you can select the channel to highlight it, then choose Duplicate from the Channel pop-up menu. You can enter a name in the dialog box or leave it as "[your original channel] copy" after your original channel's name.

Several documents may be merged into one, provided that they are the same size, although the resolution of the files can be different. You access the Merge Channels command from the fly-out menu on the Channels palette. Channels are great for saving any selection, especially a large, time-consuming selection.

## TAKE NOTE

### ALTERING CHANNELS

Photoshop automatically creates the color Channels appropriate to your file based on the color method chosen. You will not be able to alter these channels in any real way beyond turning the Eye icon off and on to view your work in progress. Any additional Channels you create, also known as Mask or Alpha channels, are your storage pockets for graphic information in this specific file. You may reshuffle and delete at will.

**CROSS-REFERENCE**

For more on using filters, see Chapter 14.

**FIND IT ONLINE**

For more advanced channeling stuff, see http://axesgw.axes.co.jp/~hisashin/tips-tricks/mam03/mam0306.html.

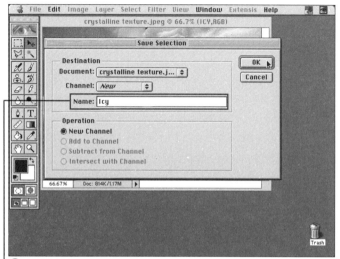

**1** *Save your selection by choosing Save Selection from the Selection menu. Give the selection a name. Deselect the selection by pressing Command (Ctrl)+D.*

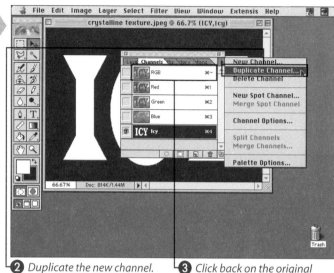

**2** *Duplicate the new channel.*

**3** *Click back on the original channel and apply a blur to it. Click the RGB Channel.*

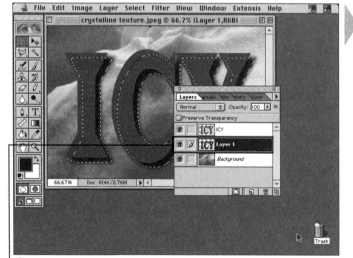

**4** *Load the original selection (channel) and move it down and to the right. Create a new layer between background and the text. Then press Option (Alt) delete to fill with black.*

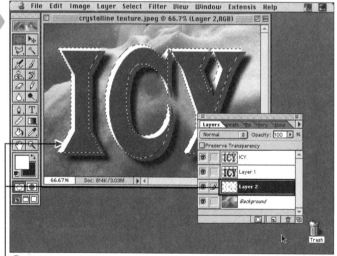

**5** *Load the duplicate selection (channel) and move it up and to the left. Click the background layer to activate it, then press Delete to fill with white.*

# Fading with Channels

Use the Channels Palette in much the same way you use the History and Layers Palettes—to watch how changes are affecting your image and to manage existing Channels and create new ones.

The Channels Palette shows you all of the Channels currently in your document. Changes to this palette are reflected right away.

You can click the eye icon to the left of the small representation of the image in the Channels palette to view a Channel individually. The color channels are represented in grayscale, like a printer's plates. You can see at a glance precisely how much visual "ink" is used of the color mentioned in order to create that particular color "plate."

You can Duplicate Channels from within the Channels Palette. If you do so, however, you'll note that when the top level Channel icon is selected, only the Channels that make up an essential part of the image are highlighted. Photoshop knows the difference between the Channels essential to making up its image and those that have been added.

Photoshop's Channels are only maintained if you save in certain formats: Photoshop, PICT, TIFF, Raw, and DCS2. If you must, or want to, save in any of the other formats available to Photoshop, your channel information will be lost.

To preserve your channel information individually you can break down an image's channel information for reconstitution at a later date or a different place. To do this, you have to start with a flattened image, or one that had no layers in the first place. Then choose the Split Channels command from the Channels Palette. The result will be several new files on your computer screen, with the one you split nowhere in sight. Each new file represents a single channel of the original file. They will have been named accordingly: horse_b for the Blue plate, horse_g for the green plate, and so on.

To bring these all back together again, the whole thing is done in reverse. With the files you want to merge open in Photoshop, you simply select Merge Channels from the Channels palette. In a dialog box, you then specify the number of channels as well as the color mode. You're left with a single file composed of the previously separated one.

## TAKE NOTE

### WORKING ON INDIVIDUAL CHANNELS

You can work on Channels individually. Simply highlight the Channel you wish to edit in the Channels Palette. If you're working on more than one, click the first desired with your mouse, then press Shift and click the next one, until done.

### CROSS-REFERENCE

For more on layer effects, see Chapter 11.

### FIND IT ONLINE

For a smoother fade effect, see **http://www.adobe. com/studio/tipstechniques/phsfade/main.html**.

**1** Click the Green channel in the Channels palette to activate it.

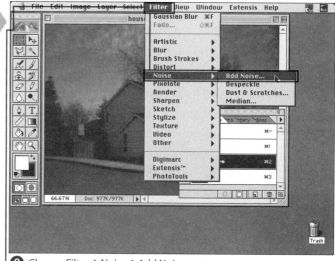

**2** Choose Filter ➪ Noise ➪ Add Noise.

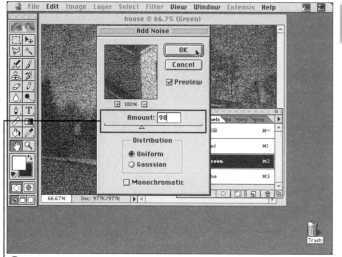

**3** Drag the Amount slider to a high amount to create a grainy look to the Green channel.

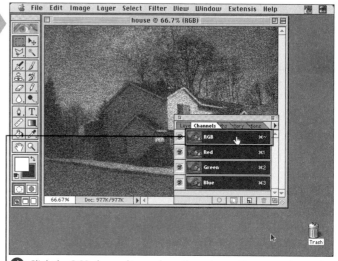

**4** Click the RGB channel to see how the noise on the green channel affected the whole image.

# Using Masks

Photoshop's Masks and Quick Masks act like the frisket a traditional artist uses to paint on a selected part of an image while protecting the rest. If you were a water colorist, you'd use a liquid frisket that you paint over the stuff you're protecting and remove after completion, or an acetate frisket that you cut into shape and stick over the stuff you want untouched.

Photoshop's masks work in just this same way—without, of course, the need to get all that sticky frisket on your hands! Photoshop lets you create three distinct types of Mask:

▶ The Quick Mask is a temporary mask that can be edited exclusive of the Channels palette. The main advantage to using a Quick Mask is that the Quick Mask is, itself, not a Selection. That leaves you free to use almost all of Photoshop's tools on your Quick Mask including the Selection tools.
▶ The Layer Mask enables you to create a Mask for a single layer.
▶ Alpha Channel Masks enable you to load an existing Selection and use it as a Mask.

As in other areas of Photoshop, one type of Mask isn't inherently better than the others, just different. As such, they have different purposes and different things they're good at.

An overview of Photoshop's Masks:

▶ Store masks in channels to use whenever needed.

▶ You can do anything to an eight-bit mask that you can do to an RGB or CMYK image: edit masks with any of the painting and editing tools; paint using black, white, plus 254 shades of gray; apply fills and gradient blends; and feather selections.
▶ Use masks to select specific parts of an image, which you can then edit using all the painting and editing tools as well as filters and other special effects.
▶ Use the quick mask mode to create a mask or edit a selection—without necessarily saving it in a mask channel.
▶ Change Mask options with the Mask Options dialog box. Double-click the Quick Mask icon to open this.

### TAKE NOTE

▶ **CHANNEL COLORS**
Photoshop automatically creates the color Channels appropriate to your file, based on the color method chosen. You will not be able to alter these channels in any real way beyond turning the Eye icon off and on to view your work in progress. Any additional Channels you create, also known as Mask or Alpha channels, are your storage pockets for graphic information in this specific file. You may reshuffle and delete at will.

**CROSS-REFERENCE**
For more on layer masks, see Chapter 11.

**FIND IT ONLINE**
To create a backlight, see **http://axesgw.axes.co.jp/ ~hisashin/tips-tricks/mam04/mam0410.html**.

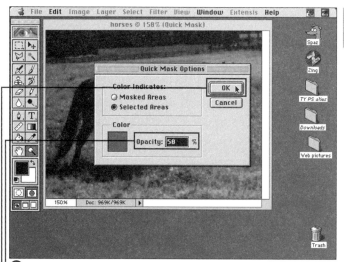

**1** Double-click the Quick Mask icon to activate the Quick Mask dialog box. We like to set the Opacity to 50% so we can still see the image underneath. You can also set the color by clicking the Color box to activate the color picker if you wish.

**2** Click OK.

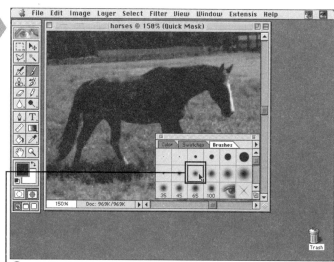

**3** Choose a brush size and style.

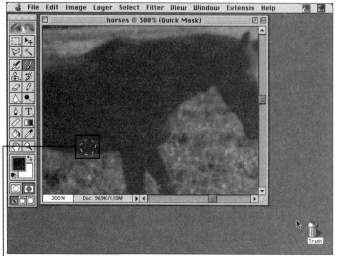

**4** Start painting in the image. If you go outside of the object you want to select, then press the X key and erase out the errors. Remember to press the X key again to start painting in.

**5** Once you are done painting in, click the Edit in Standard Mode button to see your selection.

# Using the History Palette

One definition of the word *history* is *A chronological record of events* [*American Heritage*]. That definition also sums up Photoshop's new History command quite well. Unlike a multiple undo, which Photoshop lacks and some other programs have, the History palette gives you a visual overview of at least the last 20 things you've done to alter your image. Again, unlike undo, you don't have to remember what you did six steps ago. You just punch up the History palette and it's all there for you, including the tools you used and the action you took.

The default is set to 20 for your system resources. If your machine is loaded with RAM and you figure you can allocate a bit more space to history, you can increase the number of steps. Even if you'd just like to see farther back, you can increase the number of steps back you're able to see and access by upping the default History Options, found in the pop-up menu of the History palette.

This History palette has been well located in Photoshop 5: it's found on the same Palette as Layers, Channels, Paths, and Actions, so a single keystroke will return the History palette to the screen if you're working with any of these others.

Unfortunately, neither your file's History nor any Snapshots you might take are remembered by Photoshop once you've closed the program. This is too bad: a semi-permanent visual history of a file would be a very good thing in some cases. This is something I, for one, would love to see in future versions of Photoshop.

Not everything you do to a file gets registered in your History palette, only things that directly affect the image. If you change your Preferences, color settings, or apply an Action, it will not be reflected in the History palette. This is because these are things that affect the overall program, not your work file.

## TAKE NOTE

### DON'T FORGET UNDO

The easiest way to change the very last thing you did is still the Undo command. You access Undo from the Edit menu or by selecting Command+Z or Ctrl+Z. Pressing Command or Ctrl+Z brings the undone thing back again.

**CROSS-REFERENCE**
For more on Paths, see Chapter 10.

**FIND IT ONLINE**
For better embossing techniques, see **http://axesgw.axes.co.jp/ ~hisashin/tips-tricks/mam03/mam0303.html**.

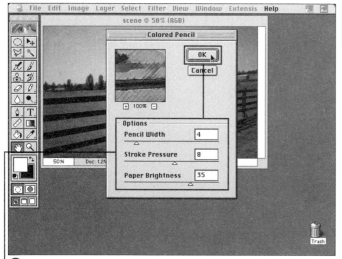

**1** *Choose Filter ➪ Artistic ➪ Colored Pencil. Adjust the sliders to your preferences, then click OK.*

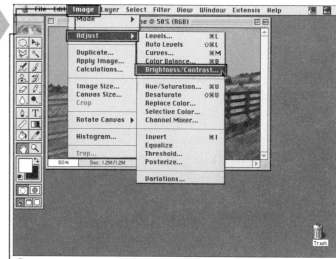

**2** *Choose Image ➪ Adjust ➪ Brightness/Contrast.*

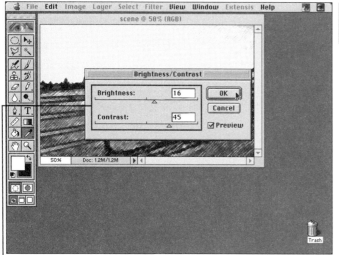

**3** *We increased the Brightness and Contrast to make this image snappier.*

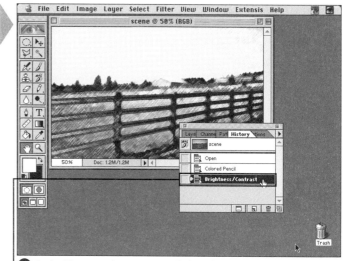

**4** *In the History palette you can click on the Colored Pencil to turn off the Brightness/Contrast and see if you like the change. If you don't like the change, you can drag the activity into the little trashcan icon at the bottom of the History Palette.*

# Controlling the History Palette

The History Palette is a new amazing addition to Photoshop. The History Palette is the answer to the much needed question: Can we have more undo's? It isn't necessarily an undo palette. The History Palette records each function you do in Photoshop as a separate step. You can remove steps, and do it between steps if you wish. You can also click a step to turn off the step below.

Let's say you opened an image and made a selection, applied a blur, and used Levels to correct the lights and darks. The History palette will list each of those changes from your selection to the blur filter and Levels. The History palette does not remember some aspects of Photoshop, such as Palette, preference, color changes, and anything recorded by the Actions palette.

The History palette stores 20 steps or states. You can change the default to more, but it will affect Photoshop's performance unless you set a lot of RAM to Photoshop. If you leave the default at 20 and keep creating more operations, the oldest ones get removed to make space for the newer ones. If you really want to keep a certain step or state, you can make a snapshot of it.

To make a snapshot of a state, after you create the state, click the paper icon at the bottom of the History palette. You can give it a name by double-clicking the snapshot at the top half of the History palette. The History palette consists of two separate halves. The top is for snapshots and the bottom is for states. The states are named by whichever command was used. If you click a state, the ones beneath the state are turned off temporarily so you can view how just that particular state looked.

If you click a state in the middle and change that state, all of the later states are deleted, so keep that in mind. You can remove a state by dragging it to the trashcan icon at the bottom of the History palette.

The areas of the History palettes are as follows:

▶ The top area is the Snapshot area. This is where the History brush references to paint from. You click the snapshot you want to use, then paint back the areas you want.
▶ The History State area shows each task you have done in Photoshop.
▶ The History State slider shows you the active or selected state.
▶ The first button at the bottom makes a new document from the selected state button.
▶ The next button (which looks like a piece of paper) makes a new snapshot from the current state of the image.
▶ The last button (the trashcan) lets you remove a state or snapshot by dragging it to that icon.

### TAKE NOTE

#### REMOVING A STATE

Keep in mind if you click a state, the lower states are dimmed and not visible. If you remove a state in the middle, the lower states are not removed.

### CROSS-REFERENCE

For more on third-party filters, see Chapter 14.

### FIND IT ONLINE

To make a quick woodgrain texture, see
http://axesgw.axes.co.jp/~hisashin/tips-tricks/mam04/mam0406.html.

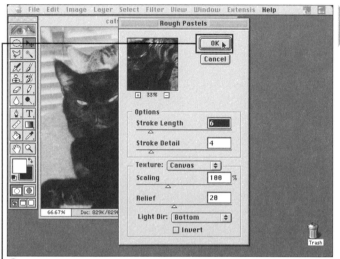

**1** *Apply an effect to your image. We chose to apply Rough Pastels from the Artistic filters to this image.*

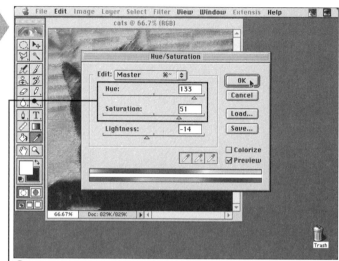

**2** *Adjust the Hue/Saturation of your image. Make a snapshot of this stage.*

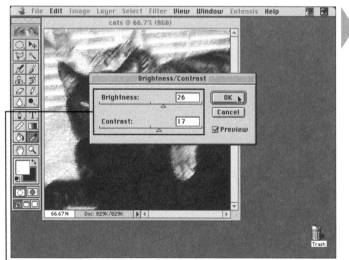

**3** *Adjust the Brightness/Contrast of your image. Make a snapshot of this stage.*

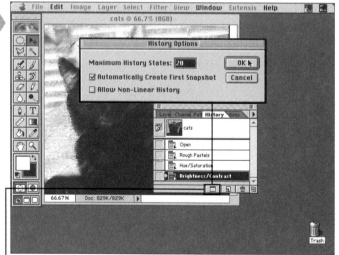

**4** *Check out the History palette to see each snapshot of the image and each stage. Choose History Options from the History palette pop-up menu to check out what you can change.*

# Personal Workbook

## Q&A

**1** How many channels can a single document have?

_____

_____

_____

**2** Why would you split a channel?

_____

_____

_____

_____

**3** When would you use a mask?

_____

_____

_____

**4** How is a mask like a channel?

_____

_____

_____

**5** What is the History command?

_____

_____

_____

_____

**6** How many undo's can you undo?

_____

_____

_____

_____

**7** What is a snapshot?

_____

_____

_____

_____

**8** Can you move stages around in the History palette?

_____

_____

ANSWERS: PAGE 340

## EXTRA PRACTICE

**1** In any file you've been working with for a while, open the History palette and click backward on various points in the file's recent history. Watch your file.

**2** Use the Snapshot command from the pop-up menu in the History palette. Make a mental note to remind yourself to make occasional Snapshots of images in progress, to help you get quickly back to crucial points in a document's history.

**3** With an image open in Photoshop, open the Channels palette. Create a New Channel from the Channels palette's pop-up menu and play with it a bit.

## REAL-WORLD APPLICATIONS

✔ You've been working on a file for hours. Just as you add the third filter and manipulate the blue Channel, you realize that the Selection you made 16 steps ago wasn't quite what it should have been. You use the History palette to backtrack to the point of Selection, then go on without losing all of your work.

✔ You use a Quick Mask to make a very complicated Selection. It took so long that you never, ever want to make this Selection again, yet you know it's one you're going to have to come back to in the future. You turn the Quick Mask into an Alpha Channel. You now have a permanent way of accessing the very same Selection.

## Visual Quiz

How was the painterly effect added to only parts of this image?

_____

_____

_____

_____

_____

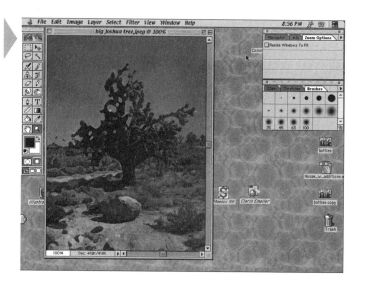

CHAPTER **13**

MASTER
THESE
SKILLS

▶ **Using Actions**
▶ **Creating an Action**
▶ **Automating Tedious Tasks**

# Automating Photoshop

Now that you are cruising through Photoshop, you realize there are many daily routine tasks you do over and over again. Well, Photoshop has an answer to that: *Actions*. Actions are the high-octane macros of the Photoshop environment. Simply put, Actions allow you to record a series of editing steps in an Action list that you can later apply to a selection, file, or multiple files by using the Automate command. The Actions palette offers a set of Default Actions as well as the opportunity to create your own actions.

Photoshop 5.0 is the second version of the program to contain the Actions command. If you used Photoshop 4.0, you might have played with Actions, might even have found some use for the command, but that earlier version had some fairly significant limitations. Though the Actions command is used in precisely the same way as it was in 4.0, it's a much more powerful tool with a wider range of capabilities. Because of this, you can use any of the Actions you might have used in Photoshop 4.0 in 5.0. However, the addition of some extremely cool features in Photoshop 5 means that Actions aren't backward compatible. In other words you can't develop an Action in Photoshop 5.0 and then play it in 4.0.

Photoshop 5.0 ships with a set of default Actions. Most of them are geared to creating 3D effects suitable for Web graphics use. Both Actions and Automation add a wider range to your Photoshop capabilities.

New to 5.0 is the ability to do some pretty serious large-scale graphics automation. The Batch Processing command gives the ability to instruct Photoshop to perform Actions on a whole bunch of files while you go for a walk, grab a bite to eat or sneak in a nap. While Photoshop 4.0 lets you process a Batch directly from the Actions menu, Automate now has its own menu under the File menu. This move is more than a physical one: You can now not only process Actions by the batch, but Photoshop can also be told to process batches of mode changes, or process multiple images from a digital camera or a scanner that's been fitted with a document feeder.

# Using Actions

ctions are found in the same palette that lets you access Layers, Channels, Paths, and History. The Actions palette is reminiscent of a tape recorder, with these familiar commands: stop, start, play, and record. The pop-up menu, accessible from the right-arrow on the Actions palette, provides access to more commands than the quick command icons located at the palette's bottom. These icons are Stop playing/recording, Begin recording, Play current selection, Begin new set, and Delete selection.

The pop-up menu for the Actions palette gives you a larger set of choices.

New Action lets you create a new action, and you'll be prompted to enter a name for that action and then start recording. The New Set creates a new heading for the next set of actions you want to record; it keeps them organized in a set so you can access that set easily. Duplicate makes a copy of an Action. Delete removes an Action, and Play plays an Action.

Rather than use the record button at the bottom of the Actions palette, choose Start Recording from the pop-up. Use Record Again to add to an existing Action. You can insert a Menu Item, Stop, or Path by choosing the appropriate one from the pop-up menu. The Playback Options let you determine how you want your Action played. You can accelerate the action, have it go step by step, or make it pause for so many seconds in between steps. The Action Options

let you rename the action, change the location to another set, assign a Function key with or without using the Shift or Command (Ctrl), and assign a color to the Action.

The next set of options is adjustment options. Clear Actions deletes or removes the selected Actions. You can Reset Actions back to the Default set. You can Load any saved Action or Save any Action. You can also Replace an Action with another Action. The last option is Button Mode, which displays the Actions as a rectangular button with only the name showing. While Button Mode is the easiest to use, you can't stop or alter the action while in Button Mode.

Using and creating Actions is as simple as using a tape recorder. Try opening an image file and playing the Wood Frame action from the Default Actions set. It's fun to watch Photoshop do all the work for you. Increase your productivity by leaps and bounds by using Actions to do the tedious, repetitive work for you.

## TAKE NOTE

### ▶ LIMITATIONS OF ACTIONS

There are some Action limitations. For example if you use Brush, Pencil, Airbrush, or toning tools on your image, accessing the tool will be recorded, but not actually drawn. To fix this, you may want to insert a stop, so you can paint as you'd like, then start recording again.

## CROSS-REFERENCE

Actions work great with filter effects; for more on filter effects, see Chapter 14.

## FIND IT ONLINE

For some freebie actions, check out **http://www. ultimate-photoshop.com/actions/archive.html.**

■ Create a wood frame around your art.

**①** If the Actions palette isn't visible, choose Window ⮕ Show Actions. Click the triangle to open the set of Default Actions in the Actions palette.

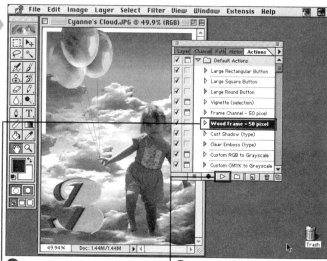

**②** Click the wood frame once to highlight this action.

**③** Click the Play button to start the Action.

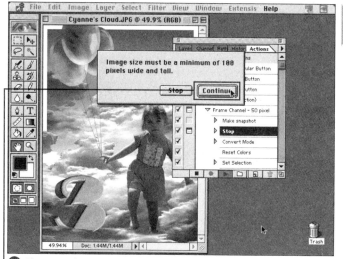

**④** If you get the warning dialog box, click Continue. The Action will add the space needed to complete this command.

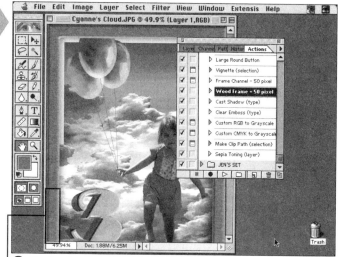

**⑤** The final result is amazing, with no work at all to create this masterpiece.

# Creating an Action

It's pretty easy to create your own Actions. Simply perform the Action once with the Record button depressed. While you work, you'll see the Actions palette remembering each step you took. When you're done, stop recording and the Action is complete. It doesn't get much simpler than that.

You can't record everything Photoshop does, simply because some things contain variables that require human intervention. Photoshop functions that require interaction with a Dialog Box, for instance, cannot be recorded because you need to make the decision that spurs the dialog. In these cases, it is still possible to record the desired command and then insert a Modal Command after the Action has been recorded. Modal controls are toggled on the Actions palette, directly to the left of the text describing the Action. When the Modal control icon is visible, it is on; if it's not visible, it's off.

If Modal control is on when an Action is played, it pauses over the dialog boxes until you input your keystroke. For other types of nonrecordable Actions, you can also use the Insert Menu Item command to insert keystrokes and menu items.

If there is a restriction to the number of commands that can be contained by a single Action,

we haven't found it. It is possible to create very complex and complicated Actions using the Actions command.

## TAKE NOTE

▶ **SETTING ACTION SPEED**

Sometimes you want an Action to occur quickly. Other times, however, you want to slow things down so you can see each part of the Action as it plays. This is especially useful in debugging a complicated custom Action that isn't playing quite right. To change the speed at which Actions are played, choose Playback Options from the fly-out menu on the Actions palette, then choose the performance speed from the three options available.

▶ **EDITING YOUR ACTIONS**

Once you've recorded an Action, remember that it's not written in stone. You can go back and change one thing or several. You can change the order of the steps within an Action just by dragging them to a new position as you would in any other palette, and add new commands to existing Actions. You can also Duplicate commands and even entire Actions, add and delete Modal commands to accommodate dialog, and reset Actions back to their default if you've changed them a lot and are unhappy with the changes.

**CROSS-REFERENCE**

For more on using Photoshop for Web page creation, see Chapter 16.

**FIND IT ONLINE**

For downloadable actions, see this Web site: **http://www.elated.com/toolbox/actionkits/actionkit1.zip.**

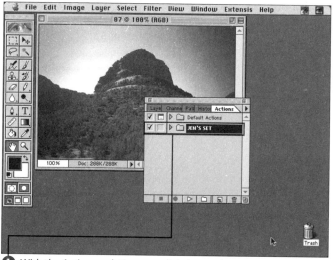

**1** With the Actions palette open, click the set that you want to add your new Action to. This activates that set.

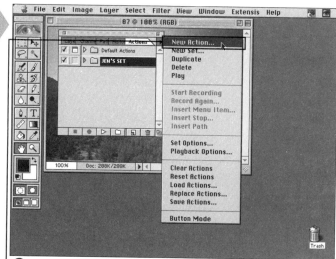

**2** Choose New Action from the pop-up menu.

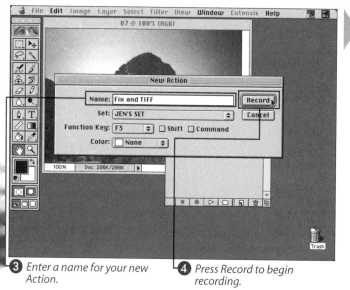

**3** Enter a name for your new Action.

**4** Press Record to begin recording.

**5** Edit and save your image as you normally would. When you are done, press the Stop button.

■ Note that the steps taken are shown in the palette.

# Automating Tedious Tasks

The Automate command is new in Photoshop 5.0 and opens the door for a lot of wonderful possibilities. At present, all Batches are set up through the Actions command, and the duo work rather well together. Batching allows you to set an Action to be performed on a folder with multiple files. That way, you can set it up, go take a break, and all will be done when you come back. This is great if you have to save a bunch of files in a certain way that can be quite tedious. You record the desired Action in Photoshop, then specify a Batch with the Automate command.

The Automate command can do a few other things as well. Through a dialog box accessed from the Automate command, Conditional Mode Change switches a document's color mode to the mode you specify.

We like Contact Sheet a lot. Choosing it from the Automate command produces thumbnail previews of all of the images in a designated folder. You end up with a printable, sendable Photoshop file of images, all on one sheet. The images you put on a Contact Sheet must be closed before this one will work.

Fit Image resamples the image to a size that fits within parameters you set. This is one you'd likely use most often with the Actions command; embedding Fit Image within an Action when resizing a Selection is difficult or impossible.

Only Adobe could make the Multi-page PDF to PSD command because it involves a couple of their very own formats. This could be a handy one, so

remember where it is; you're not likely to use it every day. The command lets you open a Portable Document Format (PDF) file and open it in the Photoshop (PSD) format. PDF files are often downloadable from Web pages. You need a special piece of software called Adobe Acrobat Reader, which is available free from Adobe, to read these files.

Processing a Batch of files with Photoshop's automate command is easiest if you place all of the files you're going to process into a single folder on your hard drive. If the Action you've chosen is one that will make permanent changes to a file, it can also be wise to have a destination folder ready to take the new files. That way, if something goes wrong, you can toss the new ones and begin again. After the Batch has been successfully processed, it's an easy matter to go into your hard drive and discard the originals if desired.

**CROSS-REFERENCE**

For more on third-party filters, see Chapter 14.

**FIND IT ONLINE**

Go to Adobe's Web site at **http://www.adobe.com** to download Adobe Acrobat Reader.

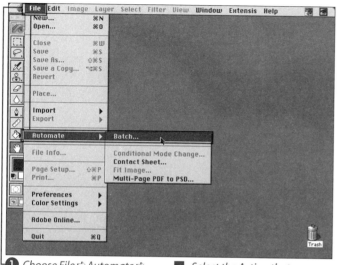

**❶** *Choose File ⇨ Automate ⇨ Batch to start the Automate process.*

■ *Select the Action that you want to automate from the appropriate set.*

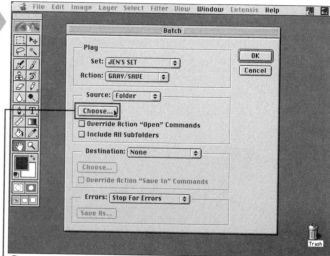

**❷** *Click the Choose button to select the folder to which you want to apply the Automate process.*

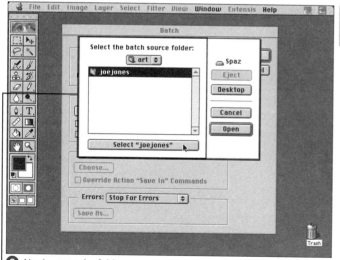

**❸** *Navigate to the folder you want to use and press Select "folder name".*

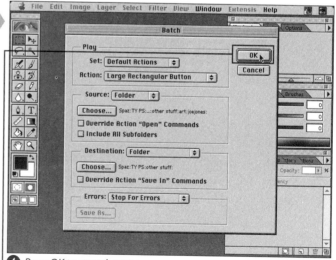

**❹** *Press OK to start the process.*

# Personal Workbook

## Q&A

**1** Where do you access the Actions palette?

_____

_____

_____

_____

**2** What is a *set*?

_____

_____

_____

_____

**3** Can you make your own actions?

_____

_____

_____

_____

**4** What is a *modal control*?

_____

_____

_____

**5** Can you change the pace at which actions are played?

_____

_____

_____

**6** Where do you access automation in Photoshop?

_____

_____

_____

**7** Can you do anything with automation besides process batches of actions?

_____

_____

_____

ANSWERS: PAGE 354

## EXTRA PRACTICE

**①** Open the actions that ship in Adobe Photoshop's goodies folder. Run through a few of them, as many as you have time for.

**②** Lay some type and run through the actions that say "type" behind the name. Open an image file and apply some image-appropriate actions to images. In other words, play with the actions in a non-pressure way when you're not on deadline. That way, when deadline comes, you'll be ready.

**③** Think about the repetitive things you do or are likely to do in Photoshop. Create your own action to do one of these tasks, even if it's a fairly simple one.

## REAL-WORLD APPLICATIONS

✔ You're redesigning your Web page and want to create some distinctive buttons to help people navigate your site. You use the Round button action in the default actions and you're on your way.

✔ One of your client's logos has a complicated facet and shadow that must be duplicated every time you recreate the logo, which is often, as they are forever making changes and fine-tuning for various different uses. You're tired of redoing the silly thing every time they ask. You create an action that does it for you. But you still bill the same. Life is good.

## Visual Quiz

All of these action sets ship with Adobe Photoshop 5.0. Can you find the extra ones on your hard drive?

_____

_____

_____

_____

_____

_____

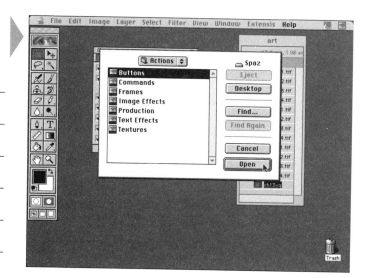

CHAPTER **14**

**MASTER THESE SKILLS**

▶ **Using Blur and Sharpen Filters**

▶ **Creating with Artistic Filters**

▶ **Altering Your Image with Distort Filters**

▶ **Applying Noise to Your Image**

▶ **Creating Clouds with the Render Filter**

▶ **Adding Pizzazz with Stylize Filters**

▶ **Making Your Life Easier with Extensis PhotoTools**

# Working with Filters

Filters are probably the coolest of all of Photoshop's features. Where else can you choose an effect and have it instantly applied? Filters make life easier when applying any effect. You can apply your basic effects like Sharpen and Blur, or more sophisticated artistic effects. The filters you have to choose from are Artistic, Blur, Brush Strokes, Distort, Noise, Pixelate, Render, Sharpen, Sketch, Stylize, Texture, Video, Other, and Digimarc. If you have loaded any third-party filters, they would show up at the bottom half of the Filter menu. Some third-party filters actually create a new pull-down menu of their own.

Filters make fixing images and creating effects easy. Many Photoshop filters are used to fix images. The Blur and Sharpen filters seem to repeat the Blur and Sharpen tools. The Blur and Sharpen tools enable you to apply the blur and/or sharpen effect like a brush. The Blur and Sharpen filters will apply the effect to the whole image, or to a certain selection. You can use the Add Noise filter to add some slight texture to your image or selection. The Noise filter pull-down menu also has the Dust and Scratches filter, which can fix any images that have been scratched or scanned in with a dirty scanner glass.

Photoshop provides us with so many choices under the Filter menu. Each section is grouped by effects. If these filters aren't quite enough for you, there are many third-party developers that have given even more possibilities for Photoshop. Extensis has a great line of third-party filters from Mask Pro 2.0, Intellihance Pro 4.0, PhotoFrame 1.0 to PhotoTools 3.0. MetaCreations has just upgraded KPT (Kai's Power Tools) from 3.0 to 5.0. There are a ton of new things to see and do with KPT now. Alien Skin Software offers Eye Candy 3.01, which has some pretty cool special effects.

Photoshop filters can fix or enhance images. You can also use the selection tools to apply effects to certain parts of your image. The Layer palette can also be quite useful in applying effects to certain areas. One more area not to forget is that you can apply filters directly to existing channels or new channels; this can make for some really interesting effects as well. You can then load a channel and apply a combined effect to your image.

# Using Blur and Sharpen Filters

There are so many effects you can create with the Filter menu. The two main filters that you will use time and time again are the Blur and Sharpen filters. Typically, as you use the Blur filter more often, you'll come to depend on using Gaussian Blur to add a blur to your image. Gaussian blur is much more subtle than the other blur effects, and you control how much of a blur you are creating. The more you use Sharpen, you'll find that Unsharp Mask is the one you need. Unsharp Mask offers you the opportunity to enter the values that you want, rather than do a predetermined amount automatically. The Motion and Radial Blurs are great for creating special effects.

**Blur.** The Blur filter applies a preset blur amount to your image or selection.

**Blur More.** This filter applies an even greater preset blur amount to your image or selection.

**Gaussian Blur.** The Gaussian Blur filter brings up a dialog box where you can choose the Radius of the blur. The higher the radius, the greater the blur.

**Motion Blur.** This blur filter lets you choose an angle as well as a distance (in pixels) for your blur. The blur will drag the pixels at the angle and distance that you enter.

**Radial Blur.** The Radial Blur dialog box has a few more options than the others. You choose the Amount of your blur (in pixels), the Blur Method (Spin or Zoom), and the Quality of the blur (Draft, Good, or Best). In the Blur Center box, you can click or click and drag a new center point. The Spin Method will simulate a water drop ringing outwards. The Zoom method simulates a perspective movement.

**Smart Blur.** This blur option will accurately apply a blur. You set the Radius, Threshold, Quality, and Mode of the blur and have total control on your outcome.

**Sharpen.** The Sharpen filter, similar to the Blur filter, will apply a predetermined amount to your image or selection.

**Sharpen Edges.** This filter will locate the pixels with the greatest difference in color and sharpen them. This tends to be the edge of an object in an image.

**Sharpen More.** Sharpen More will apply an even greater Sharpen amount that is preset to your image or selection.

**Unsharp Mask.** This is the Sharpen filter most professionals use. This is the chosen one because you have the control over the Amount, Radius, and Threshold.

---

### TAKE NOTE

#### USE MOTION BLUR TO ADD MOVEMENT

The Motion Blur filter is a great way to add movement to an object. By selecting your object, then selecting inverse, you can apply a Motion Blur to the background to make it look like your object is moving.

---

### CROSS-REFERENCE

For more on making selections, see Chapter 3.

### FIND IT ONLINE

Go to **http://www.aquariumsoftware.com.au/ photoshop/glass.htm** to follow a step-by-step example on how to make a glass effect.

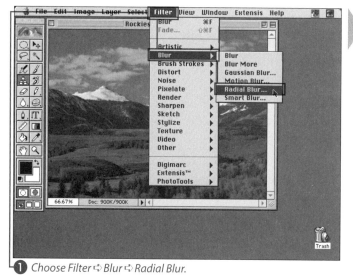

① *Choose Filter ➪ Blur ➪ Radial Blur.*

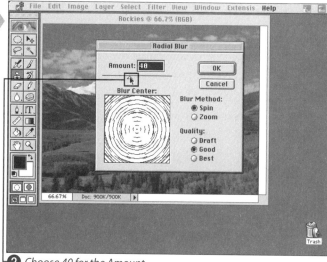

② *Choose 40 for the Amount.*

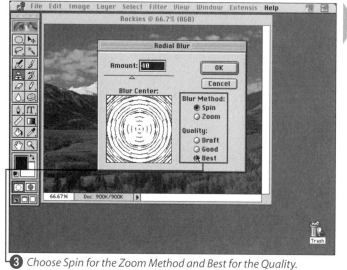

③ *Choose Spin for the Zoom Method and Best for the Quality.*

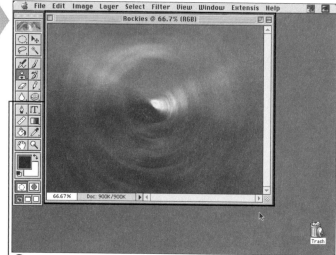

④ *After you press OK, see the results. If you want to apply the filter again at the same settings, press Command (Ctrl)+F.*

# Creating with Artistic Filters

The Artistic filters mimic effects that can be created by using traditional drawing/painting means. The success of the Artistic filters lies in the quality of the image with which you are starting. These filters can be quite stunning in combination with a photo because of the artsy look to the filter. You can pull out an object or a background to apply the filters to rather than the whole image.

**Colored Pencil.** The selected parts or whole image is rendered using a crosshatch colored pencil effect. The edges are emphasized, while the more solid areas retain their color.

**Dry Brush.** This filter paints using a brush effect on the edge (edges are defined by different colored pixels that are beside each other). The colors are reduced to combine colors to a similar color.

**Film Grain.** This filter can be used to remove banding between colors. This happens mostly when importing an Illustrator (vector) image that has used a gradient and creates lines between the colors. The Film Grain filter creates a pattern in the shadow and midtone areas.

**Fresco.** This filter applies paint to the image in quick, hurried brush dabs.

**Neon Glow.** The Neon Glow filter creates a glow to the edges of your objects. The color of the glow is based on the chosen color in the Glow box (found in the Neon Glow dialog box).

**Paint Daubs.** Paint Daubs lets you choose from a 1-pixel to a 50-pixel brush and from six different brush styles.

**Palette Knife.** This filter shows a canvas-like texture with a painted overlay.

**Plastic Wrap.** This filter simulates plastic stretched over your image or selection.

**Poster Edges.** The Poster Edges filter changes the number of colors to the number you enter in the Posterization field. Then you enter the thickness and intensity of the edge that will outline the main colors.

**Rough Pastels.** This cool filter makes your selection or image look like it was drawn with pastels on a textured canvas.

**Smudge Stick.** The Smudge Stick filter creates a blurred or smudged short stroked lines in the darker areas. The light areas fade out.

**Sponge.** This filter makes your image very contrasted and textured.

**Underpainting.** This great filter will make your image textured, then repaint the image again over the texture.

**Watercolor.** This filter simulates actual watercolor. The image or selection will be flooded with water and color and softened with a brush.

**CROSS-REFERENCE**

For more on advanced selecting, see Chapter 4.

**FIND IT ONLINE**

This Web site at **http://www.adscape.com/eyedesign/ photoshop/four/filters/artistic.html** shows you an example of each of the artistic filters found in Photoshop.

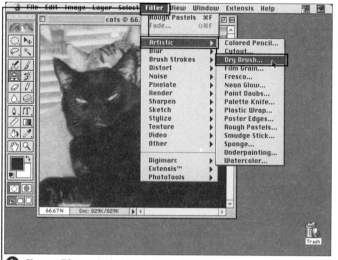

① Choose Filter ➪ Artistic ➪ Dry Brush.

② Click OK.

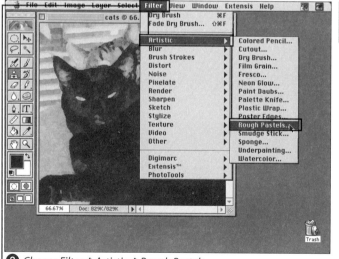

③ Choose Filter ➪ Artistic ➪ Rough Pastels

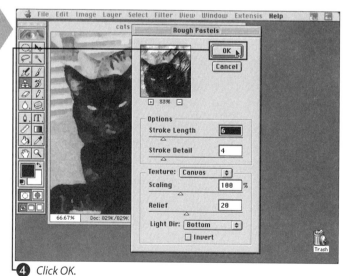

④ Click OK.

# Altering Your Image with Distort Filters

The Distort filters create a variety of effects to any selection or whole image. This is one of the filter groups that tend to use up a lot of memory. The Distort group of filters twists, pinches, ripples, bends, zigs, zags, and more to your image.

**Diffuse Glow.** Diffuse Glow makes your image look like you are seeing it through a soft, fuzzy, white glowing light.

**Displace.** This filter uses a map that you create and bends the image to that map's shape in 3D. If you create a worm shape as your map, then your image will wrap around that shape.

**Glass.** The Glass filter looks as if you are viewing your image through a glass. Your glass choices are Blocks, Canvas, Frosted, and Tiny Lens, or you can load a texture.

**Ocean Ripple.** The Ocean Ripple filter makes your image look like water with wind blowing over it.

**Pinch.** This filter is actually two filters in one. If you drag to the positive numbers, your image appears to have been pinched or pulled inward. If you drag to the negative side, your image will bulge outward.

**Polar Coordinates.** The Polar Coordinates will change your image from Polar to Rectangular points and from Rectangular to Polar points.

**Ripple.** This filter is very similar to the Ocean Ripple filter without the water. The effect is still like the moving pattern that the wind makes on a wet surface.

**Shear.** This filter gives the illusion of your image bending back in 3D. You base the distortion on a curve setting that you define in the Shear dialog box.

**Spherize.** Spherize will wrap your image around a circular shape. You specify the amount that the circle bulges out. If you drag to the negative numbers, you create a Pinch. Spherize is the opposite of Pinch.

**Twirl.** Twirl will rotate your image or selection around a center point. The inner area will be tighter and have more movement than the outer areas.

**Wave.** The Wave filter is similar to the Ripple filter. With the Wave filter, you can do even more things to distort your image. You can adjust the type of wave, length of wave, height of wave, and even choose a randomize effect.

**ZigZag.** ZigZag creates a variety of distortions. If you choose Pond Ripple, your image will ripple from the top to the bottom. The From Center option will look like you dropped a rock in the center of your image and it is rippling out. The Around Center option will create ripples and twirl them around a central point.

## TAKE NOTE

### FIXING A SPHERIZED IMAGE

The Pinch filter can't undo the damage of the Spherize filter. If you apply a 100% Spherize, then apply a 100% Pinch, it won't look like it did originally. You are better off removing the filters in the History palette.

## CROSS-REFERENCE

For more on advanced selecting, see Chapter 4.

## FIND IT ONLINE

The Web site at **http://www.adscape.com/eyedesign/photoshop/four/filters/distort.html** shows you an example of each of the distort filters found in Photoshop.

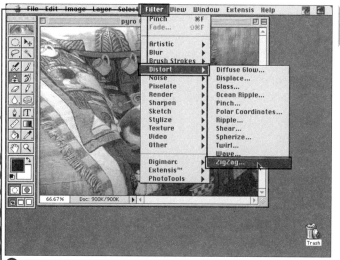

**①** *Choose Filter ⇨ Distort ⇨ ZigZag.*

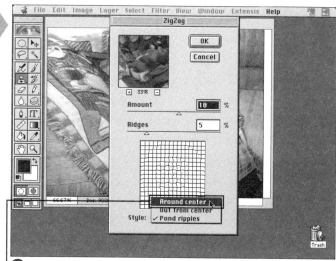

**②** *Change the Style pop-up menu to Around Center.*

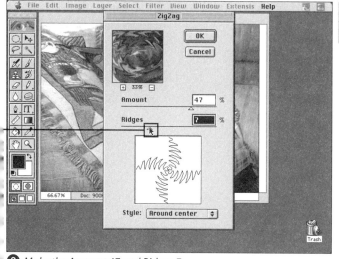

**③** *Make the Amount 47 and Ridges 7.*

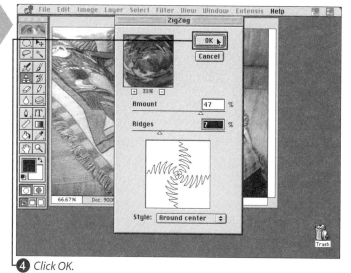

**④** *Click OK.*

# Applying Noise to Your Image

The Noise filters let you add or delete randomly placed pixels. This filter creates a blend by adding pixels or fixes scratches on an existing image.

**Noise.** This filter does what it sounds like; it adds a white noise to your image. This filter can be used to fix lines between areas of color that you want to blend. Uniform creates a more subtle effect. Gaussian creates an all-over noise effect. If you check the Monochromatic box, only the colors in the image will be used rather than random colors inserted.

**Despeckle.** Despeckle will blend the interior areas and leave the edges intact.

**Dust & Scratches.** The Dust & Scratches filter fixes scratches or irregular pixels in your image or selection. The filter looks for the odd pixel and blends in the surrounding colors.

**Median.** This filter takes out the random pixels by finding a midtone pixel range to replace the odd pixels with.

**Pixelate.** Pixelate filters create a pattern in your image by arranging and grouping like pixels together. The different choices you have will create wildly different effects. Keep in mind that these filters will totally change your image or selection from a realistic photo to a dotted pixel artsy effect.

**Color Halftone.** Color Halftone creates the effect of a halftone screen being applied to each different channel of your image or selection. In the dialog box, you enter the radius of the circle to be used, and you can change the screen angles of each channel or stick with the default. If you are only working with an RGB image, then only use channels one through three. If you are working with a CMYK image, then use all four channels.

**Crystallize.** The Crystallize filter creates a polygon shape in which pixels that are alike are grouped together.

**Facet.** This filter groups like pixels in a box shape. This can really simulate a painterly look to your image.

**Fragment.** Fragment will duplicate the pixels, then offset them to make a shattered effect. This effect is what your image would look like after you have consumed 20 beers.

**Mezzotint.** The Mezzotint filter changes the image into your selected method of dots, lines, or strokes. There are 10 types to choose from, and all produce a different effect. The three main groups are the dots, lines, and strokes.

**Mosaic.** This filter simulates an actual mosaic. The pixels are grouped into squares. You enter the square size. The larger the square, the more detail you'll lose.

**Pointillize.** Pointillize simulates the works of Monét. This filter will make your image look like it has been created using random dots.

**CROSS-REFERENCE**

For more on layers, see Chapter 11.

**FIND IT ONLINE**

For an example of each of the noise filters found in Photoshop, browse **http://www.adscape.com/eyedesign/photoshop/four/filters/noise.html**.

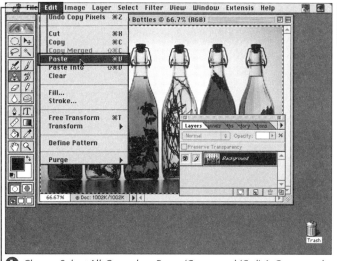

**1** Choose Select All, Copy, then Paste (Command (Ctrl) A, Command (Ctrl) C, Command (Ctrl) V).

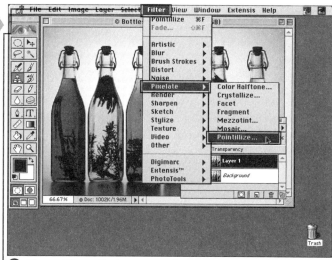

**2** Choose Filter ➪ Pixelate ➪ Pointillize.

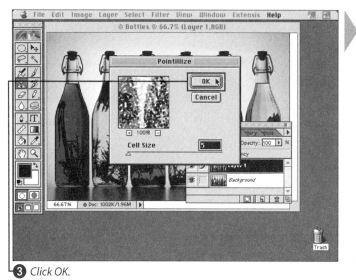

**3** Click OK.

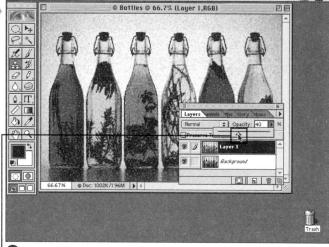

**4** Drag the transparency slider in the Layers palette back for a more subtle effect.

# Creating Clouds with the Render Filter

The Render filters create three-dimensional effects using shadows and light. You can create clouds, lens, lighting, and texture effects with these filters.

**3D Transform.** This filter really lets you do some amazing things. You can map your image around a cylinder, cube, or sphere.

**Clouds.** The Clouds filter creates a cloud effect based on your foreground and background color found in your toolbox.

**Difference Clouds.** Difference Clouds will create a cloud pattern based on the opposite colors found in the foreground and background colors.

**Lens Flare.** Lens Flare creates a light flare as if you are getting a light shining across your camera.

**Lighting Effects.** The Lighting Effects filter creates different effects using a variety of light sources. You can choose the light style, type of light, and properties of light.

**Texture Fill.** Texture Fill will fill the whole image or a part of your image with an existing texture or a texture that you create.

**Sketch.** The Sketch filters add a human touch to your image. These filters create a hand-drawn feel to your whole image or any part of it.

**Bas Relief.** This filter creates a carved feel to your image.

**Chalk & Charcoal.** This filter draws your image using chalk for highlights and charcoal for shadows and midtones.

**Charcoal.** The Charcoal filter draws your image using different angles for charcoal-like strokes.

**Chrome.** The Chrome filter makes your image look like it was made out of Chrome.

**Conté Crayon.** Conté Crayon draws your image resembling the smooth soft edges of using a waxy conté crayon.

**Graphic Pen.** This filter simulates an ink sketch style to create your image.

**Halftone Pattern.** The Halftone Pattern filter creates a dot pattern as your image.

**Note Paper.** Note Paper makes your image look like it was created with paper.

**Photocopy.** This filter will make your image look like it was copied on a photocopier.

**Plaster.** The Plaster filter uses the dark and light areas of your image to create a 3D plaster effect.

**Reticulation.** Reticulation creates murky shadows and textured highlights.

**Stamp.** Stamp simulates a rubber or wood-carved stamp of your image.

**Torn Edges.** Torn Edges simulates creating your image using ripped pieces of paper.

**Water Paper.** This filter is the only one that retains your color image. This simulates your image being painted on a water-soaked paper.

**CROSS-REFERENCE**

For more on history, see Chapter 12.

**FIND IT ONLINE**

For an example of each of the render filters found in Photoshop, go to **http://www.adscape.com/eyedesign/photoshop/four/filters/render.html**.

**1** Choose Duplicate Layer from the Layers pop-up menu. Enter a name for the layer.

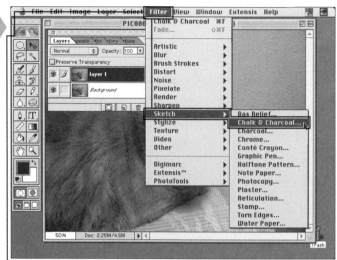

**2** On that new layer choose Filter ➪ Sketch ➪ Chalk & Charcoal.

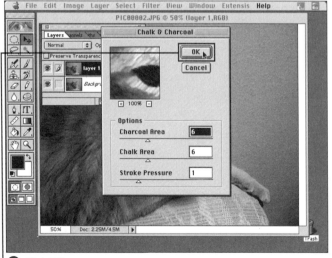

**3** Click OK.

**4** Change the opacity of that layer in the Layers palette so you can see some of the color showing through the hand-drawn effect.

# Adding Pizzazz with Stylize Filters

The Stylize filters are also in the grouping of filters that produce artistic painterly effects. These filters emboss, diffuse, glow, extrude, tile, and trace your image or selection. The effects can be thought of as impressionist art.

**Diffuse.** Diffuse creates a fuzzy, not blurry, edge to the pixels. It is as if your image has a bad case of static electricity. You can choose from Normal, Darken, or Lighten modes. Normal will affect the whole image. Darken affects the shadows and Lighten affects the highlights.

**Emboss.** The Emboss filter creates a 3D look by using highlights and shadows. The image will be filled in gray and appear to have a raised feel to it with highlights and shadows added to the edges. You choose the Angle of the emboss, the height of the raised areas, and the amount you want it to be embossed. The higher the amount, the more intense the emboss.

**Extrude.** This filter extrudes your image in either a block or a pyramid shape. You choose the size of the blocks or pyramids, how deep the extrude will be in pixels, and whether the shapes will be level or random based.

**Find Edges.** Find Edges actually creates an outline around your image. This filter reads where there is an edge (created by different colored pixels against each other) and draws a dark outline. The inside areas are filled with white. This is a great way to create a line art of your image.

**Glowing Edges.** Glowing Edges will find the edges of your image and create a glow around the edge. The options you choose are the Width of the glow, the Brightness of the glow, and the Smoothness of the lines. Opposite of Find Edges, the background is filled in with black.

**Solarize.** Solarize will create the effect of a film negative and positive combined together.

**Tiles.** The Tiles filter breaks the image into squares. You set the number of Tiles and the percentage of the Offset. You also choose whether the background behind the tiles will be filled in with the Foreground color, Background Color, Inverted image, or Unaltered image.

**Trace Contour.** This filter looks for the brightest colored areas and places an outline around the edge. The outline is made up of the Channel colors (RGB or CMYK). The background area is filled with white.

**Wind.** The Wind filter makes your image look like a windstorm has blown the pixels in a direction. You choose either Wind, Blast, or Stagger for your style of wind. The direction choices are either from the Left or from the Right. This filter will drag our horizontal likes from your image to simulate the blown effect.

**CROSS-REFERENCE**

For more on channels, see Chapter 12.

**FIND IT ONLINE**

See **http://www.adscape.com/eyedesign/photoshop/four/ filters/stylize.html** for an example of each of Photoshop's stylize filters.

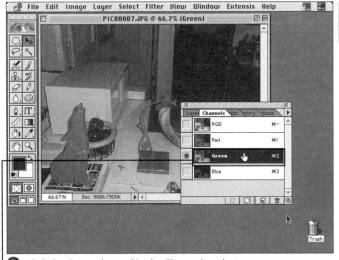

**1** *Click the Green channel in the Channels palette.*

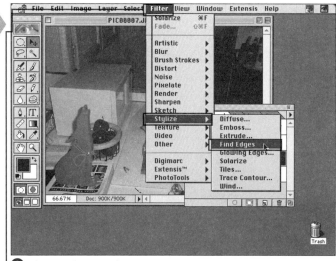

**2** *Choose Filter ⇨ Stylize ⇨ Find Edges. Click OK.*

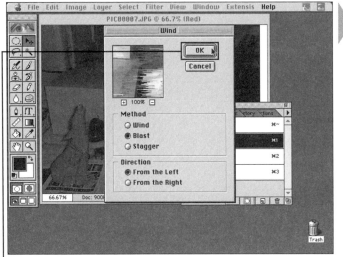

**3** *Click the Red channel then choose Filter ⇨ Stylize ⇨ Wind. Choose the Blast and from the Left, click OK.*

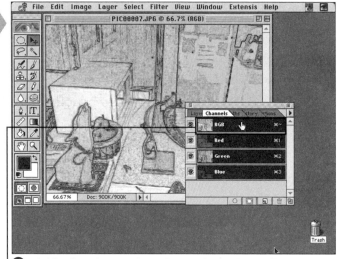

**4** *Click back on the RGB channel to see the combined effects.*

# Making Your Life Easier with Extensis PhotoTools

Extensis PhotoTools 3.0 is a bundle of filters that create textures, buttons, bevels, and shadows. Included with PhotoTools is PhotoAnimator. You run PhotoAnimator by itself to create animations that you can use GIF or Photoshop documents to start with.

**PhotoBars.** PhotoBars takes many of the pull-down menu options and puts them into easily accessible buttons. You can customize your own bars and even put a folder of frequently used images as a button to access quickly. The bars can be stand-alone or tag onto the top, bottom, left, or right side of your screen.

**PhotoBevel 3.0.** PhotoBevel creates a bevel based on your input. You choose the Bevel type, shape, edge tolerance, width, softness, balance, highlight intensity, shadow intensity, angle of the bevel, and highlight and shadow colors. You have the choice to save any bevel you create or to choose from a variety of preset options.

**PhotoButton 3.0.** PhotoButton lets you create a button instantly. You input exactly the way you want your button to look and can see the preview of the button before you hit Apply. You choose the Shape, Bevel, Color, and Texture of the button. There are preset shapes to choose from or you can edit a shape to create your own.

**PhotoCastShadow 3.0.** This filter creates one or multiple cast shadows on your object. You choose from the style of shadow. The styles include Blur, Perspective Blur, Opacity, Noise, Blend mode, and Color. The Shape tab lets you choose how far the shadow is offset in the x and y direction, the angle, length, invert selection, and create shadow only.

**PhotoEmboss 3.0.** PhotoEmboss creates an emboss with such ease and great results, nothing is quite like it. You choose the Emboss type, amount, softness, contrast, highlight, shadow, direction, and highlight and shadow colors.

**PhotoGlow 3.0.** This filter creates a neon glow around your selection or image. You choose the type of glow (either Edge or Solid), the Stroke shape, Stroke width, Radiance, Opacity, Blend mode, and Color of glow.

**PhotoGroove 3.0.** You can create a groove or bevel using PhotoGroove. PhotoGroove makes the image or selection appear to be 3D. You set the shape and space of the groove, the bevel width, bevel height, material type, highlight angle, and highlight color.

**PhotoTexture 3.0.** To create textures to any degree quickly and easily, use PhotoTexture. This filter creates textures based on your input or image. You choose the tile tab or the preview tab. In the tile tab, you can choose from Effects (which gives you a starting point for a texture) and Filters (to alter the effect). You can repeat effects and filters as well as combine them. You can also choose the color of the textures with a background and foreground color.

**CROSS-REFERENCE**

For more on automating Photoshop, see Chapter 13.

**FIND IT ONLINE**

Order PhotoTools right from the Extensis Web site at http://www.extensis.com

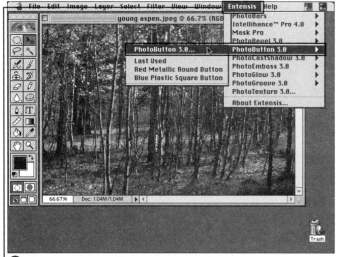

① Choose Extensis ➪ PhotoButton 3.0 ➪ PhotoButton 3.0.

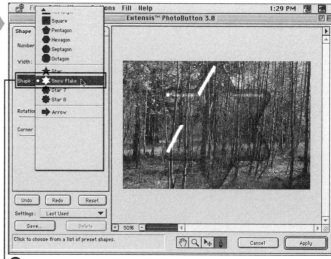

② Choose the shape of the button. We chose snowflake.

③ Choose a color by clicking the color swatch and finding a new color.

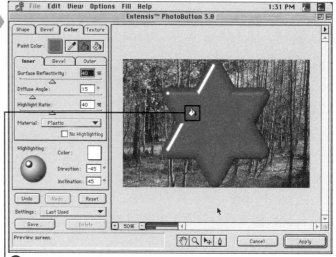

④ Using the Paintbucket, fill in the button to your new color. When done, click the Apply button.

# Personal Workbook

## Q&A

**1** Which blur filter do you use to apply an effect that you control?

_____

_____

_____

**2** What is the best way to crisp up (sharpen) an image?

_____

_____

_____

**3** What filter do you use to blend away banded colors?

_____

_____

_____

**4** How can you fix a scratch in a photo?

_____

_____

_____

**5** What filter creates a sky to a plain background?

_____

_____

_____

**6** Which group of filters changes your image to a grayscale from color?

_____

_____

_____

**7** How can you create a quick and easy button for the Web?

_____

_____

_____

**8** What plug-in lets you create custom textures?

_____

_____

_____

ANSWERS: PAGE 342

## EXTRA PRACTICE

1. Select people out of a group and sharpen them to make them stand out.

2. Use the Blur feature to create motion on an object by selecting everything but that object.

3. Use the Distort filters to create a pond ripple effect on your image.

4. Create a more exciting sky by selecting a plain sky and using the Clouds filter. Try holding the Option [Alt] key for a more dramatic result.

5. Create an artistic effect with your image by combining a semi-transparent image that has a Stylize filter applied to it over the original color image.

6. Create a texture in PhotoTexture, then use that texture on a button that you create using PhotoButton.

## REAL-WORLD APPLICATIONS

✔ Your client loves the photos that you fixed, but wants the sky to be more exciting to show that the hotel resort always has great weather. You use the clouds filter and instantly insert fluffy white clouds over a big blue sky.

✔ You get a batch of photos back from the processing studio and find that all of them have the same scratch across the left side. Use the Dust and Scratches filter to fix them.

✔ Use the Sharpen filter to pop out an object and the Blur filter to blur the background out.

✔ PhotoTools comes in handy when you are creating a whole web page for an important client. You use PhotoTexture to create some amazing backgrounds, and PhotoButton to create some great buttons.

## Visual Quiz

How was only the black channel affected with this filter?

_____

_____

_____

_____

# PART

# V

Contents of 'Desktop'

Name

My Computer

Network Neigh

Internet Explor

Microsoft Outloo

Recycle Bin

My Briefcase

3252-9

3259-6

3261-8

3262-6

3281-2

3296-3

DE Phone List

Device Manager

In

Iomega Tools

# Finishing Touches and Version 5.5

# CHAPTER 15

# Printing and Managing Colors

If you've spent any time with Photoshop, by now you'll have thought of two essential parts of the program: How do I get images into Photoshop, and how do I get them out when I am done? This chapter looks at colors and printing and how best to do these in Photoshop.

The paperless office of the future is still a long, long way off. Almost any proofing stage — both for our own perusal and for clients — can require the printing of multiple copies. You often need hard copies of final art for approval or permanent files. Printing in Photoshop is not unlike printing in other programs, but there are some sophisticated twists that can make all the difference in your final results.

If you are looking to get multiple Photoshop files printed on separate plates, then you may want to consider using another program like Adobe PageMaker or QuarkXPress. You can easily import your files from Photoshop into these programs as pages, then print separations. A separation is when your image prints out each color on its own page. If you have a full-color image and want to print it on four plates to show Cyan, Magenta, Yellow, and Black, then each color in the image will print out on its respective plates. If you are printing an image that only has one color or a spot color, then you'll only have two pages or plates printing. This chapter will discuss printing separations.

Since computer screens only view in RGB and you print in CMYK, sometimes it is a good idea to send a test file to your printer to see if the colors are looking the way you want. This may seem to cost a bit more, but in the long run, you will be thankful. Sometimes an image you prepare will go beyond being printed on your own laser or inkjet printer. For example, you may need to send files to a service bureau for high-quality output, or you may send it to a printer who will use your computer art to generate a plate with which to reproduce your graphic on a larger scale. For these cases, there are many considerations. Some of the things you need to know about are registration, crop marks, halftone requirements, and emulsion orientation. All of these things need to be taken into consideration in order to present your work in the best possible light.

# Cross-Platform Gamma and Monitors

The powers-that-were-hardware-designers have determined that the correct gamma setting for a Macintosh monitor is much different than that for a Windows system. This is true for other computer platforms as well. Different systems pump different amounts of light to the user through the monitor. Gamma, then, is the difference in the appearance in tonality of your images based on the way your computer looks at light and compensates for it. In short, gamma is the way your monitor gauges brightness and then translates it.

In the natural course of design, this doesn't affect us. Once you have everything nicely calibrated, off it goes to output; that is, until your output is targeted for Web distribution rather than hard printing.

Put more simply, what looks like a perfectly color-corrected image on a Web browser on your Mac will look very dark on your Window's browser. The reverse is not true for Windows users because, due to their monitor's gamma settings, they have already made the image lighter than the Macintosh's monitor would have done.

What you must do, as a designer whose work may be viewed on many computer platforms, is to find a good average of light and brightness that will ensure that all viewers get the full impact of your images.

If you are a Windows user, it might be good to ignore the entire gamma issue because an image that is slightly lighter than perfect is better to view than an image that is too dark. Images that are corrected

for Windows gamma will look too light on the Macintosh, and the images corrected on the Macintosh systems will look too dark on the Windows system. Plus, a larger percentage of Web surfers use a Windows-based system, so images corrected to your gamma will look good to most people.

Keeping in mind that the most common gamma setting on a Windows system is 2.5 and 1.8 on the Macintosh, the easiest way to compensate for the way your images will be seen is to "shoot the gamma gap." What this means is that at home you'll set your own gamma at around 2.2. This solution is easy but not perfect because you end up with images that aren't intended to be perfect on *any* system. In the rough-and-tumble world of present-day Web graphics, however, perfect is a little much to shoot for.

## TAKE NOTE

### ▶ MONITORS

Nowadays, the Macintosh computers can use any monitor (Macintosh or Windows) successfully without any special software.

### ▶ GAMMA AT A GLANCE

Gamma is the type and amount of light that comes through your monitor. The standards that determine your system's gamma are loose, at best.

Graphics viewed on a Macintosh will appear darker than the same graphics when viewed on a Windows system.

**CROSS-REFERENCE**

For more on image adjusting, see Chapter 8.

**FIND IT ONLINE**

Macintosh users can find a useful gamma correction tool at **http://www.flash.net/~rolandg/thanks/**. GammaToggleFKEY is freeware created and distributed by Roland Gustafsson.

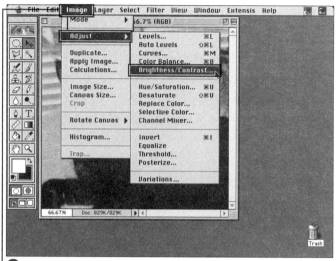

**1** *Choose Image ⇨ Adjust ⇨ Brightness/Contrast.*

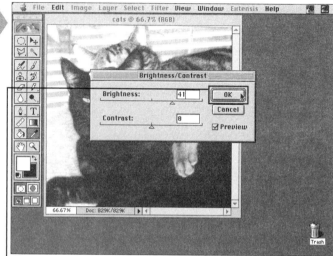

**2** *With the Preview box checked, adjust the sliders to make the image slightly lighter (for the Macintosh). Click OK.*

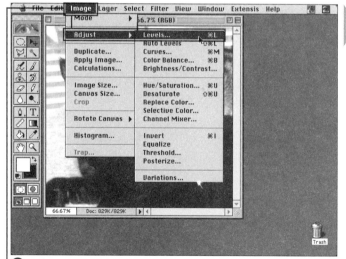

**3** *To lighten an image globally, choose Image ⇨ Adjust ⇨ Levels.*

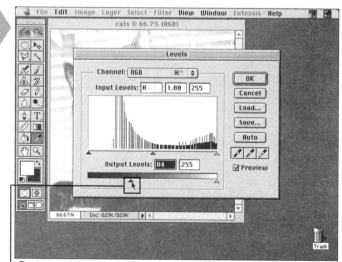

**4** *Drag the black slider in the Output Levels (at the bottom of the dialog box) towards the right to lighten the whole image. We like to do this to dim an image for putting text overtop.*

# Color Settings

Unless you are planning on working exclusively in RGB mode, you need to learn to convert images from one image type to another. That way they can be printed professionally or published on the Web. If a lot of your work is output-based, the most common conversion you will encounter will be to change images from RGB mode to CMYK mode. When you perform this conversion, the colors that are expressed in terms of their red, green, and blue channel components are first converted to three channels of luminance, an A component, and a B component in the lab mode. Following this, they are further converted into the four channels of the CMYK mode: cyan, magenta, yellow, and black.

Remember that because you're converting from an additive color mode to a subtractive mode, the colors will not be exactly the same and there's no going back once values have been changed. Always keep a copy of your original file before you do an intermode conversion. That way, if you don't like the results, you can begin again.

Converting an image from one mode to another is easy: You simply select the new mode from the pop-up menu found under Image ⇨ Mode. The only exception to this is when you convert an image to the indexed color mode, in which case you have a number of different options to deal with.

The Color Setting found under the File menu houses the setup dialog boxes RGB, CMYK, Grayscale, and Profile setups. The RGB Setup, Grayscale Setup, and CMYK Setup dialog boxes let you define the native color space for editing RGB, Grayscale, and CMYK images. The settings in these dialog boxes are used for three things. The first is to convert images between standard color modes (such as from RGB to CMYK). The second, when opening an RGB, Grayscale, or CMYK file, is to compare the file's color space to the color space defined in the appropriate Setup dialog box. If the two color spaces are not the same, you can convert the file. The last, when viewing a file on-screen, is to convert the file to the monitor's color space. This only affects the display, not the file — Photoshop assumes that the file's true color space is the one defined in the appropriate Setup dialog box.

Changes to the Setup dialog boxes do not affect the pixel values of open images. However, the on-screen appearance may change, because Photoshop then displays the image assuming a different native color space.

For example, suppose your file was created in the sRGB color space and you use the RGB Setup dialog box to change the color space to ColorMatch RGB. Photoshop will treat your file as a ColorMatch RGB file when it displays it online, even though it is not changing the actual pixel values in the file.

**CROSS-REFERENCE**
For more on changing color modes, see Chapter 2.

**FIND IT ONLINE**
This Web site shows you Photoshop tips:
http://www.andyart.com/photoshop/index.html

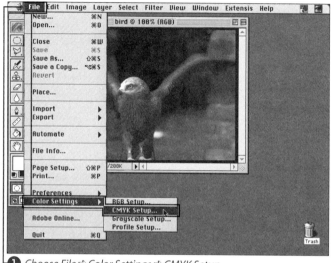

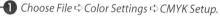

**1** Choose File ➪ Color Settings ➪ CMYK Setup.

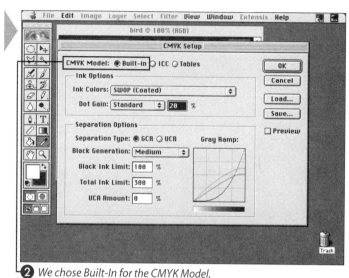

**2** We chose Built-In for the CMYK Model.

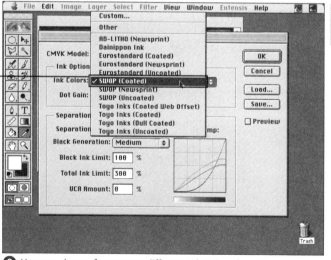

**3** You can choose from many different Ink Colors from the pop-up menu. We chose SWOP (Coated).

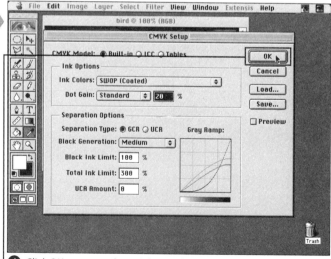

**4** Click OK to accept these Color Model Settings.

# Trapping Colors

You may be wondering when to specify screen angles of your image. You set the angle of the screen when printing a CMYK image. Each color gets a slightly different angle. This is so that the dots are laid down in such a way that the color of the resulting image looks blended.

This also affects how the halftone will look, especially when working with colors that may create a moiré pattern. You usually want to avoid getting a moiré pattern in any image. The only danger of setting your own screen angles to avoid a moiré pattern is that the printer you send it to may override your settings. It is better to let your printer know how you want the screen angles if moiré patterns are a problem. We have only run across moiré patterns when we use a client's specified color palette using an overprinting and it makes a pattern. A moiré pattern is a distinctive pattern that is created when two or more colors overlap and the screen values of those colors have been changed. Typically the inks print out with black at 45 degrees, magenta at 75 degrees, yellow at 90 degrees, and cyan at 105 degrees. When you change any of these values you run the risk of your colors creating an obvious pattern rather than a smooth color.

When you have any two colors that overlap or butt up against each other, you need to think about how you'll trap the colors. When two colors are against each other without a trap, there is a really good chance that when you send the image to the printer, you'll get an uneven white edge where the colors meet. This happens because the printer "shifts" when printing. The print gets shifted because of the color plates not getting placed perfectly, or there are irregular-sized negatives. There isn't a whole lot you can do about the shifting, but you can correct it on your image so if there is a shift, then there is color overlapping instead of butting.

The first thing you need to know in trapping is how much. To determine this, ask your printer. They will be able to tell you what would cover their presses. In a vector-based program, trapping is much easier. You usually use a stroke to create the trap. Because Photoshop is pixel-based, trapping is a little harder. You want to create a spread or choke when you trap. Which one depends on whether your trap uses the color of the object or background.

Photoshop provides a trapping option for you, found under the Image menu. The image first has to be converted to CMYK for the Trap option to be available. Once you activate the Trap dialog box, you simply enter the number in pixels of the trap that your printer suggested you use.

To manually trap your image, you can select the spot color in the Channels palette, make it an active selection, choose either Contract or Expand from the Modify menu, then delete to push the pixels out or in. Typically you'll trap any yellows outwards so you don't see an edge in the yellow areas.

**CROSS-REFERENCE**
For more on colors and images, see Chapter 8.

**FIND IT ONLINE**
This Web site shows you Photoshop resources: **http:// www.algonet.se/~dip/photoshop/PS_index.htm**

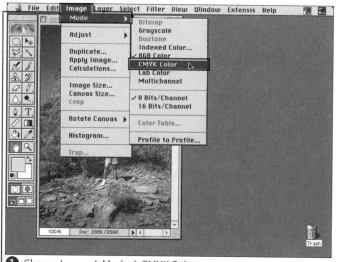

① *Choose Image ⇨ Mode ⇨ CMYK Color.*

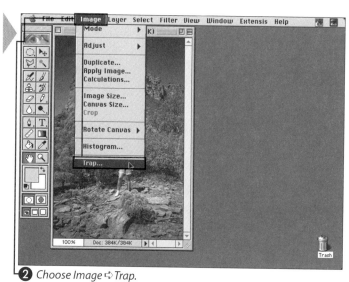

② *Choose Image ⇨ Trap.*

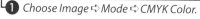

③ *Enter the value that your printer suggests. We used the highest value of 10 so you could see the trap.*

④ *This image shows you the result after applying a 10-pixel trap.*

# Making Color Separations

When you are creating a color print-out of your image and want to check how the color is on each plate, you can separate the plates out when you print. You need to have your image converted to CMYK first. In the Print dialog box, there is a Space pop-up menu where you'll choose separations from the list. When you do this, you'll get four pages that print. We recommend that if you have many files to print separations, then use a program like QuarkXPress into which you'll dump the files, and print one time.

If you are working with a file for the Web, you don't have to worry about creating a color separation. After choosing Indexed Color, you can choose Color Table from the Mode submenu of the Image menu. Five different types of color tables are accessed under the Color Table pop-up menu. The Black Body color table shows a range of colors based on the colors emitted as a black body radiator heats up. The gradient proceeds from black to red, orange, yellow, and white. The Grayscale color table shows the full range of 256 grayscale tones from 0 (black) to 255 (white). The Macintosh System displays the Macintosh's color palette, with 256 choices. The Spectrum color table shows the rainbow of colors in the visible spectrum. The Windows System color table shows the Windows System color palette, with 256 choices. Color tables can be saved and loaded. Use the Save and Load buttons in the Color Table dialog box.

You can change the color table associated with an indexed color image, thereby changing the colors represented in the image. RGB, CMYK, and grayscale image color tables can be edited when the image is converted to indexed color.

Grayscale images do not have to be printed with only black ink. When they're printed using colored ink, they are called monotones, duotones, tritones, or quadtones, depending upon the number of inks used. Monotones are printed with one color of ink that is not black. Duotones, tritones, and quadtones are printed with black ink plus one, two, or three additional colors.

Although a grayscale image might contain much subtle detail, when it is printed using black ink in a single pass on a press, only about 50 gray levels are reproduced. Sometimes two passes of black ink are used, or occasionally, one pass each of black and gray ink, to increase the tonal range. Another alternative is to print that second pass using a colored ink. This gives the image a slight tint and creates an image of much greater depth.

Although duotones can look somewhat like tinted color images, they are not created in the RGB or CMYK mode. Instead, they are converted from grayscale to duotone mode by selecting Duotone from the Mode menu. Duotones begin with one channel, like grayscale images, although additional mask channels can be added in which to save selections.

**CROSS-REFERENCE**

For more on colors see Chapter 7.

**FIND IT ONLINE**

Visit **http://desktoppublishing.com/photoshop.html** more information on Photoshop:

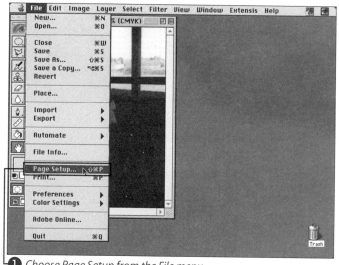

**1** Choose Page Setup from the File menu.

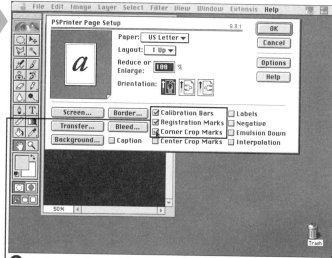

**2** On the Page Setup dialog box, check the Calibration Bars, Registration Marks, and Corner Crop Marks.

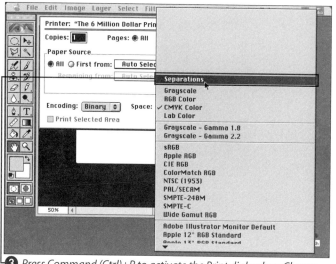

**3** Press Command (Ctrl)+P to activate the Print dialog box. Choose Separations from the Space pop-up menu.

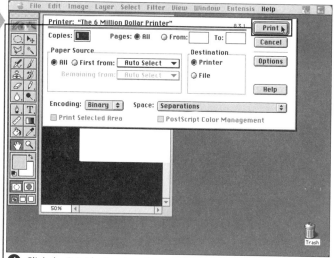

**4** Click the Print button to print out the separations.

# Using Printing Options

Photoshop makes many printing variables possible and easily accessible. Prior to printing, set your options by using the Page Setup command under the file menu. While Photoshop will produce acceptable results using the default settings in most cases, understanding the full range of printing possibilities can be beneficial to creating really great final results in the program.

The Page Setup dialog box you see on your screen will probably look different from the one illustrated in this task. That's because the content on the top half of the dialog, paper size, orientation, and so on, is generated by the print driver software, not Photoshop. However, whatever your printer type, the bottom half of the dialog box will include the same options:

▶ **Screen.** Sets the halftone screen.
▶ **Transfer.** Transfer functions are not used often in Photoshop because the program allows more effective places to adjust for dot gain.
▶ **Background.** Allows specification of a background color that will be printed around your image when working from a color printer.
▶ **Border.** Prints a black release in a width you specify around your image.
▶ **Bleed.** Lets you print crop marks inside an image for when you're trimming something out of a larger piece.

▶ **Caption.** Prints the caption you set using the File Info command.
▶ **Calibration Bars.** Prints an 11-step grayscale bar under your image, allowing you to fine-tune your system calibration.
▶ **Registration Marks.** Help keep the plates aligned so that the image is reproduced properly.
▶ **Corner Crop Marks/Center Crop Marks.** Indicate where a document is to be trimmed.
▶ **Labels.** Prints the document name and channel name on the image.
▶ **Negative.** Converts the output to a negative image.
▶ **Emulsion Down.** The most common film output choice, although some publications may request emulsion up.
▶ **Interpolation.** Applies only to PostScript Level 2 and 3 printers.

---

**TAKE NOTE**

▶ **NO PAGE SETUP WITHOUT A PRINTER**

If you do *not* have a printer installed, you won't be able to access the Page Setup dialog. Photoshop checks to see what driver is coming when the request is made. If none is detected, Photoshop tells you so.

---

**CROSS-REFERENCE**

If you aren't printing your images and are going straight to the Web, see Chapter 16.

**FIND IT ONLINE**

The Photoshop Guru's home page (**http://gurus.i-us .com/**) has lists of cool stuff as well as links to other Photoshop sites.

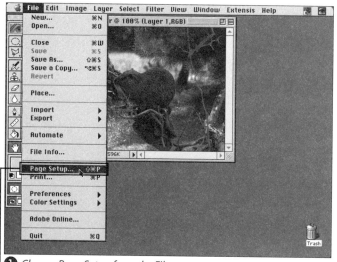

**1** Choose Page Setup from the File menu.

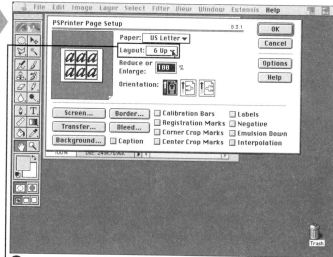

**2** If you are printing business cards, then choose the Layout. We chose 6 Up. You can see a display of how it lays out to the left of the Layout pop-up menu.

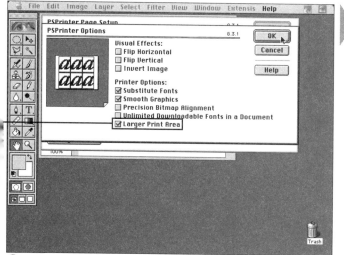

**3** Click the Options button to choose some other page setup options. We like to choose Larger Print Area so you get more area to work with.

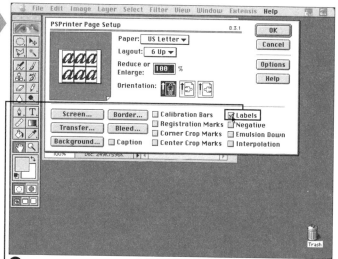

**4** We like to check the label check box so we can see the name of the file on the printout.

# Preparing a Halftone Screen

Traditionally prepared photographs are continuous tone images, meaning that you don't see dots in the image. Photographs you see in newspapers and magazines have been halftoned. Before computers were in use for publication pre-press, photos were re-photographed with a screen over them to create a series of dots that the eye perceives as tones and that duplicates the visual feeling of the original continuous tone image.

Because computer graphics are made of dots of light (pixels), they are already more like a halftone than a continuous tone photograph. When images are viewed in Photoshop, you're already seeing something that is very like a halftone. If you zoom in on a section of an image by 1,600 percent you'll get a feel for the pixels that make up the image. A halftone is very similar to a bunch of pixels that together end up looking like your image.

Dithering creates colors that are not in the designated color table. If you're using the System palette, the following three dithering options are available:

▶ **None.** Colors are not dithered. Missing colors are replaced with the closest nearby colors. This can create a somewhat posterized effect with abrupt transitions between image colors.

▶ **Diffusion.** Pixels are added without obvious patterning.

▶ **Pattern**. Pixels are added at random to simulate missing colors. The pattern is pronounced and looks like a needlepoint cross-stitch.

If you are using an Adaptive, Custom, or Previous palette, only Diffusion and None are available. If you are using an Exact palette, there are no missing colors in the table (since 256 or fewer are being used), and consequently there is no need for dithering.

When you go to print that computer image, still more transformation is required. This is especially true if the graphic you are preparing is going to be printed by someone else or is going to be incorporated in a newspaper or magazine layout. An image being printed in black and white on newsprint, for instance, will need to be screened very coarsely. On the other hand, if it's a brochure cover you're preparing that's going to be printed on a glossy stock by a careful craftsman, you're going to need a much finer screen; detail will be everything.

This being the case, it's important to establish a dialogue with the people doing the work any time an image is leaving your hands for final reproduction. Increasingly, professional printers and other outside agencies are getting used to dealing with designers who work on computers. When asked, they can often give you a list of their requirements as well as what form they prefer to get their material in (on a Zip, Jaz, film, etc.).

**CROSS-REFERENCE**

For more on softening a halftone image using Blur, see Chapter 6.

**FIND IT ONLINE**

Photoshop Org at **http://www.photoshop.org/** is an organization dedicated to teaching Photoshop.

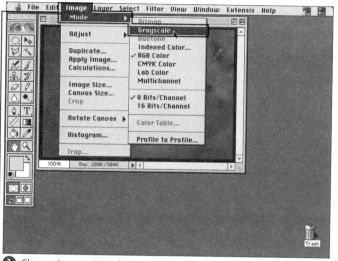

① *Choose Image ⇨ Mode ⇨ Grayscale if you are working with a color image.*

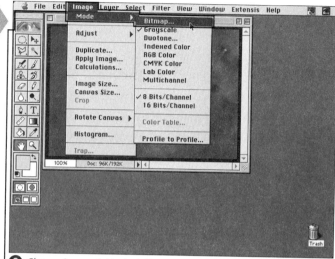

② *Choose Image ⇨ Mode ⇨ Bitmap to create your halftone screen.*

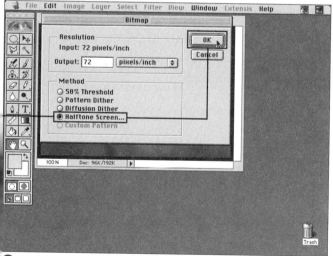

③ *Click the Halftone Screen button, then click OK.*

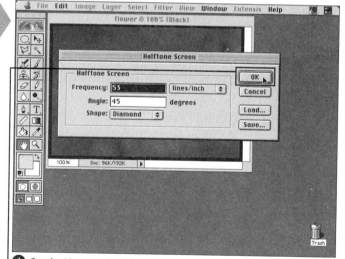

④ *Set the Lines per inch (according to your printer), angle, and shape of the dots, then click OK to see your halftone screen.*

# Previewing an Image and Printing

Before you print, sometimes it's good to check that you have all of the elements in place for your print job to be successful. A utility built into the bottom of the image window on the Macintosh and at the bottom of the screen on a Windows system lets you quickly check your page orientation, as well as any other things you might have added to the document for execution at the printing stage.

Print Selected Area (Macintosh) or Selection (Windows) will only be available if you have a current Selection in the document. If you do, and the option is selected in the Print dialog box, only the selected item will be printed. This can be very helpful when printing a proof for your own use. This is especially helpful for an image that's very large, very complicated, or both. In that case, printing only the selected area can save time, system resources, and paper.

Photoshop also allows you to print to a destination other than the printer. When selecting the destination, the PostScript File option will result in the creation of an EPS file with all of your print specifications in place rather than an actual hard copy. This can be useful if you're sending a file out on disk, to a client, or for publication, but you still want to indicate crop marks, registration marks, or other things determined in Page Setup. Printing to destination lets you do this.

You can determine the type of encoding: Binary, ASCII, and JPEG. As a general rule of thumb, Binary is best because it's very fast, but not all printers understand it in this form. ASCII is safe, because all PostScript printers understand it. JPEG is the fastest, but JPEG is a less accurate form of compression so your results are likely to not be as good as one of the other two methods.

Depending on the output device you're using, you'll be able to select either PostScript Color Management (for PostScript devices) or Printer Color Management. You only need to select this alternative if you're printing to an RGB-based printer or if the document hasn't been converted to the printer's color space.

You use the Color Space profile when you want to send the printer mode information that is different from what you're actually sending. That means, you send a file in CMYK mode, but it's really RGB or you want to print it with a different Gamma than what was on your system. With the appropriate selection made from the Space pop-up menu, the file will print as though it was in the mode specified.

## CROSS-REFERENCE

For more on gamma, see the beginning of this chapter.

## FIND IT ONLINE

Lots of Photoshop tips at **http://desktoppublishing.com/photoshop.html** in Photoshop Paradise.

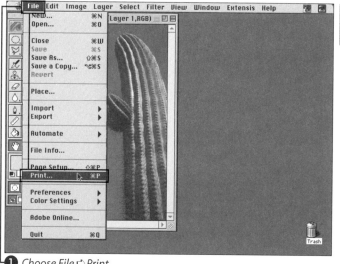

**1** Choose File ⇨ Print.

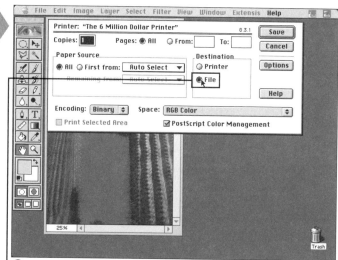

**2** Click the File button in the Destination area to print your image to a file.

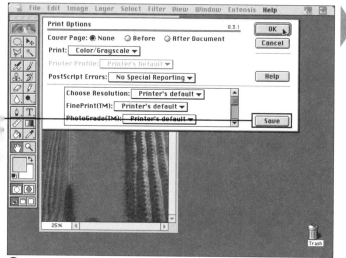

**3** Choose your option under the Print pop-up menu. We chose Color/Grayscale, but if you only want to print a color image in black and white, then choose that option. Click the Save button.

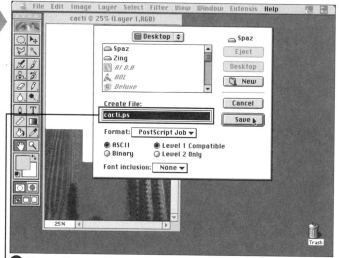

**4** Enter a filename if you want it different from the defaulted one. You can choose the Format, as well as Font Inclusion if there are any fonts in this image.

# Personal Workbook

## Q&A

**1** Will your Macintosh saved image look the same viewed on a Windows system?

_____

_____

_____

**2** Where do you access the Color Tables?

_____

_____

_____

**3** Why do you need to trap an image?

_____

_____

_____

**4** Can you trap the image in Photoshop?

_____

_____

_____

**5** How do you make a Color Separation of your document?

_____

_____

_____

**6** How do you get more paper space when printing?

_____

_____

_____

**7** Why do you need to make a halftone screen (in what cases)?

_____

_____

_____

**8** Can you print your image to a file?

_____

_____

_____

ANSWERS: PAGE 342

300

## EXTRA PRACTICE

1 Save the same image as a JPEG, PNG and GIF. Examine the differences in file size and quality.

2 Look at the resulting images in as many different Internet browsers as possible in order to see how your changes will be viewed by others.

3 Create a piece of art that contains both photographic and typographic elements. Find the best Web format.

4 Create a separation of a CMYK image including label, registration marks, crop marks, and a calibration bar.

5 Instead of printing your file, try printing the document to a file.

## REAL-WORLD APPLICATIONS

✔ You want to take a favorite image from your portfolio and put it on a Web site. Because this is an image you created to be printed, you have to rethink the way it will be viewed because you want it to look just as good on the Web as it did in hard copy.

✔ You have an image that includes both type and photographic elements. You find the best way to display it on the Web.

✔ A client wants you to translate a printed brochure to material to be used on a Web site. You determine what will be better re-created for Web use and what you can scan and resave in Web file formats.

✔ You need to send your printer a document, but you want to double-check for any overprinting or knockout errors, so you print out separations to check it out.

## Visual Quiz

What method of halftoning was done to create this image?

_____

_____

_____

_____

_____

# CHAPTER 16

MASTER
THESE
SKILLS

▶ **Preparing an Image for the Web**

▶ **Creating a GIF File**

▶ **Creating a Button for the Web**

▶ **Adding a Digital Watermark**

# Using Photoshop for Web Creation

In the not-so-distant past when we talked about image manipulation software like Photoshop, the talk was exclusively about manipulating images for reproduction in some hard format like offset printing, laser printing, or some other type of printing where you end up with a hard copy in your hands. But things have changed. These days, you are just as likely to have some use for your image that doesn't involve output and that will entail others seeing your work in the very medium in which it was either created or manipulated: the computer screen.

The latest version of Photoshop includes features for publishing as well as for presenting your images in their best light on the World Wide Web and other electronic media. Despite the best efforts of many, Photoshop is still an unbeatable tool for preparing Web graphics.

Many features of the most recent versions of Photoshop lend themselves to efficient - electronic publication. These include:

▶ Easy GIF89a, PNG, and JPEG image conversion for Web use

▶ The Actions command (covered in chapter 13), which allows a series of commands including image mode and file type conversion to be executed quickly and for large batches of files.

▶ Digital watermarking to provide authorship information and help protect your creations from theft on the Internet

▶ A specifiable Web color palette for converting an image to an indexed color

There is good news about saving files that you don't plan on printing: You save a ton in file size. Since you are only viewing it on screen, you only need a resolution of 72 dots per inch. Other than saving files for the Web, you can transfer files over the Internet to keep long-distance family members up to date with your baby's progress. You can send invoices, documents, artwork, anything you'd like across the Internet. If you have a scanner, your options are expanded. Using your scanner with Photoshop, you can work with images from existing photographs and send them to whomever you'd like.

# Preparing an Image for the Web

Whenever you create an image, you generally think in terms of final output as well as about how others will view it. If the image is for a print magazine layout, you have to think about how to prepare the image so that when it's output to film, the printer will be able to reproduce the image as closely as possible to the original version and intention. You also have to check with the printer about the printer's resolution before you even create your image.

In Web use, final output is several steps closer and almost entirely in your control. Output will be computer screens, potentially all over the world. Because Internet data is still mainly carried by telephone lines, the smaller the file size, the more quickly the file will transfer. Also, because your image will be viewed on different computer platforms and different browsers, you have to try to correct in advance for potential discrepancies in lighting and color delivery.

Essentially, any file you save in any Web graphics format will be useable on a Web page. It's important to remember this, as it allows you to play a bit. In the beginning, it's not essential that your files be perfect examples of the format: Being seen is good enough. And even your early files will be viewable if correctly saved in JPEG, GIF, or PNG formats.

After a while, you'll want to make better and better Web graphics: smaller, perhaps. Cleaner. Or both. Remember, experimentation is key to making good Web graphics. A file saved in any of the Web formats will work on the Web. Don't be afraid to play! A perfect Web graphic is one that both looks good and downloads quickly. Don't let pictures stop you; after getting the hang of creating an image for Web graphics, create your own buttons, text, arrows, and more.

**CROSS-REFERENCE**

For more on saving files, see Chapter 2.

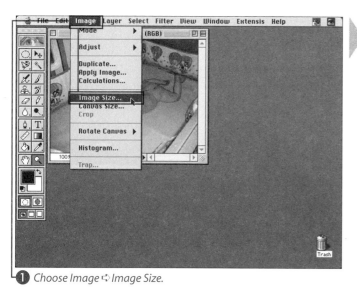

❶ Choose Image ➪ Image Size.

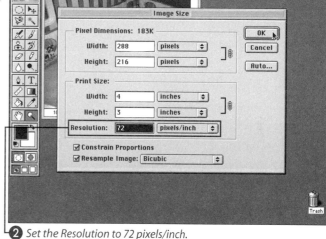

❷ Set the Resolution to 72 pixels/inch.

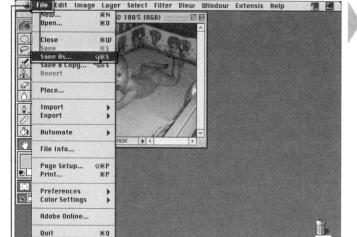

❸ Choose File ➪ Save As, and in the next dialog box, save the file in JPEG format by choosing JPEG from the pop-up menu. Click the Save button to access the JPEG Save dialog box.

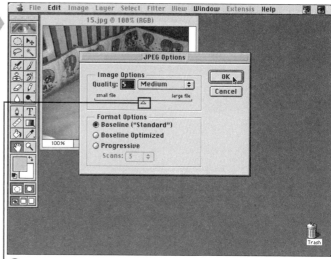

❹ Set your Image Options Quality slider.

■ Choose small or medium, depending on your purpose. Small files are easy to download and e-mail, but they won't look very good printed.

# Choosing the Best File Format

It is best to choose a format that will make your files small and easily downloaded, most accessible to the widest number of browsers, and shown to best advantage. There are three basic file types for delivery of still images via the Internet: GIF, JPEG, and PNG. Photoshop 5 supports all three.

Most images you view on the Web are saved as GIFs (Graphics Interchange Format). GIF allows 1-bit transparency and a palette of a maximum of 256 colors. When you save an image as a GIF file, you can specify how the image will load. If you select Interlace from the file options, the image will download gradually in ever-increasing detail. All Web browsers support GIF compression, so you can safely include GIFs on your Web page and know that people will be able to view them. So, when in doubt, use a GIF because most people will be very likely to view it.

Use a GIF file when your finished art contains a lot of solid color surfaces, or is mainly art rather than photographic based. To save as a GIF89a format, you need to choose Export from the file menu rather than the Save As options. When you save a file as JPEG (Joint Photographic Experts Group) you retain all of the color information of an RGB image. GIF does not. The downside is that JPEG compression works by tossing out information not deemed necessary to rendering the image. This makes for an imperfect compression because data lost can't be recovered, so the file you save will be inferior to the one you started with. On the whole, though, JPEG files tend to be slightly smaller than GIF files and the format is just as widely accepted. Choose the JPEG format when the image you're dealing with is photographically based images, but since data will be lost when you save to this format, remember to save an uncompressed backup of the file in a different format.

The PNG (Portable Network Graphics) file format is being developed as an alternative to the GIF format for displaying images on the Web. PNG not only retains all color information of the original file, but also retains the alpha channels. PNG is a lossless compression method so none of your valuable bits of data get dropped in the translation. Browsers are only beginning to support the PNG file format. Once it becomes widely accepted, we predict we'll be seeing a lot more of this format on the Web. Photoshop's PNG support is not very good. Photoshop *will* enable you to make a PNG file, but Photoshop's PNG files are flawed because they are much larger than they should be.

## TAKE NOTE

### GIVING YOUR GIF A TRANSPARENT BACKGROUND

If you have a file for which you want the background transparent, click with the eyedropper on the color you want to be transparent in the GIF 89a dialog box. To access the GIF89a dialog box, choose File ⇨ Export ⇨ GIF89a. In that dialog box, you'll see the eyedropper to choose your transparent color.

## CROSS-REFERENCE

For more on file types, see Chapter 2.

## FIND IT ONLINE

You can find good information on creating Web graphics and other things relating to Web pages at **http://www.techbabes.com.**

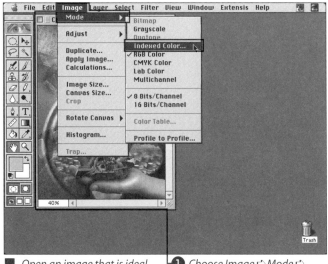

■ *Open an image that is ideal for saving as a GIF.*

❶ *Choose Image ➪ Mode ➪ Indexed Color.*

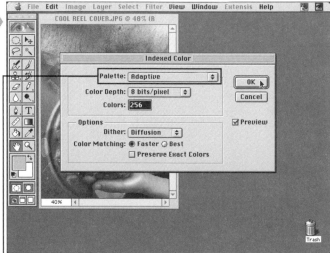

❷ *Choose Adaptive from the Palette menu. That way your image will display as much color as the system of the person who is viewing your image.*

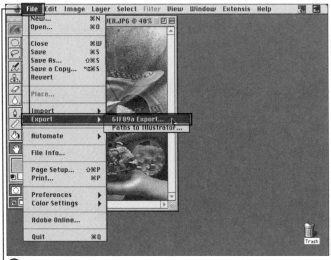

❸ *Choose File ➪ Export ➪ GIF89a Export.*

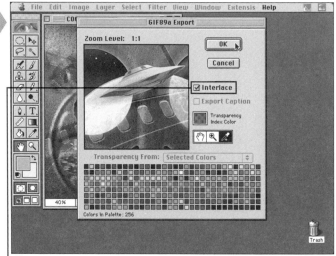

❹ *Check Interlace so the image will display more detail as it is being downloaded.*

# Creating Web Page Buttons

You can now use Photoshop to create your Web page graphics. The key to creating a button is knowing what you want that button to look like. You can make a three-dimensional button, a button with a drop shadow, a flat color button, and so on. What is really cool about creating buttons is that you can start from scratch, or use an existing image. You can also create fantastic backgrounds for buttons.

The key things you need to know when creating a button are making a selection, creating a shadow, and giving a button depth. (Making selections is covered in Chapters 3 and 4.) You can make buttons of any shape, using any or all of the selection tools. If you want to start basic, use the Ellipse marquee for a round button or the Rectangular marquee for a square one. To round the corners of a squared button, use the Feather command. The higher the Feather the more rounded the corners.

A really great button creation program is Extensis' PhotoTools 2.0. This Photoshop plug-in takes the guesswork out of button creation. PhotoTools' PhotoButton feature lets you create multiple buttons in many shapes, sizes, and colors and save any or all of your settings. Just pick what you want from the dialog box, and you're done!

Under PhotoTools' Shape tab, you choose how many buttons you want to appear horizontally and how many appear vertically on your Web page. Then you can select from Preset shapes or alter one to be exactly like you want. After choosing the shape, you can adjust the Rotation Angle, Corner Radius, Inner Height, Bevel Height, Bevel Width, and Bevel Curve. You can save settings, delete, or use one of the presets.

PhotoTools' Color tab lets you choose a color and fill it in. Style options include Inner, Bevel, and Outer button style, Surface Reflectivity, Diffuse Angle, and Highlight Ratio. For Highlighting, you can move the light source, change the highlight color, direction, or inclination, or opt to have no highlighting. As with the Shape tab, you can save, delete or use a preset option.

Other options that PhotoTools gives you include PhotoBars, PhotoBevel, PhotoEmboss, PhotoCast-Shadow, and PhotoText.

## TAKE NOTE

### EASY BUTTONS

If you want a quick and easy button, stick to the presets. As you delve more into PhotoButton, you'll create many new presets of your own.

**CROSS-REFERENCE**
For more on PhotoTools, see Chapter 14.

**FIND IT ONLINE**
Check out PhotoTools and other Extensis products at http://www.extensis.com.

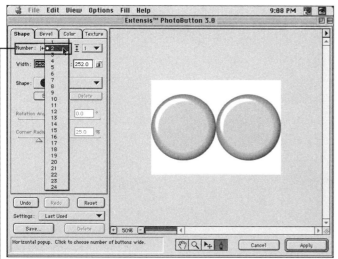

■ This exercise requires Extensis' plug-in for button creation, PhotoTools.

■ We chose two horizontal buttons with a width of 250 and a height of 250.

**1** Choose PhotoTools ⇨ PhotoButton, select number of buttons.

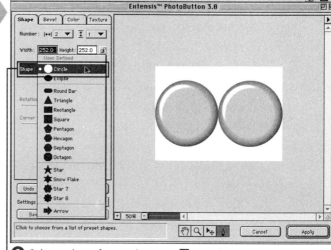

**2** Select a shape for your button here.

■ We chose a basic Circle shape, but as you can see, there are many shapes to choose from.

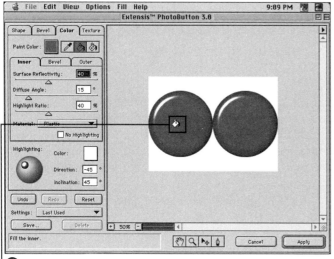

**3** After choosing a color, we used the Paint Bucket tool and clicked the buttons to fill with the color.

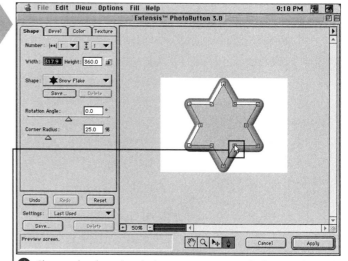

**4** Change the shape by placing your cursor over the button; the path and anchor points automatically appear, and you can drag the anchor points to change the shape. When you create a new shape, you have the option to save it. Under the pop-up shape menu, use the Save button. You can also rotate the shape and change the corner radius to vary the appearance.

# Adding a Digital Watermark

For as long as people have been "publishing" their images on the Web, artists have been concerned with people stealing their work — and not without some justification. An image that can be viewed on a browser can be lifted just about as easily as it's looked at, and this opens a whole can of creative worms.

While there continues to be no easy answer, the latest version of Photoshop has tried to address this concern. Working with the Digimarc Corporation, Photoshop 5.0 includes a filter that enables you to embed an electronic watermark into your image. What is a watermark? If you hold a nice piece of letterhead paper up to the light, you'll see the paper's watermark: the paper company's logo or even the paper variety's name are embedded into the paper during its manufacture. The watermark is an intrinsic part of the paper.

In theory, an electronic watermark works in just the same way. Digimarc's entry adds your personal code as noise to your image's lightness channel. This watermark is invisible and doesn't mess with the image's integrity. When a watermarked image is loaded into Photoshop, the copyright symbol is displayed, letting the would-be Web thief know that this is a protected image.

Electronic watermarks make it possible not only for you to prove your authorship of the image, but also enables prospective clients who have access to your image and watermark to contact you. That's the theory, anyway. The reality is that only time will tell.

There are several organizations and companies that have been cooking up watermarking systems to help protect artists and those who produce other types of creative works. By including Digimarc's watermark in Photoshop, Adobe gives a nod to the company's system. This endorsement of their watermark is important for Digimarc, and something you should consider. Watermarking can't be highly effective without a lot of market support.

## TAKE NOTE

### IMAGE THEFT

No one knows the true extent of image theft on the Web. While there is no guaranteed way of protecting your work from theft other than not showing it to people, digital watermarking offers a solid possibility if enough people get behind it.

### CREATING A CUSTOM BUTTON

To create a custom button that lets you embed the Digital Watermark, use PhotoTools Custom Buttons. Choose Extensis ⇨ PhotoBars ⇨ Customize Toolbars. Select Custom Button. Here you can choose Menu Item and drag to the Embed Digital Watermark option. Then you can choose an icon by clicking Choose Icon. Click the Done button. To add the new custom button to your PhotoTools toolbar, drag the icon to the toolbar. Now you only have to click the button to access the Embed Digital Watermark dialog box.

---

**CROSS-REFERENCE**

For more on other tasks that PhotoTools can help you with, see Chapter 14.

**FIND IT ONLINE**

You can find information on the Digimarc Watermarking system on the Web at **http://www.digimarc.com**.

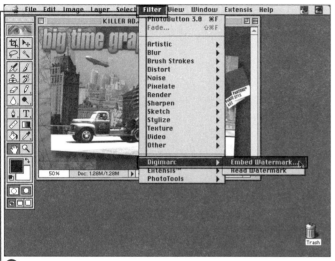

**1** With an image open, choose Filter ➪ Digimarc ➪ Embed Watermark.

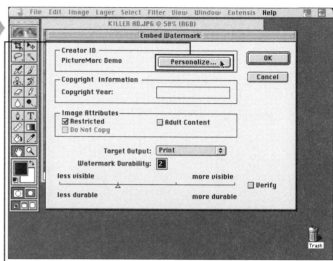

**2** Click the Personalize button to get your own ID and register your watermark. You'll have to have Internet access up and running to do this. The other options you have available are Copyright year, Image Attributes, Target Output (Monitor, Web, Print), and the visibility of the Watermark.

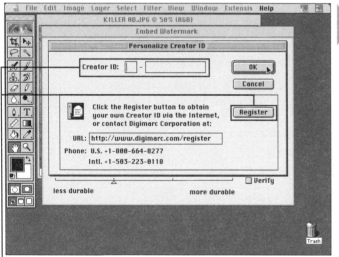

**3** When you click the Personalize button, you'll need to click the Register button to access Digimarc's web page. That is where you'll receive an ID number from Digimarc. There are two options: One you pay for, the other is free. Once you choose the Basic (free) option, you'll have to accept the restrictions to get your ID.

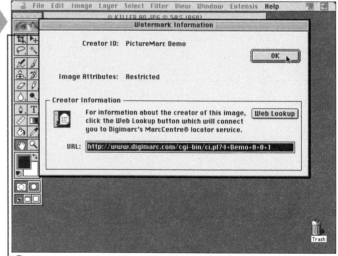

**4** To view your watermark information, choose Filter ➪ Digimarc ➪ Read Watermark.

# Personal Workbook

## Q&A

**1** What are the three Web graphics file formats?

_____

_____

_____

**2** How would you choose what type of format to use for a specific image?

_____

_____

_____

**3** What is the smallest file size you can save as?

_____

_____

_____

**4** How can you make a basic Web button?

_____

_____

_____

**5** How can you make multiple buttons at one time?

_____

_____

_____

**6** What is a _watermark?_

_____

_____

_____

**7** How can you check for your watermark that you embedded?

_____

_____

_____

**8** Why would you need to think about protecting your artwork?

_____

_____

_____

ANSWER: PAGE 343

## EXTRA PRACTICE

1. Save the same image as a JPEG, PNG and GIF. Examine the differences in file size and quality.

2. Experiment with the various settings in the format's Dialog Box. Save files with different names at different settings (for example, test1.gif, test2.gif, and so on) to see how both the quality and file size are affected.

3. Look at the resulting images in as many different Internet browsers as possible to see how others will view your changes.

4. Create a piece of art that contains both photographic and typographic elements. Find the best Web format.

## REAL-WORLD APPLICATIONS

✔ You want to take a favorite image from your portfolio and put it on a Web site. Since this is an image you created to be printed, you have to rethink the way it will be viewed because you want it to look just as good on the Web as it did in hard copy.

✔ A client wants you to translate a printed brochure to material to be used on a Web site. You determine what will be better re-created for Web use and what you can scan and resave in Web file formats.

✔ You want to make sure your work can't be pilfered on the 'Net. You find the best way to protect it.

## Visual Quiz

How did this image get a transparent background?

_____

_____

_____

_____

_____

_____

CHAPTER **17**

MASTER
THESE
SKILLS

- ▶ **Extracting to Make a Mask**
- ▶ **Erasing the Background**
- ▶ **Creating with the Art History Brush**
- ▶ **Making a Contact Sheet and Jumping to Other Applications**
- ▶ **Saving for the Web**

# Photoshop 5.5

Adobe upgraded Photoshop 5.0 to version 5.5. This upgrade addresses many of the features users of Photoshop have wanted for a while. ImageReady 2.0 ships bundled with Photoshop. ImageReady 2.0 is still a stand-alone application that gives you many more features including animation for creating Web pages. (This application is only sold along with Photoshop in this version.) Faux styles are also a new addition to Photoshop 5.5. Now you can easily apply bold, italics, and underline styles to text that may not have had those particular text styles. The Type tool has added more features like Crisp, Strong, Smooth for Anti-aliasing choices as well as a check box for Fractional Widths to the dialog box. These features make it possible for you to do your text additions in Photoshop and not have to copy and paste from another program.

Masking is a big feature that has been added, and makes a great leap forward in creating a good clean mask with little effort. Photoshop has added an Extract function that is found under the Image menu. It is perfect for creating a mask with an image that has a fuzzy or unclear edge. Along with the masking features is a new Background Eraser tool. The Background Eraser tool is perfect for removing a background or foreground from an image that has a clear defined edge.

Photoshop 5.5 also provides an Art History brush. This type of brush lets you paint as you would by hand. You can simulate painting on different types of canvas and control the brush styles that fit with actual hand painting.

Contact sheets are also available in Photoshop 5.5. Now you can create a catalog of your images for easy reference. Along with contact sheets, you can also use this feature to create picture package and galleries. A Jump-To feature enables you to quickly move between applications without losing any document information.

The last feature Photoshop has added is a Save for Web dialog box. This fantastic upgrade feature lets you choose various ways and settings to save your images for the Web.

# Extracting to Make a Mask

asking in Photoshop has been a daunting task in previous versions. Photoshop experts turned to third party software to fulfill their masking needs. Version 5.5 of Photoshop finally addresses the need of good masking in Photoshop. Adobe looked at the third-party software and enhanced their masking abilities.

Found under the Image menu, the Extract function takes you into a dialog box to create your mask. In the Extract dialog box, you'll find some new tools to make your mask. The Extract feature is the best to use on images that don't have a very clear edge. By using Extract rather than the old methods of masking, you'll save a ton of time. In the Extract dialog box, you'll find some new and old tools. The new tools are described for you here.

**Edge Highlighter tool.** Use this tool to define the edge of the area you are masking. The best way to use this tool is to include some outside and inside pixels to totally cover the edge of what you are masking. You can change the brush size in the Tool Options area found on the right side of the dialog box. If you make a mistake in creating your edge, you can use the Eraser tool to remove the highlight. You can adjust the Brush size and Highlight options. You can enter a brush size numerically (it is registered by pixels), or you can drag the slider found at the arrow to the right of the Brush Size box. The Highlight pop-up box lets you change the Edge Highlighter tool's. The Highlight color choices are Red, Green, and Blue; or you can create your own custom color.

**Fill tool.** The Fill tool can only be used after defining the edge with the Edge Highlighter tool. To fill the area you want to keep, just click with the Fill tool in that area. To remove a filled area, click again in that same area.

**Eraser tool.** The Eraser tool works the same in the Extract dialog box as it does in Photoshop. The Eraser tool removes the highlight created by the Edge Highlighter tool. You can use this tool to clean up the edges or open up areas that have been filled in too closely. The only option you can choose for the Eraser tool is the Brush Size.

**Eyedropper tool.** This tool is available only if you check the Force Foreground box in the Extraction area of the Extract dialog box. It lets you choose the Foreground color from your image.

*Continued*

## TAKE NOTE

 **RESETTING YOUR IMAGE**

As with most Photoshop dialog boxes, if you totally mess up you can always hold down the Option (Alt) key to activate the reset button.

**CROSS-REFERENCE**

For more information on third-party masks see Chapter 4.

**FIND IT ONLINE**

For information on the new masking features see
http://www.adobe.com/prodindex/photoshop/masking.html.

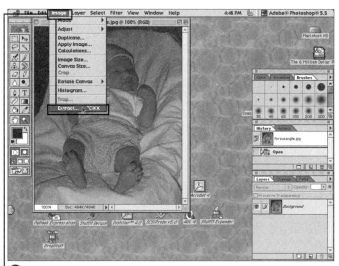

**1** Open an image to extract. Choose Image ➪ Extract.

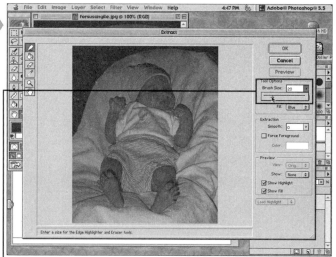

**2** To change the brush from the default size, either drag the slider or enter a value in the Brush Size field.

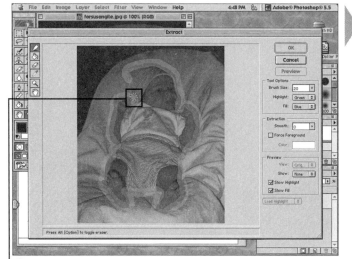

**3** Using the Edge Highlighter tool, drag around the edge of the area you want to extract. Be sure to include a little of the inside and outside pixels in your selection.

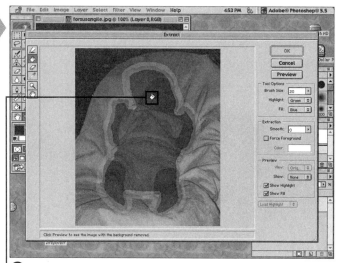

**4** With the Fill Tool click the area you want to keep. In this case we clicked the inside area.

# Extracting to Make a Mask

*Continued*

**Zoom tool.** The Zoom tool magnifies or reduces the viewing area. If you click, you'll zoom in, If you Option (Alt) click, you'll zoom out.

**Hand tool.** The Hand tool lets you pan around your image.

There are other options found in the Extract dialog box that let you fine-tune the tools and settings. The Tool Options are Brush Size, Highlight, and Fill. The Extract function also creates a partially transparent pixel edge so you can seamlessly blend your extracted image with a new background.

You can enter or drag the slider to change the brush size of the Edge Highlighter tool and the Eraser tool. You can also change the Highlight and Fill colors to Red, Green, or Blue; or you may pick your own custom color.

The Extraction options are Smooth, Force Foreground, and Color. The Smooth option will fine-tune the edges of your selection. When you click a color for the Force Foreground, the color shows up in the color swatch area.

The last area is Preview. In the View pop-up menu, you can choose two views, the extracted view and the original. The Show pop-up menu lets you choose a background color for previewing. You can choose a Black, White, or Gray matte, or choose a color of your own. You can also choose to show the mask. If you choose None for Show, you'll get a transparent preview for your mask. Keep in mind that this is only for preview purposes in the Extract dialog box. When you click OK, the background will be transparent.

## TAKE NOTE

### FLATTEN YOUR IMAGE

When you use the Extract function, your image automatically goes to Layer 0. That means your only option for saving the file is as a Photoshop file. You can choose Flatten Image from the Layer menu to have more saving options.

**CROSS-REFERENCE**

For more information on layers, see Chapter 11

**FIND IT ONLINE**

To read about the new features in Photoshop 5.5 see
http://www.adobe.com/prodindex/photoshop/main.html.

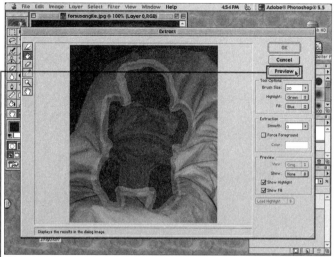

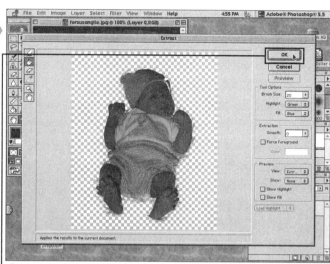

**5** To see the mask, click the Preview button. If you don't like the mask, press the Option (Alt) key to reset the dialog box, adjust the settings, and try again.

**6** When you get the mask you like, click OK.

■ If you need to touch up the mask, remove any offending pixels with the Eraser tool. If some of your image is missing and you want it back, use the History brush.

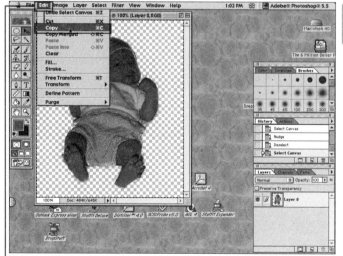

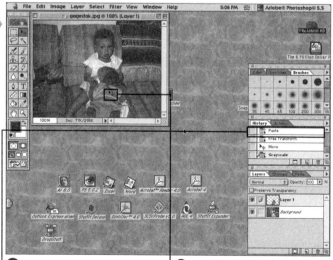

**7** Choose Select ⇨ Select All. Then Choose Edit ⇨ Copy.

**8** Go to another image that you want to paste it into and choose Edit ⇨ Paste.

**9** Move the image in place with the Move tool.

# Magically Erasing the Background

The other two wonderful new additions to Photoshop's masking abilities are the Background Eraser and the Magic Eraser tools. Found in the same pop-up menu with the Eraser tool, the Background Eraser and Magic Eraser tools are used best on images with a crisp and clear edge. The old method of removing a background from an image that has a clear edge would have been to select the background with one of the selection tools and then to press delete to fill with white. Now you can quickly remove the background in one step.

The Magic Eraser tool removes pixels based on similar valued pixels to your first click, or pixels similar in value and contiguous to your first click. The Magic Eraser is like the other Magic tools in that you can set a tolerance. The tolerance lets you adjust how closely you want to match the original selected pixel. The Magic Eraser tool's options are Tolerance, Opacity, Use All Layers, Anti-aliased, and Contiguous. If Use All Layers is checked, the color can be chosen from any layer for your first click, rather than just the active layer. You can adjust the Magic Eraser tool's tolerance to determine how closely the pixel's values must be to become transparent.

The Background Eraser tool works almost exactly like the Magic Eraser tool, except instead of clicking to remove pixels, you drag to remove pixels. You can set the Tolerance on how closely the pixels match your original selection. You also set whether the pixels will be contiguous (next to each other). Both the Magic Eraser and Background Eraser tools remove pixels to a transparent background. From a pop-up menu in the Background Eraser Options palette, you determine how far the erasing will be. In this pop-up menu, you choose Discontiguous, Contiguous, or Find Edges. Another option you set is whether the pixels are determined from a contiguous, once, or the background swatch sampling. The Tolerance setting is where the edge style will be determined. The lower the number, the harder the edge between the transparent background and the edge of the area you are keeping. The higher the number, the softer or fuzzier the edge will be between the background and area you are keeping. Another really great feature of the Background Eraser tool is that it will create a slightly transparent edge to the pixels you are keeping so you won't get a haloed edge to your image. That way if you put in a different background, or copy and paste the image to another background, it will blend nicely

**TAKE NOTE**

**ERASING TO THE BACKGROUND COLOR**
The original Eraser tool erases to the background color only, unless you start with the Magic Eraser or Background Eraser tool first to establish the transparent background.

**CROSS-REFERENCE**
See Chapter 12 for more on the History palette.

**FIND IT ONLINE**
See some of the frequently asked questions on Photoshop 5.5 at
**http://www.adobe.com/prodindex/photoshop/faq.html#q1.**

① Open the image whose background you want to remove in Photoshop.

② To access the Magic Eraser, click and hold on the Eraser tool to see the pop-up additional tools. Then drag over to the Magic Eraser tool.

③ Click the blue part of the sky to remove it. Then click the white clouds to remove that color as well. You can see how wonderful this tool works around the palm fronds.

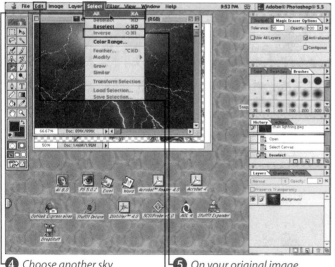

④ Choose another sky background for this image and copy it to the clipboard by selecting the whole image (Select ➪ Select All), and copying (Edit ➪ Copy).

⑤ On your original image choose Select ➪ Select All, then Select ➪ Inverse.

⑥ Choose Edit ➪ Paste Into.

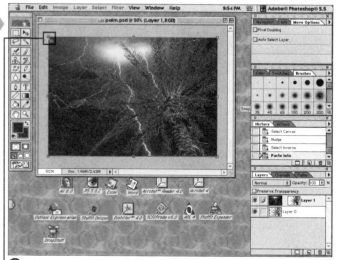

⑦ Choose Edit ➪ Free Transform to move, rotate, or scale the pasted image.

# Creating with the Art History Brush

Photoshop has added another brush to its toolbox. This fantastic new brush called the Art History Brush is housed with the History Brush. The Art History Brush lets you expand your mind by allowing you to paint in Photoshop as if on a canvas by hand. This cool new feature lets you create an array of painterly effects on any or parts of an image with very little effort.

The Art History Brush's effects are based on a selected history state or snapshot. The brush uses this information for your painting style. This way, you don't have to change colors to create your painterly effect.

The Art History Brush options are

**Painting Mode.** The painting modes or blending modes are Normal, Darken, Lighten, Hue, Saturation, Color, and Luminosity. Normal blends between the base color to make it the result color. Darken chooses the darker color (between the base and the blend colors) and makes that the result color. Lighten chooses the lighter color and makes that the result color. Hue takes the base color's luminance and saturation and combines them with the blend color's hue to make the result color. Saturation creates a result color based on the combination of the luminance and hue of the base color and the saturation of the blend color. Color creates the result color from the blend of the base color's luminance and the blend color's hue and saturation. Finally, the Luminosity blends the base color's hue and saturation with the blend color's luminance for the resulting color.

**Opacity.** The Opacity determines how much color is applied. The higher the number, the more opaque you paint. A lower number lets more of the background show through.

**Painting Style.** The Painting Style has a pop-up menu that lets you choose the shape of the paint stroke. You can choose from Tight Short, Tight Medium, Tight Long, Loose Medium, Loose Long, Dab, Tight Curl, Tight Curl Long, Loose Curl, and Loose Curl Long.

**Fidelity.** The Fidelity option controls how much the color will vary from the original. The lower the Fidelity setting, the more you get a variety of colors. The higher the setting, the more closely colors resemble the original colors.

**Painting Area in Diameter.** This option determines how large an area is affected (different than brush size). If you choose a large diameter, you'll get more brush strokes in that particular area.

**Tolerance.** Tolerance lets you adjust the slider to restrict where the brush strokes will be. A low number lets you paint pretty much anywhere. A high number only paints in areas of contrast.

## CROSS-REFERENCE

For more information on the History Brush, see Chapter 6.

## FIND IT ONLINE

Find out more about the Art History Brush at http://www.adobe.com/prodindex/photoshop/arthistory.html.

① Open a file in Photoshop to apply the Art History Brush to.

② To access the Art History Brush, click and hold the History Brush. Then drag to the Art History Brush and release.

③ To access the Art History Brush Options palette, double-click the Art History Brush tool.

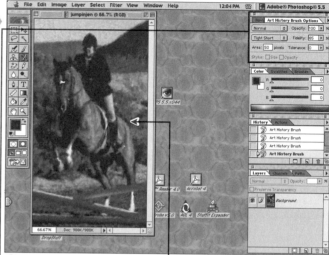

④ To apply a painterly effect to the whole image, we chose the Tight Short style with an 85% Fidelity. The Area was set to 75 pixels and the Tolerance at 0.

⑤ We chose a medium brush and dragged the brush over the entire image.

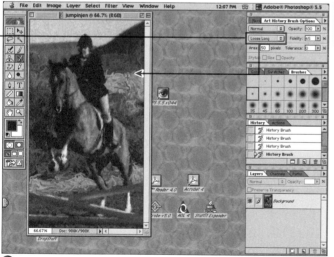

⑥ In the Art History Brush Options palette the style was changed to Loose Long and the Art History Brush was dragged over the grass and dirt areas to give a rough sketchy look.

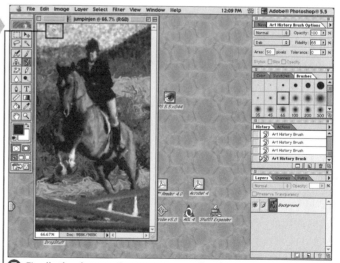

⑦ Finally the sky was given more texture by changing the style to Dab and making the Fidelity 65% so more colors were added to the sky colors.

# Making a Contact Sheet and Jumping to Other Applications

The Contact Sheet is another feature new to Photoshop 5.5. The Contact Sheet shows multiple small previews of your images on a page. The Contact Sheet is a cool way to group images together for quick reference. With the Contact Sheet, you can move images from one page to another to make cataloguing them easier. Contact Sheet II is found under the Automate submenu of the File menu. After specifying the particulars of your Contact Sheet, you can sit back and relax while Photoshop automatically creates the sheet of thumbnails for you. The options found in the Contact Sheet II dialog box are

**Source folder.** Here is where you choose the folder that you want Photoshop to pull the images from to create your Contact Sheet. If you check Include All Subdirectories, any images inside folders within the originally chosen folder will be made into thumbnail images for your Contact Sheet.

**Document.** In the Document area, you choose the Width, Height, Resolution, and Mode of the Contact Sheet.

**Thumbnails.** Here you choose whether the images will be placed across or down. Here you also choose the number of columns and rows. You can check the box to have the filename used as the caption on the Contact Sheet. The fonts that are available will show up in the pop-up menu and will be used for the captions in the Contact Sheet.

Jumping to other applications has just become easier thanks to Photoshop 5.5. You can still drag and drop, but Jumping To retains the image's original layers, effects, type, channels, and more. Your file is automatically updated in both programs. When you are working so diligently on those Web files, you can use ImageReady to do some editing, but for the more involved changes, simply jump back to Photoshop and fix away. The bottom of the toolbox has two new buttons. These are the Jump To buttons to make moving between programs even easier. At the time of this writing, Jump To works with Photoshop 5.5 and ImageReady 2.0. Adobe will surely add this wonderful feature to other major programs like PageMaker and Illustrator.

## TAKE NOTE

### JUMPING VERSUS DRAGGING

You may wonder what the difference is between jumping to and dragging and dropping. When you drag and drop an image from another program into Photoshop and want to make any changes, you have to drag and drop the image after corrections. This can be tricky if you have done a bunch of stuff to the image. With Jump To, you fix the image in its original program, and it will update it in the Photoshop file.

## CROSS-REFERENCE

To read more on drag and drop, see Chapter 5.

## FIND IT ONLINE

For product information on Photoshop 5.5's Contact Sheet, see **http://www.adobe.com/prodindex/photoshop/contact.html**.

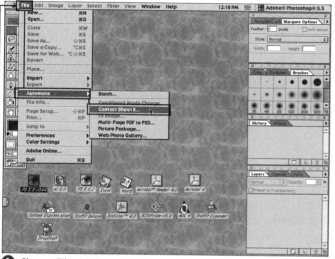

❶ *Choose File ▷ Automate ▷ Contact Sheet II.*

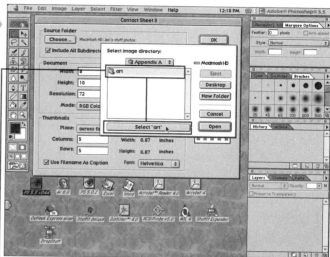

❷ *Click the Choose button to select the folder that has the art for which you want to make a Contact Sheet. Click the folder icon and then click the Select Folder button to choose that folder.*

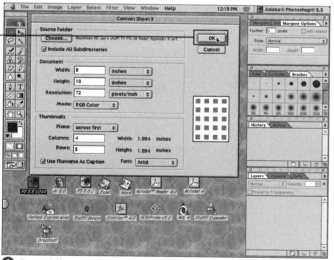

❸ *Enter different values Document and Thumbnails areas if different from the default; then click the OK button.*

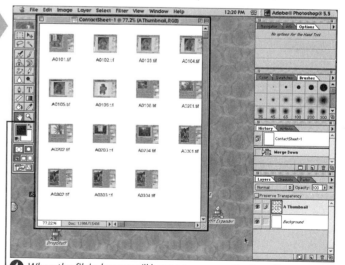

❹ *When the file's done, you'll have one or more Contact Sheets depending on the amount of images you had in your folder. These Contact Sheets will make for a quick reference and they can also be printed.*

# Saving for the Web

Photoshop 5.5 has added a Save for Web feature that lets you save images for the Web easily. The Save for Web dialog box offers you many options. Four tabs at the top of the dialog box let you view the Original image, the Optimized image, 2-Up views showing the Original on one side and the Optimized on the other side, and 4-Up views showing the original and three other settings for Optimized images. Your file choices for saving are variations of GIF, JPEG, and PNG formats. At the bottom of the dialog box, you can change the zoom level from the pop-up presets, or type in a numeric value. Another setting at the bottom of the dialog box is the Select Browser menu. You can choose from the pop-up options or choose Other to select a browser from your hard drive.

Beneath the Options, there are two more tabbed areas. One tabbed area shows the Color Table for the optimized image based on the settings above it. The other tabbed area shows the Image Size. The Image Size tab lets you view the original size and allows you to change it. You can change the Width and Height in pixels, or the Percent of the image. The Constrain Proportions chec kbox keeps the image proportionate or, if unchecked, alters the image according to the input values. The Quality pop-up choices are Smooth (Bicubic) or Jagged (Nearest Neighbor). When any of these values are changed, you have to click the Apply button to see the new values.

Photoshop has put in default settings for each of the save settings for GIF, JPEG, and PNG. Within each of these settings you can leave the default or alter it. With the GIF settings you can save as GIF 128 Dithered, GIF 128 No Dither, GIF 32 Dithered, GIF 32 No Dither, GIF 64 Dithered, GIF 64 No Dither, or GIF Web Palette. With any of the settings, you can save or delete as necessary. The GIF settings are

**Lossy.** This adjusts how much lossiness will be allowed for compression. A lossy file retains information with some compression, little file loss, and smaller files.

**Colors.** The Colors setting includes the pop-up menu to the left that lets you choose the palette from Perceptual, Selective, Adaptive, Web, Custom, Mac OS, or Windows. You can drag the slider or enter a value in the Colors field for the maximum number of colors you want available for the color table.

**Dither.** The Dither setting includes the pop-up menu to the left that lets you choose the type of Dither. You can choose from Diffusion, Pattern, or Noise. Drag the Dither slider higher or lower to have a bigger or smaller dither, or enter a value in the Dither text box. Dithering reduces any banding between colors.

## TAKE NOTE

▶ **DELETING A DEFAULT SETTING**

Fear not if you delete a default setting by accident. You can throw out the preferences file in Photoshop and all of the settings will be returned.

**CROSS-REFERENCE**

For more on saving in Photoshop, see Chapter 1.

**FIND IT ONLINE**

To find out more about Photoshop 5.5 Web optimization, see **http://www.adobe.com/prodindex/photoshop/preview.html**.

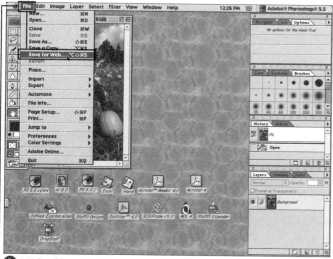

**1** With a file open, choose File ➪ Save for Web.

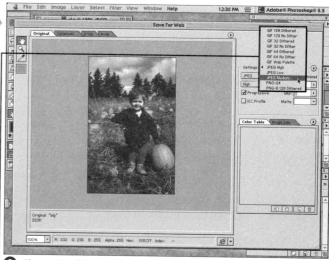

**2** Choose the file type from the Settings pop-up menu. Here, JPEG Medium was chosen.

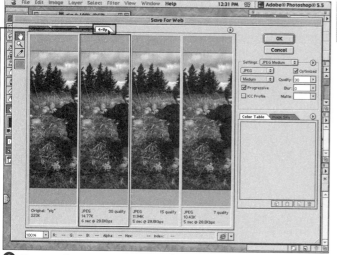

**3** To see various ways to save your file, click the 4-Up tab.

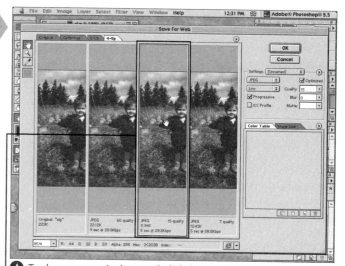

**4** To change a particular panel, click the panel first to activate that panels settings.

# Saving for the Web
*Continued*

**Matte.** Here you choose the color with which the transparent pixels will be blended. The Matte choices are Eyedropper Color, White, Black, or Other. Other brings up the Color dialog box so you can choose any color or custom color.

**Web Snap.** This snaps colors to match the Web palette. The slider adjusts the tolerance. The lower the number the less tolerance, and the higher the number the more colors will snap because of the higher tolerance. You enter a value in the text box, or drag the slider.

**Transparency.** The Transparency check box, if checked, makes a color transparent based on the eyedropper color.

**Interlaced.** The Interlaced check box, if checked, displays a lower resolution file while the higher resolution file is downloading. You get a larger file when the option is checked.

JPEG file choices are JPEG High, JPEG Low, and JPEG Medium. With JPEG files your settings are

**Optimized.** When the Optimized box is checked, you can save a smaller file, but there is a chance that it won't be compatible with other applications or browsers.

**Quality.** The Quality setting includes the pop-up box to the left. You can choose High, Medium, or Low quality, or you can enter a value or drag the slider in the Quality text box. The higher the quality, the larger the file; the lower the quality, the smaller the file.

**Blur.** The Blur option enables you to choose how much an image blurs when downloaded. The higher the number, the more of a Gaussian blur is applied.

**Matte.** The Matte option is the same as with the GIF files.

**Progressive.** The Progressive option downloads and images in sections. This results in a nicer-quality image, but takes up more memory (RAM) when downloading. It also may not be compatible with other applications or browsers.

**ICC Profile.** This check box downloads the ICC Profile from Photoshop with the file. Not all Web browsers accept ICC Profiles, but if they do, your image is viewed with that profile.

PNG file options are PNG-24 or PNG-8 128. The PNG file settings are

**Interlaced.** The Interlaced check box if checked will display a lower-resolution file while the higher-resolution file is downloading. This creates a larger file when the option is checked. The Interlaced option cannot be used with the Lossy or Dither options.

**Matte.** The Matte option is the same as GIF and JPEG files.

**CROSS-REFERENCE**

See Chapter 2 for more information on file types.

**FIND IT ONLINE**

For more on Photoshop file types, see Adobe's Web site at **http://www.adobe.com/supportservice/ custsupport/NOTES/d702.htm.**

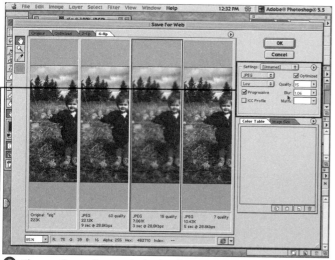

**5** Change the settings as desired in the Settings area.

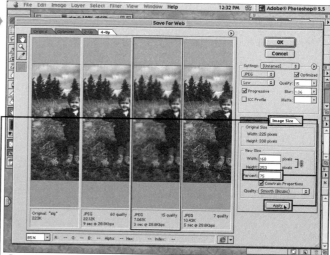

**6** To change the Image Size, click the Image Size tab. Enter a new value for the Image Size, here a value of 75% was chosen. Click Apply to see the new size.

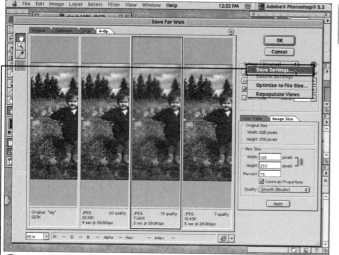

**7** If you want to keep the settings, choose Save Settings in the upper right of the dialog box. Enter a name and a location for the file, and then click Save.

**8** When finished, click OK to activate the Save Optimized As dialog box. Enter a name and a location for this optimized file then click Save.

# Personal Workbook

## Q&A

**1** You have an image with a wispy background; which new Photoshop 5.5 feature do you choose: Extract, Background Eraser, or Magic Eraser?

_____

_____

_____

**2** If you choose a black Matte in the Extract dialog box preview area, will the area be black behind your extracted image when you click OK?

_____

_____

_____

**3** What is the difference between the Magic Eraser and the Background Eraser?

_____

_____

_____

**4** How can you create a painterly effect without using Photoshop filters?

_____

_____

**5** When painting with the Art History Brush, how can you make more colors that what the image actually has?

_____

_____

_____

**6** How do you easily create a collection of your images?

_____

_____

_____

**7** If you are saving an image for the web and aren't sure of how you want to optimize the file, do you choose Export, or Save for Web?

_____

_____

_____

**8** You have an image with a lot of line art in it, what Web file format do you choose?

_____

_____

ANSWER: PAGE 344

## EXTRA PRACTICE

1 Open an image with a person who is on a background that is similar to their hair color and use the Extract function to create a mask.

2 Quickly remove a sky in an image using the Magic Eraser.

3 Change the color of someone's eyes by using the Background Eraser to remove the color first, and then use a paintbrush to fill in a new color.

4 Create a fun, textured background by using the Art History Brush.

5 Create a family album of your pictures by scanning in your relatives and then using Contact Sheet to make the album.

## REAL-WORLD APPLICATIONS

✓ You need to combine that image of a lion in a zoo scene, so you use the Extract feature to mask out the lion's furry head and add your new background.

✓ Create a quick reference for your client of their images using Contact Sheet.

✓ The Art History Brush can be used to create a soft painterly effect for making posters or advertisements.

✓ Save a file for the Web using the Save for Web function and show your client various ways the image will look when saved differently.

## Visual Quiz

How was this cat given a perm?

_____

_____

_____

_____

_____

_____

# Personal Workbook
# Answers

## Chapter 1

see page 4

**❶ How do you separate a palette from its group?**

A: Click the tabbed name of the palette and drag it away from the group. Let up on your mouse, and it is separated.

**❷ How do you access the pop-up tools?**

A: To access the pop-up tools or menu, click and hold the arrow in the upper right of the palette to see more options/tools/menu.

**❸ What color mode does a computer monitor display?**

A: RGB

**❹ What is a quicker way to access some pull-down menu options?**

A: Use the key commands listed next to the pull-down menu options. Once you learn them, life gets so much easier.

**❺ What kind of files can Photoshop open?**

A: Photoshop, Photoshop 2.0, Adobe Illustrator Paths, Amiga IFF, BMP, CompuServe GIF, Photoshop EPS Photoshop DCS 1.0, Photoshop DCS 2.0, Generic EPS,EPS PICT Preview, EPS TIFF Preview, Filmstrip, JPEG, Kodak ICC Color Photo CD, PCX, Photoshop PDF, Generic PDF, PICT File, PICT Resource, Pixar, PNG, Raw, Scitex CT, Targa, and TIFF.

**❻ How do you save a document for the Web?**

A: Choose Export GIF89a from the File ⇨ Export menu.

**❼ What is the best way to save a document for a page-layout program?**

A: A TIFF file is the best way to save a document for a page-layout program.

**❽ How can you change the guide line color?**

A: Access the Guides & Grids preferences from the File ⇨ Preferences ⇨ Guides & Grids. In that dialog box, pick a new color or create your own color.

### Visual Quiz

Q: **How did we make this large all-encompassing palette, and how do we change it back?**

A: We dragged and dropped all of the individual palettes into one palette. To change it back to default, choose File ⇨ Preferences ⇨ General. Then click the button that says Reset Palette Locations to Default.

## Chapter 2

see page 28

**❶ What does ppi abbreviate?**

A: PPI stands for Pixels Per Inch. That refers to your monitor. DPI or Dots Per Inch refers to your printer. These numbers (PPI, DPI) are the same except that one refers to how your screen views and the other refers to how your printer prints.

# Personal Workbook Answers

**2** **Why is it important to start with an image close to the size you need it?**

A: By starting with an image close to the size you need, you have little room for printing error because of resolution. If you change the size around, you may print out a pixelized or even an overly saturated image.

**3** **What is resampling?**

A: Resampling is the process of changing resolution and image size at the same time, so that individual pixels are either replaced with more or less pixels. Resampling typically degrades an image, regardless if the image is resampled up or down.

**4** **When would you use the Image Size command?**

A: To either change the physical size of an image or its ppi.

**5** **Can you scan straight into Photoshop?**

A: You can scan straight into Photoshop using the Twain Acquire module (in the File menu) or by using a plug-in supplied from your scanner manufacturer.

**6** **Where does the scanner plug-in module go?**

A: In the Plug-ins folder in your Photoshop application folder.

**7** **How would you get Photoshop paths into an Illustrator file?**

A: By copying and pasting, dragging and dropping into Illustrator from Photoshop, or by opening up an image saved as an EPS with a clipping path.

**8** When would you use File Information?

A: When you want to use a caption, keywords, or special instructions.

**9** **How are Preferences accessed?**

A: You can access Preferences from the Preferences sub-menu in the File menu or by pressing Command (Ctrl)+K.

## Visual Quiz

Q: **How did this image become blurry and pixelized without using any filters?**

A: This image was changed to a low resolution and when viewed at 100% it becomes blurry and pixelized.

# Chapter 3

see page 62

**1** **Name the Selection tools.**

A: Rectangular Marquee tool, Elliptical Marquee tool, Row Marquee tool, Column Marquee tool, Freeform Lasso tool, Straight Line Lasso tool, Magnetic Lasso tool, and Magic Wand tool.

**2** **How are selections and paths related?**

A: Selections can be created from paths, and paths can be created from selections.

**3** **What's the easiest way to make a square selection?**

A: Using the Rectangular Marquee tool, press the Shift key and drag.

**4** **How does the Magic Wand work?**

A: It selects contiguous pixels that are close to the pixel(s) you clicked in terms of brightness and color value.

**5** **What tool would be the correct one to use to outline a specific shape from a Photograph?**

A: Mask Pro 2.0 from Extensis. Or, if you don't have it, you should go and get it from **http://www.extensis.com**. If you absolutely can't afford it, you can always slum it by using the Magnetic Lasso in Photoshop, but it's not all that useful.

**⑥ What are the keyboard shortcuts for adding to a selection?**

A: Pressing the Shift key before making a selection will add the new selection to the current one.

**⑦ What is the keyboard shortcut for subtracting from a selection?**

A: Pressing the Option (Alt) key before making a selection will subtract the new selection from the current one.

**⑧ Which is more accurate, the Rectangular Marquee or the Crop tool, for cropping an image?**

A: The Crop tool, because it enables you to fine-tune the size of your image prior to cropping.

## Visual Quiz

Q: Look at the before and after of this image. How was the black line edge removed?

A: Before this image was pasted onto the background, the Select ⇨ Modify ⇨ Contract was used. Only a small amount of 2 pixels was needed to remove the black edge from the original background.

# Chapter 4

see page 86

**① When should you use Color Range?**

A: To select a similar color within an image, specifically in non-contiguous areas.

**② How do you remove a black edge from your selection?**

A: Use the Remove Black Matte option.

**③ What Photoshop plug-in creates a great mask selection even with an image of a person with wispy hair?**

A: Mask Pro 2.0 from Extensis corporation.

**④ What is a font?**

A: A set of characters, including numbers, letters, and symbols, all designed with certain unique common characteristics.

**⑤ What is the difference between Type and Vertical Type?**

A: Type appears in horizontal rows, while Vertical Type appears in vertical columns.

**⑥ How do you change Type orientation?**

A: Choose Vertical from the Type submenu.

**⑦ Why are type layers a good thing?**

A: Type layers contain fully editable text.

**⑧ Since Photoshop type cannot be edited after it is rendered, what should you do if you want to make changes?**

A: Don't render the type unless you are sure it is okay, or re-do the type.

## Visual Quiz

Q: How was this lion's fine wispy hair selected from the original background and put so effortlessly on the new background?

A: This image utilized Extensis' Mask Pro 2.0 to get all of the wispy hair from the background.

# Personal Workbook Answers

## Chapter 5

see page 112

**❶ Where does a copied or cut object go?**

A: To the Clipboard.

**❷ How many items can the Clipboard hold?**

A: One.

**❸ What is a "floating" selection?**

A: A selected set of pixels that haven't been burned into the current layer.

**❹ What can happen when you drag and drop between documents?**

A: The image will change resolution to the resolution of the document it is being copied into. That means the image you are copying could be noticeably larger or smaller depending on how different the resolutions are.

**❺ When would be a good time to use the Paste Into command?**

A: When you want to create a Masked section to your image.

**❻ What are the differences between the transform and the free transform?**

A: Transform lets you choose individually from a pull-down menu different transformation options. Free Transform lets you scale, rotate, and move all in one step.

## Visual Quiz

Q: **The image here shows a cool cityscape stuffed inside of text. How was it done? What other options can you apply to the text? Can you do this on your own?**

A: This image utilized the Paste Into option. The text was selected using the Magic Wand tool, then the selection was saved under Select ⇨ Save Selection. The background layer was selected and cut (to reveal the white background). Click the Text layer and choose Select ⇨ Load Selection. Then you choose Edit ⇨ Paste Into and you have it! Since the text is still fully editable, you can apply any of the special text effects found under the Layer ⇨ Effects menu.

## Chapter 6

see page 126

**❶ What is the purpose of the editing tools?**

A: The editing tools enable you to lighten, darken, smudge areas that are under-/overexposed or need a little blending. You can also blur and sharpen to fix a grainy image or an image that is too blurry.

**❷ Where does the phrase "dodge and burn" originate?**

A: These phrases dodge and burn come from the traditional photographer's way of fixing a negative.

**❸ Why would you use the Smudge tool?**

A: You can use the Smudge tool to blend areas so that the color is obvious and banded, or to smooth out rough areas.

**❹ Name the retouching tools.**

A: Blur, Sharpen, and Smudge are the retouching tools.

**❺ Name the toning tools.**

A: The toning tools are Dodge, Burn, and Sponge.

**6** **When should you use the Sponge tool?**

A: You can use the Sponge tool to remove color intensity from parts of an image, or to add more color intensity to parts of an image.

**7** **How can you apply cool filter effects to text?**

A: You can apply cool filter effects to text by choosing Layer ⇨ Effects then choosing one of the special effects listed.

**8** **How does the History Brush compare to the Magic Eraser?**

A: The Magic Eraser will erase to your last saved version. The History Brush will remove or erase to your last taken snapshot of your image.

## Visual Quiz

Q: **Can you tell if this "before and after" image was an actual doctor's photograph for plastic surgery or a Photoshop creation?**

A: This image was "doctored" up using Photoshop. Actually the image on the left was doctored up, the image on the right is the original.

# Chapter 7

see page 148

**1** **What is a fill?**

A: A fill is a chosen color found in the foreground Swatch in the toolbar that is used to flood color in the whole image or a selection.

**2** **What is a gradient?**

A: A gradient is a blend of two or more colors to create a fill.

**3** **What can be filled?**

A: You can fill your whole image, or a selection.

**4** **How do you access the Custom colors?**

A: When you access the Color Picker (by clicking the Foreground Swatch in the toolbox), you then click the Custom button to access Custom colors.

**5** **How can you save a custom Swatches palette?**

A: In the Swatches palette, you can click the arrow in the upper right to access the pop-up menu. From this pop-up menu, choose Save Swatches.

**6** **When would you use a gradient?**

A: Gradients are ideal to use when you are trying to create a three-dimensional look to a fill rather than a flat color.

**7** **What is the keyboard command to fill with the foreground color?**

A: Option (Alt)+Delete is the keyboard command to fill with the foreground color.

**8** **How do you change the default gradients?**

A: If you double-click the gradient tool, you'll access the Gradient Tool Options. In this palette, you click the Edit button to edit the current gradient. To change gradients, choose a different gradient from the pop-up menu in this palette.

## Visual Quiz

Q: **This portrait image has bars made with the Gradient Editor that fades to the underneath image. How was it created?**

A: In the Gradient editor, the Transparency button was chosen and the colors to the right were given a more transparent value.

# Personal Workbook Answers

## Chapter 8

see page 166

**1 What are the eyedroppers for in the Levels dialog box?**

A: You use the white eyedropper to click the lightest part of your image. The black eyedropper is used to click the darkest part of your image. The gray eyedropper is used to click the 50% midtone of your image.

**2 How do you dim an image using Levels?**

A: You can dim an image using Levels by dragging the black Output levels slider (found at the bottom of the Levels dialog box) to the right.

**3 What is the easiest method to using Curves?**

A: By using the "S" curve method of dragging the graph to create an "S" shape.

**4 How can you fix red-eye in a photo?**

A: To fix an image with red eye is to use Color Balance. Using the Elliptical Marquee, select the red eyes, then use Color Balance to decrease the Red and Magenta (increase the Cyan and Green) and add a touch of Blue.

**5 What adjust feature do you use to increase the darks and whites in your image?**

A: The Brightness/Contrast option enables you to increase the darks and whites in your image.

**6 How can you change the color of a section of your image without filling in with color?**

A: You can change the color of a section of your image by using the Hue/Saturation adjust feature.

**7 How can you adjust color, saturation, and lighten your image all at the same time?**

A: You can adjust color, saturation, and light by using the Variations command found under the Adjust submenu of the Image menu.

**8 How can you view many variations of your image that you are adjusting using Intellihance Pro 4.0?**

A: You can view many variations in Intellihance Pro 4.0 by using the Intellihance Pro's Power Variations.

### Visual Quiz

Q: **What adjustment option was used to give this photo a poster effect?**

A: The poster effect was created using the Curves option.

## Chapter 9

see page 184

**1 What is anti-aliasing?**

A: Anti-aliasing is the effect that is created when you get a transitional pixel that blends a color into the background.

**2 How do you create your own special Paintbrush in Photoshop?**

A: To create a new brush, choose New Brush from the pop-up menu in the Brushes palette.

**3 How do you control paint opacity?**

A: If you double-click the Paintbrush tool, you'll access the Paintbrush Options palette. In this palette, you can adjust the opacity by entering a value in the opacity box, or by dragging the opacity slider.

**4 How do you draw an arrowhead with Photoshop?**

A: Before drawing a line with the Line tool, double-click the Line tool to access the Line tool Options palette. In this palette, you can choose whether you add an arrow to the beginning, end, or both ends of the line. You first set your arrowhead options, then draw a line.

**⑤ Where can you find extra brushes in Photoshop?**

A: You can access more brushes when you choose Load Brushes from the Brushes palette. The other brushes are found in the Goodies folder inside the Photoshop folder.

**⑥ When should you use the Eyedropper tool?**

A: You can use the Eyedropper tool to select a color from an open image.

**⑦ How do you add just one arrowhead to point to an object in Photoshop?**

A: In the Line tool Options palette (found by double-clicking the Line tool) choose whether you want the line to be at the start of your line or at the end, then click and drag the line out.

## Visual Quiz

Q: **How was this gunshot-through-burlap-bag effect created?**

A: This effect was created using a large soft-edged brush with the mode set to dissolve (you set the mode by double-clicking the Paintbrush tool to access the Paintbrush tool Options palette). Then you click once with the brush on your image.

# Chapter 10

see page 204

**① Name the Pen tools.**

A: The other tools are Magnetic Pen tool, Freeform Pen tool, Add Anchor Point tool, Delete Anchor point tool, Direct Selection tool, and Convert Point tool.

**② How can you add an anchor point where there wasn't one before?**

A: You can add an anchor point to any line by using the Add Anchor Point tool.

**③ What does the Magnetic Pen do?**

A: The Magnetic Pen tool will read the difference in pixel colors and draw a path according to that difference. You can set the tolerance in the Magnetic Pen tool Options palette by double-clicking the Magnetic Pen tool.

**④ What is a path?**

A: A path is a line created using the Pen tool. The actual path is like a guide, meaning that it isn't going to print out on your image. You can also make a path from an existing selection as well.

**⑤ Which gives you more saving options, saving with Paths, or saving selections as Alpha channels?**

A: Saving a file with Paths gives you more saving options than saving a selection as an Alpha channel.

**⑥ What is a clipping path?**

A: The Clipping Path lets you define a border for your image that when brought into another program, only the pixels within that border will be visible. Clipping Paths create a mask effect to your image.

**⑦ Why would you use a clipping path?**

A: You would use a Clipping Path because you have an image that you only want a portion of showing and you are going to place in another program like PageMaker. By using a Clipping Path, you can have only the parts of your image visible that you want. If you select the portion you want and make the rest white, in PageMaker, the white areas will show as white, not transparent.

# PERSONAL WORKBOOK ANSWERS

**⑧ What is a clipping group?**

A: With a Clipping Group, you use the bottom layer as a mask for the above layers and groups. A grouped layer is made in the Layers palette. Before making a Clipping Group, first make sure the bottom layer is the mask that you want to use.

## Visual Quiz

Q: **What did we use to make the person in this newsletter show without a background?**

A: The person was created in Photoshop with a Clipping Path so the background wouldn't show through.

# Chapter 11

see page 218

**❶ How do you change the order of your layers in a Photoshop file?**

A: You can change the order of your layers in Photoshop, by dragging a layer above or below another layer.

**❷ How do you copy a layer?**

A: You can copy a layer by clicking the layer first to highlight it, then choose Duplicate Layer from the pop-up menu in the Layers palette.

**❸ How do you change the size of the thumbnail images that represent each layer?**

A: In the Layers palette, you access the pop-up menu by clicking the arrow in the upper-right corner. In this pop-up menu, you can choose Palette Options to change the thumbnail size.

**❹ How can you tell how large (or small) your file size will be once you flatten the document?**

A: In every file you work on, you'll see two file size numbers. In Windows, this number can be seen in the

lower-left corner of the screen. On the Mac, it's tucked in the lower-left side of the image window. The higher number is the estimated size of the unflattened file. A flattened file is a file with one layer

**❺ What is a layer mask?**

A: The layer mask lets you control how all of the elements on a specified Layer are hidden and how they are revealed.

**❻ Why is it good to apply layer masks before saving?**

A: To keep file sizes manageable, remember to render your Layer Masks by applying them whenever possible.

**❼ What does an Adjustment Layer affect?**

A: The Adjustment Layer lets you make adjustments to a layer's color and tonality without actually affecting the image.

**❽ When can you use layer effects?**

A: You can use Layer Effects to any layered file. You can also apply Layer effects to type.

## Visual Quiz

O: **Can we save this image just as it appears as an EPS file?**

A: No, because this file has a layer.

# Chapter 12

see page 238

**❶ How many channels can a single document have?**

A: A document can have a total of 24 channels.

**❷ Why would you split a channel?**

A: You would do this if a file is too large to be manipulated as a whole. Split channels can be merged back into one document when you've finished processing each one.

**③ When would you use a mask?**

A: You use a mask when you only want a portion of your image showing. The mask will let that portion show through.

**④ How does a mask work with a channel?**

A: Alpha Channels enable you to load an existing Selection and use it as a Mask.

**⑤ What is the History command?**

A: History palette gives you a visual overview of at least the last 20 things you've done to alter your image. The default is set to 20. You can pick and choose from those actions to remove or alter and you don't have to do it chronologically.

**⑥ How many undo's can you undo?**

A: You can undo one time in Photoshop.

**⑦ What is a snapshot?**

A: The History palette stores 20 steps or states. If you really want to keep a certain step or state, you can make a snapshot of it. It is like taking a picture of the image.

**⑧ Can you move stages around in the History palette?**

A: No, you can't drag to move them, but you can remove any stage or snapshot by dragging it to the trashcan icon found at the bottom of the History palette.

## Visual Quiz

Q: **How was the painterly effect added to only parts of this image?**

A: Half of the image was selected and an artistic filter was applied to it. You can apply any filter effect to the whole or parts of your image.

# Chapter 13

see page 254

**① Where do you access the Actions palette?**

A: The Actions palette is found under the Window menu.

**② What is a set?**

A: A set is a group of Actions.

**③ Can you make your own actions?**

A: You can make your own actions by recording them.

**④ What is a modal control?**

A: A modal control lets you insert a pause in an action where you want to have a dialog box remain so you can enter a value, then when done, the action finished playing.

**⑤ Can you change the pace at which actions are played?**

A: You can change the speed of the Actions by accessing the Playback Options from the pop-up menu on the Actions palette.

**⑥ Where do you access automation in Photoshop?**

A: The Automate command is found under the File menu in Photoshop.

**⑦ Can you do anything with automation besides process batches of actions?**

A: You can make a contact sheet of all of the images you used Automate on. This is handy when you want a quick thumbnail view of your images before you send them to a printer.

# Personal Workbook Answers

## Visual Quiz

**Q:** All of these action sets ship with Adobe Photoshop 5.0. Can you find the extra ones on your hard drive?

**A:** The extra actions are found in the Goodies folder in the Photoshop folder on your hard drive.

# Chapter 14

**❶ Which blur filter do you use to apply an effect that you control?**

**A:** To control the blur, you need to choose the Blur filter from the Filter menu.

**❷ What is the best way to crisp up (sharpen) an image?**

**A:** The best way to sharpen an image is to use Unsharp Mask found under the Sharpen submenu of the Filter menu.

**❸ What filter do you use to blend away banded colors?**

**A:** To remove a banded effect, use the Blur filter to soften the edges between colors.

**❹ How can you fix a scratch in a photo?**

**A:** The Dust and Scratches filter found under the Noise filter submenu of the Filter menu is the best for fixing a scratched photo.

**❺ What filter creates a sky to a plain background?**

**A:** To create a sky to a plain background, use the Clouds filter found under the Render submenu of the Filter menu.

**❻ Which group of filters changes your image to a grayscale from color?**

**A:** Most of the Sketch filters will change your colored image to grayscale.

**❼ How can you create a quick and easy button for the Web?**

**A:** Extensis' PhotoTools has a filter called PhotoButton that lets you create custom Web buttons easily.

**❽ What plug-in lets you create custom textures?**

**A:** Extensis' PhotoTools has a filter called PhotoTexture that lets you create all kinds of cool textures.

## Visual Quiz

**Q:** How was the black channel only affected with this filter?

**A:** To affect only the black channel you first need to click that channel in the channels palette. Then a filter effect was applied to just that channel.

# Chapter 15

**❶ Will your Macintosh saved image look the same viewed on a Windows system?**

**A:** No, the Macintosh image will appear darker on a Windows system.

**❷ Where do you access the Color Tables?**

**A:** The Color Tables are accessed under the Mode submenu of the Image menu.

**❸ Why do you need to trap an image?**

**A:** You need to trap an image when printing it because printing machines tend to shift the paper and you'll get white lines and overlapping colors if you don't trap your image.

**❹ Can you trap the image in Photoshop?**

**A:** Yes. Photoshop provides a trapping option for you found under the Image menu. The image first has to be converted to CMYK for the Trap option to be available.

Once you activate the Trap dialog box, you simply enter the number in pixels of the trap your printer suggested you use.

**5** **How do you make a Color Separation of your document?**

A: You need to have your image converted to CMYK first. In the Print dialog box, there is a Space pop-up menu where you'll choose separations from the list.

**6** **How do you get more paper space when printing?**

A: The Options button in the Page Setup dialog box lets you choose other page setup options. Choose Larger Print Area so you get more area to work with.

**7** **Why do you need to make a halftone screen (in what cases)?**

A: An image being printed in black and white on newsprint will need to be screened very coarsely because newsprint is absorbent (it sucks up a lot of ink) and the speeds at which the presses run preclude precision.

**8** **Can you print your image to a file?**

A: Yes, you can choose Print to File from the Print dialog box.

## Visual Quiz

Q: **What method of halftoning was done to create this image?**

A: The Line method was chosen as the halftone for this image.

# Chapter 16

see page 302

**1** **What are the three Web graphics file formats?**

A: GIF89a, PNG, and JPEG are the three file formats for Web use.

**2** **How would you choose what type of format to use for a specific image?**

A: It is best to choose a format that will make your files small and easily downloaded, most accessible to the widest number of browsers, shown to best advantage. The most common format to use is the GIF89a format.

**3** **What is the smallest file size you can save as?**

A: The smallest file format that still retains the color information is the JPEG format.

**4** **How can you make a basic Web button?**

A: You can make any basic Web button using your Elliptical or Rectangular marquee and pasting an image into the selection, or filling the selection with color.

**5** **How can you make multiple buttons at one time?**

A: Extensis' PhotoTools has a filter called PhotoButton that lets you create multiple buttons at a time.

**6** **What is a watermark?**

A: If you hold a nice piece of letterhead paper up to the light, you'll see the paper's watermark: the paper company's logo, or even the paper variety's name is embedded into the paper during its manufacture.

# PERSONAL WORKBOOK ANSWERS

**7** **How can you check for a watermark that you embedded?**

A: You choose Filter ⇨ Digimarc ⇨ Read Watermark.

**8** **Why would you need to think about protecting your artwork?**

A: You need to protect your artwork so that you retain the rights to it. That way no one can use your art without your permission or compensation.

## Visual Quiz

Q: **How did this image get a transparent background?**

A: This image was saved as a GIF89a file so that the background would be transparent on the Web page for which it was made.

# Chapter 17

see page 314

**1** **You have an image with a wispy background, which new Photoshop 5.5 feature do you choose: Extract, Background Eraser, or Magic Eraser?**

A: You use the Extract function to mask an image with an undefined edge.

**2** **If you choose a black Matte in the Extract dialog box preview area, will the area be black behind your extracted image when you click OK?**

A: No, any extracted image will have a transparent background when you are finished.

**3** **What is the difference between the Magic Eraser and the Background Eraser?**

A: The Magic Eraser is used by clicking on areas, the Background eraser is used by dragging the mouse over areas.

**4** **How can you create a painterly effect without using Photoshop filters?**

A: You can create a painterly effect using the Art History Brush.

**5** **When painting with the Art History Brush, how can you make more colors that what the image actually has?**

A: You can create more colors by using a low Fidelity setting.

**6** **How do you easily create a collection of your images?**

A: You can create a gallery of your art using the Contact Sheet function.

**7** **If you are saving an image for the Web and aren't sure of how you want to optimize the file, do you choose Export, or Save for Web?**

A: If you choose Save for Web, you can see many different options on saving your file, so this would be a more flexible choice.

**8** **You have an image with a lot of line art in it, what Web file format do you choose?**

A: A GIF file format is the best format to use with line art.

## Visual Quiz

Q: **How was this cat given a perm?**

A: The cat was given a perm using the Art History Brush with the Area set to 5 pixels, the Threshold set to 90, and a small, soft-edged brush was chosen from the Brushes palette. Then, the brush was dragged over the catís fur to create the curly look.

# Index

## A

Acquire options, 38
actions, 255, 256, 263
  adding to, 256
  button display of, 256
  copying, 256
  creating, 256, 258
  default, 256
  deleting, 256
  heading for, 256
  loading, 256
  nonrecordable, 258
  playback of, 256
  renaming, 256
  replacing, 256
  speed of, 258
Actions command, 260, 303
Actions palette, 255, 256, 258
Add Anchor Point tool, 10, 208
Add Layer Mask icon, 222
additive colors, 34
Adjustment Layer option, 167
Adjustment layers, 170, 219, 226
  built-in Layer Masks of, 226
  inserting, 226
Adobe, 260
  online help, 12
  Web site, 12

Adobe Acrobat Reader, 260
Adobe FreeHand, 30
Adobe icon, 12
Adobe Illustrator, 30, 102
  gradients of, 160
  text creation in, 111
Adobe Online help, 12
Adobe Online window, 10
Adobe PageMaker, 285
Adobe Postscript, 30
Adobe solutions Web site, 120
Adobe Type Manager (ATM), 102
Airbrush tool, 10, 185, 196
  options for, 196
  painting modes for, 192
aliased edges, 63
aliasing, 64
Alien Skin Software, 265
Alpha Channel Masks, 246
Alpha Channels, 212, 239, 240
America Online, Photoshop SIG
  on, 118
anchor points, 208
  corner, 206
  for curves, 212
  placement of, 212
  selecting, 212
  smooth, 206
Andy's Web, 134
Angle Gradient tool, 10

animation features, 315
animations, 278
ANPA Color, 14
anti-aliased edges, 63
anti-aliasing, 64, 68, 102, 185
Apple Color Picker, 38
applications, jumping to, 324
arrow keys, 116
arrowhead, 198
Art History brush, 315, 322, 331
  Fidelity option, 322
  Opacity option, 322
  Painting Area in Diameter
    option, 322
  Painting Mode option, 322
  Painting Style option, 322
  Tolerance option, 322
Artistic filters, 265, 268
  Colored Pencil, 268
  Dry Brush, 268
  Film Grain, 268
  Fresco, 268
  Neon Glow, 268
  Paint Daubs, 268
  Palette Knife, 268
  Plastic Wrap, 268
  Poster Edges, 268
  Rough Pastels, 268
  Smudge Stick, 268

*continued*

# Index

# Index

# INDEX

# INDEX

*continued*

# Index

# INDEX

# INDEX

# Index

# my2cents.idgbooks.com

## Register This Book — And Win!

Visit **http://my2cents.idgbooks.com** to register this book and we'll automatically enter you in our fantastic monthly prize giveaway. It's also your opportunity to give us feedback: let us know what you thought of this book and how you would like to see other topics covered.

## Discover IDG Books Online!

The IDG Books Online Web site is your online resource for tackling technology — at home and at the office. Frequently updated, the IDG Books Online Web site features exclusive software, insider information, online books, and live events!

### 10 Productive & Career-Enhancing Things You Can Do at www.idgbooks.com

- Nab source code for your own programming projects.

- Download software.

- Read Web exclusives: special articles and book excerpts by IDG Books Worldwide authors.

- Take advantage of resources to help you advance your career as a Novell or Microsoft professional.

- Buy IDG Books Worldwide titles or find a convenient bookstore that carries them.

- Register your book and win a prize.

- Chat live online with authors.

- Sign up for regular e-mail updates about our latest books.

- Suggest a book you'd like to read or write.

- Give us your 2¢ about our books and about our Web site.

You say you're not on the Web yet? It's easy to get started with IDG Books' *Discover the Internet*, available at local retailers everywhere.